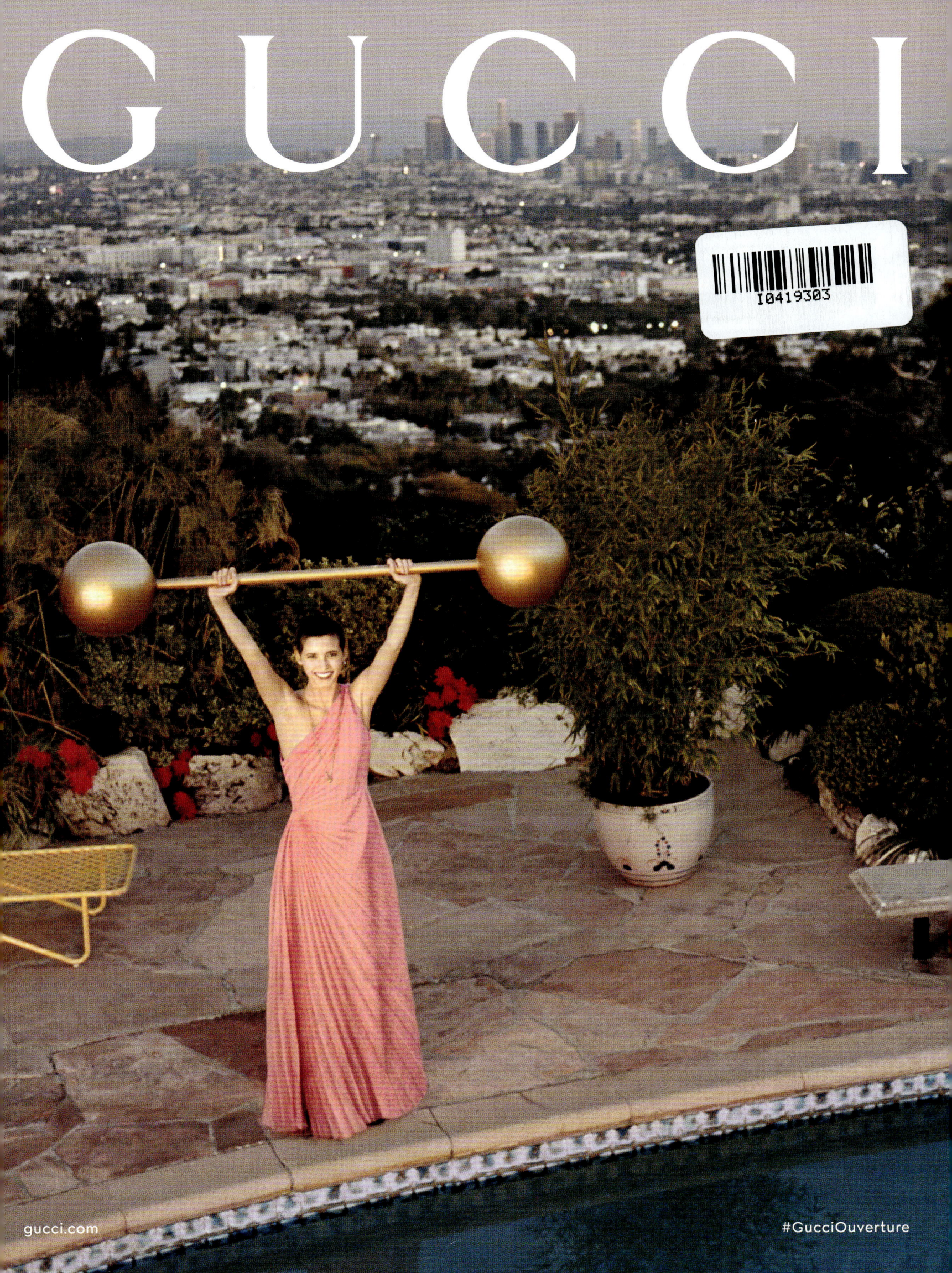

GUCCI

gucci.com

#GucciOuverture

Fall 2021
Cosmologies

Front

Back

Words & Pictures

Front cover:
Feng Li, *Good Night*, 2007–21
Courtesy the artist and Concrete Rep. Ltd
(See page 98)

Opposite:
Anne Hardy, *Into Darkness*, 2020, from the series *The Depth of Darkness, the Return of the Light*
© the artist and courtesy Maureen Paley, London
(See page 30)

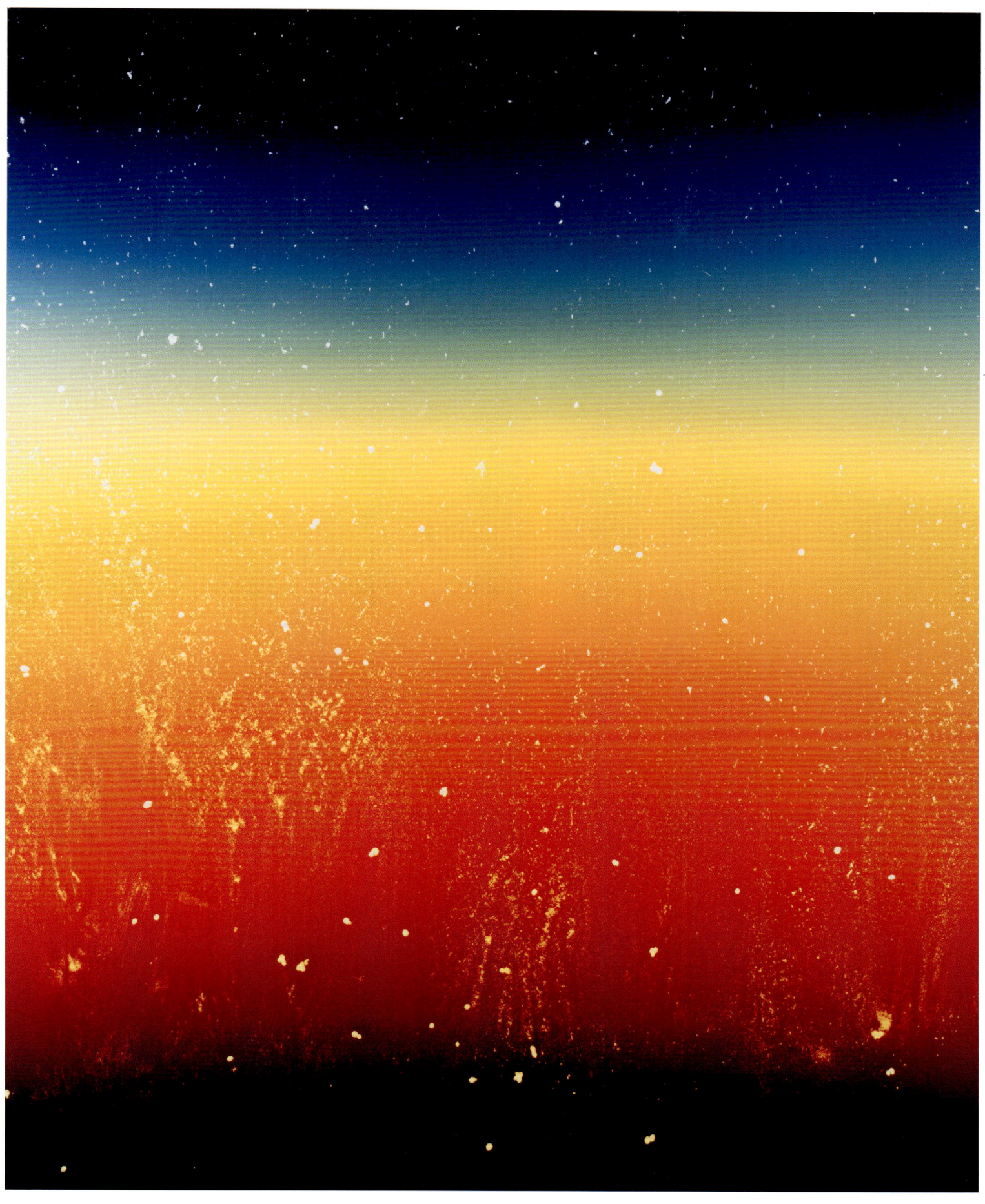

aperture

The Magazine of Photography and Ideas

Editor
Michael Famighetti

Senior Managing Editor
Brendan Embser

Assistant Editor
Nicole Acheampong

Copy Editors
Hilary Becker, Donna Ghelerter

Production Director
Minjee Cho

Production Manager
Andrea Chlad

Art Direction, Design & Typefaces
A2/SW/HK, London

Chief Operating Officer
Dana Triwush
magazine@aperture.org

Director of Brand Partnerships
Isabelle Friedrich McTwigan
212-946-7118
imctwigan@aperture.org

Advertising
Elizabeth Morina
917-691-2608
emorina@aperture.org

**Executive Director,
Aperture Foundation**
Sarah Meister

Minor White, Editor (1952–1974)

Michael E. Hoffman, Publisher and Executive Director
(1964–2001)

Aperture, a not-for-profit foundation, connects the photo community and its audiences with the most inspiring work, the sharpest ideas, and with each other— in print, in person, and online.

Aperture (ISSN 0003-6420) is published quarterly, in spring, summer, fall, and winter, at 548 West 28th Street, 4th Floor, New York, N.Y. 10001. In the United States, a one-year subscription (four issues) is $75; a two-year subscription (eight issues) is $124. In Canada, a one-year subscription is $95. All other international subscriptions are $105 per year. Visit aperture.org to subscribe. Single copies may be purchased at $24.95 for most issues. Subscribe to the Aperture Digital Archive at aperture.org/archive. Periodicals postage paid at New York and additional offices. Postmaster: Send address changes to Aperture, P.O. Box 3000, Denville, N.J. 07834. Address queries regarding subscriptions, renewals, or gifts to: Aperture Subscription Service, 866-457-4603 (U.S. and Canada), or email custsvc_aperture@fulcoinc.com.

Newsstand distribution in the U.S. is handled by CMG. For international distribution, contact Central Books, centralbooks.com. Other inquiries, email orders@aperture.org or call 212-505-5555.

Become a Member of Aperture to take your interest in and knowledge of photography further. With an annual tax-deductible gift of $250, membership includes a complimentary subscription to Aperture magazine, discounts on Aperture's award-winning publications and photography workshops, a special limited-edition gift, and more. To join, visit aperture.org/join, or contact membership@aperture.org.

Library of Congress Catalog Card No: 58-30845.

ISBN 978-1-59711-505-6

Printed in Turkey by Ofset Yapimevi

OFSET
YAPIMEVİ

Significant support of Aperture magazine is provided by The Kanakia Foundation and by Slobodan Randjelović and Jon Stryker. Further generous support is provided in part by the New York City Department of Cultural Affairs in partnership with the City Council.

Aperture Foundation's programs are made possible in part by the New York State Council on the Arts with the support of Governor Andrew M. Cuomo and the New York State Legislature.

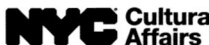
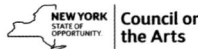

aperture.org

JUDITH JOY ROSS

GALERIE THOMAS ZANDER

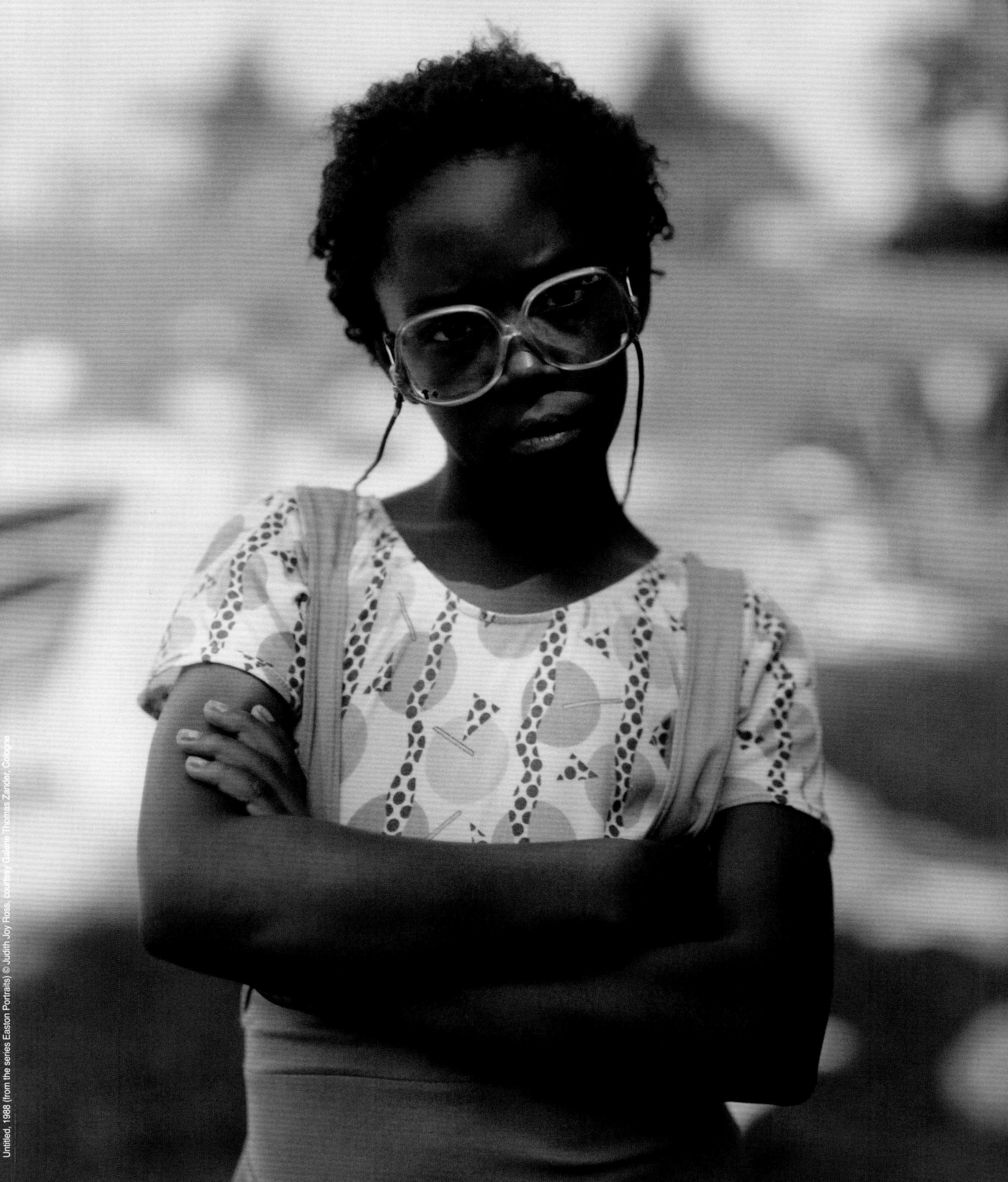

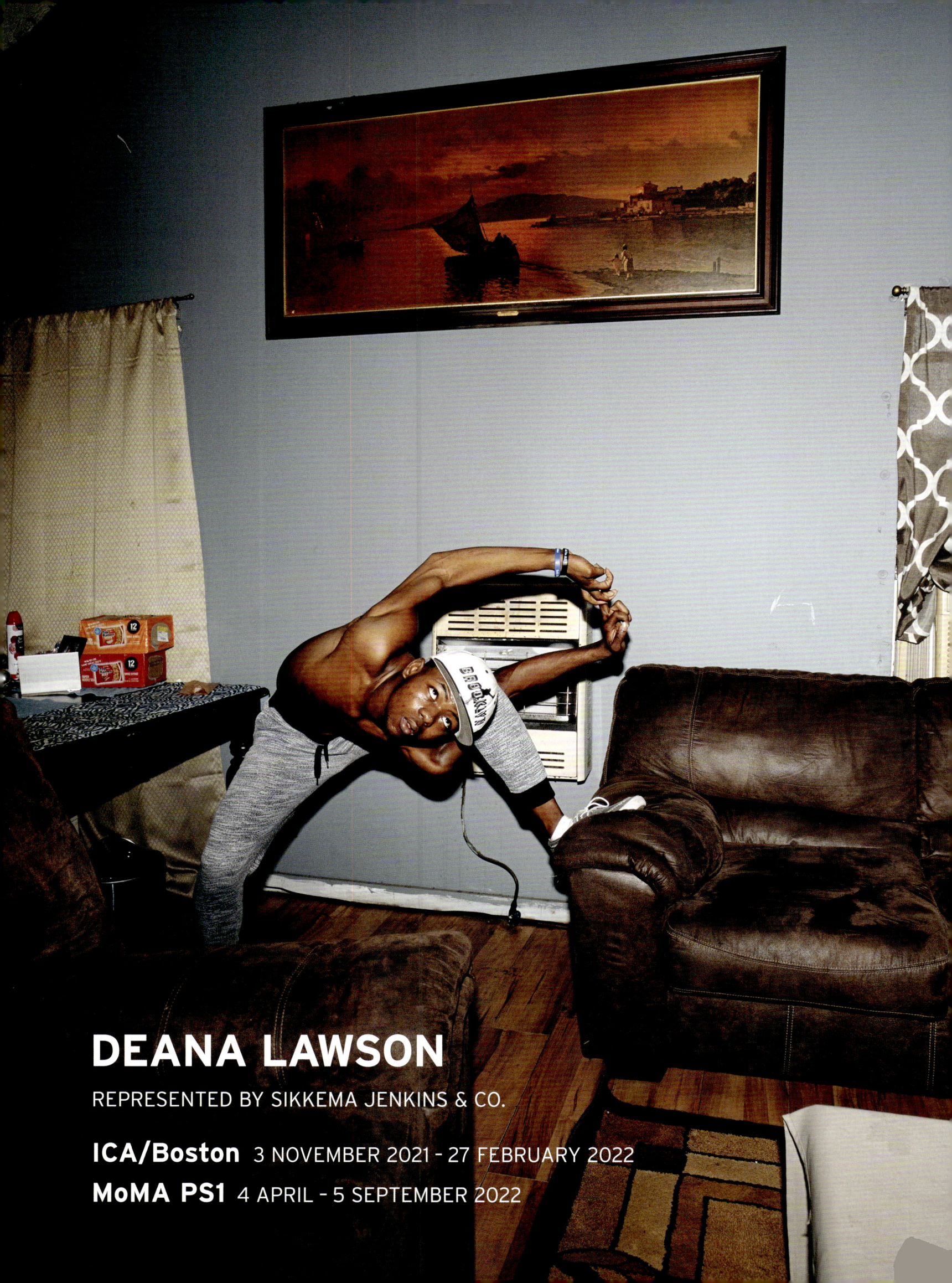

DEANA LAWSON

REPRESENTED BY SIKKEMA JENKINS & CO.

ICA/Boston 3 NOVEMBER 2021 - 27 FEBRUARY 2022

MoMA PS1 4 APRIL - 5 SEPTEMBER 2022

Agenda
Exhibitions to See

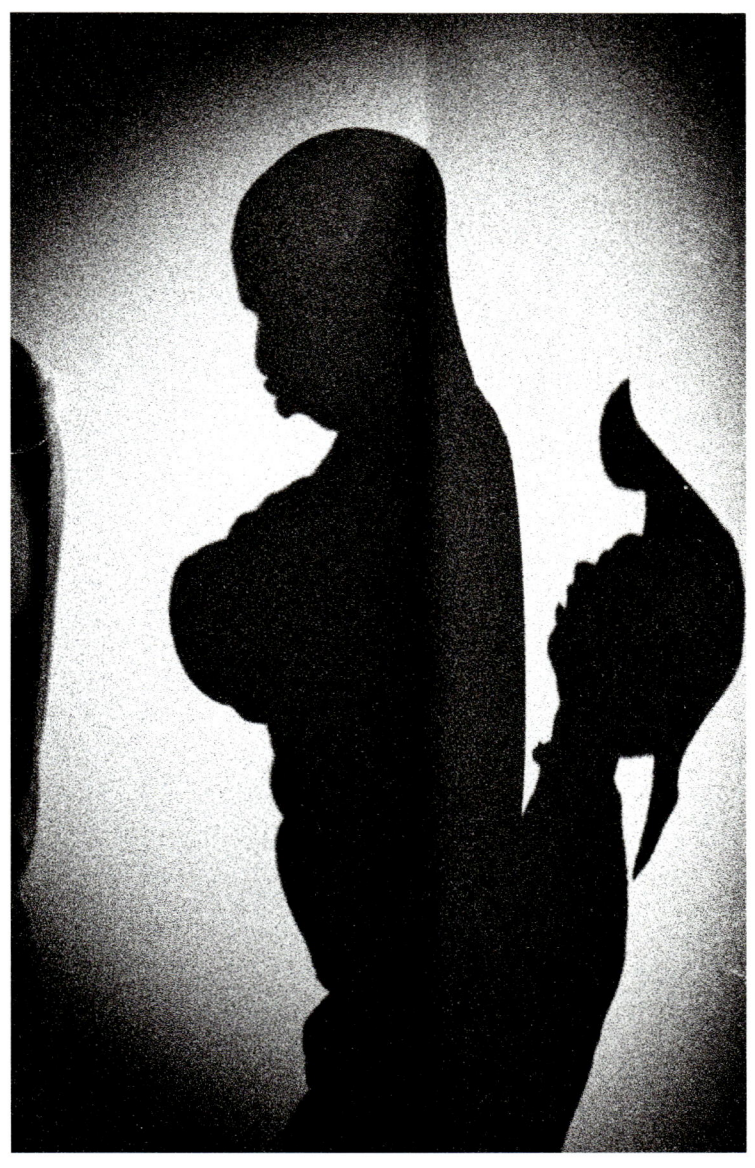

Liz Johnson Artur

"A trace of human sensibility" is what is preserved in Liz Johnson Artur's *of life of love of sex of movement of hope*, her solo exhibition at Foam that pairs photographic works with sculptural elements, all of which are calibrated to the textures and allures of everyday life. In one image, the grainy silhouette of a man in profile, his arms crossed, would appear inconspicuously commonplace if not for the shadow of a mysterious protrusion—a mythical tail? another encroaching figure? something yet more sinister?—that demands a double take and subtly destabilizes the viewer's gaze on what was almost familiar. Through a series of site-specific installations commissioned by Foam, Artur once more crafts a visual world marked by graceful, provocative poses and a delightful streak of enigma.

Liz Johnson Artur,
***of movement,* 2021**
Courtesy the artist

***Liz Johnson Artur: of life of love of sex of movement of hope* at Foam, Amsterdam, October 15, 2021–February 9, 2022**

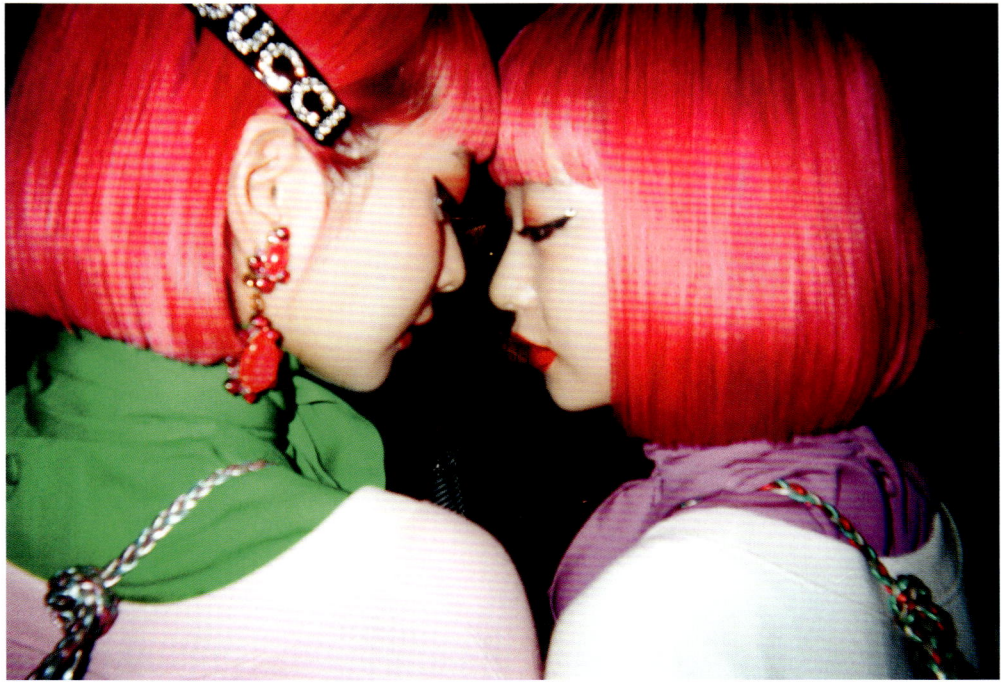

Mika Ninagawa,
***Tokyo,* from the series**
***Utsurundesu,* 2018–ongoing**
Courtesy the artist and Tomio
Koyama Gallery, Tokyo

Tokyo: Art & Photography

The University of Oxford and Tokyo have long-standing links: both the emperor and empress of Japan are former students, and the school's museum, the Ashmolean, holds a significant collection of historical Japanese art. *Tokyo: Art & Photography* presents four centuries of work that juxtaposes various eras and highlights the city's strong traditions of photography. The exhibition will feature original commissions by Mika Ninagawa, an icon of exuberant pop baroque, and the Provoke-era legend Daido Moriyama. As to why Tokyo has been such a vital artistic center, cocurator Lena Fritsch points to a history of creation in response to destruction. "Natural disasters, wars, and urban change," she notes, "have necessitated repeated regeneration and inspired artists to create powerful works of art."

***Tokyo: Art & Photography* at the Ashmolean Museum, University of Oxford, June 29, 2021–March 1, 2022**

Gillian Wearing, *Me as Meret Oppenheim*, 2019
Courtesy Maureen Paley, London; Tanya Bonakdar, New York; and Regen Projects, Los Angeles

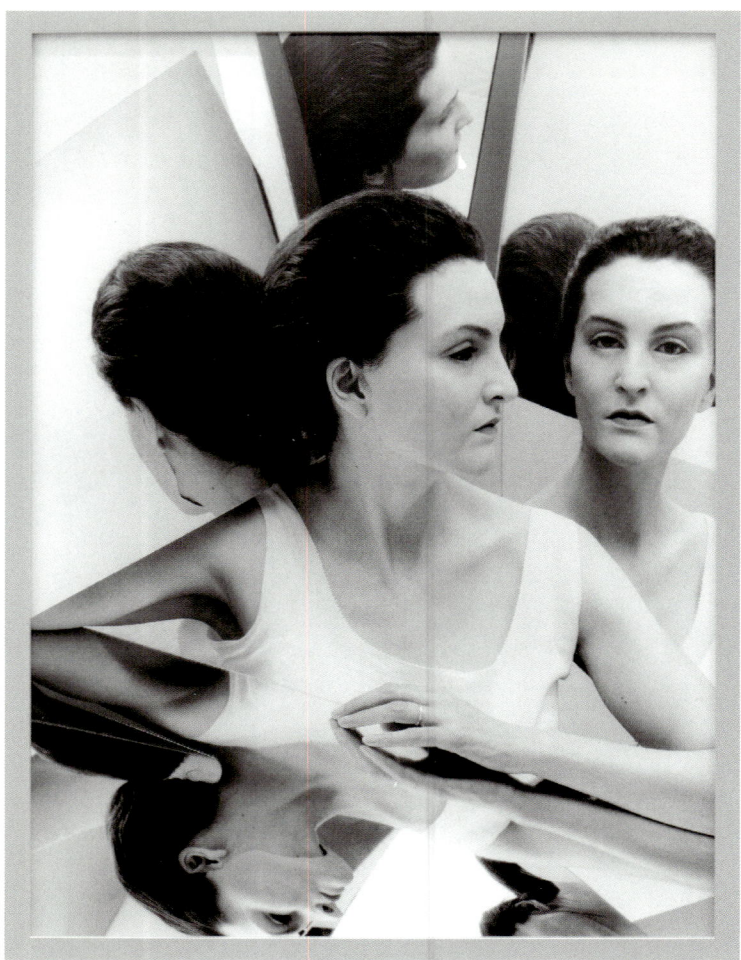

Gillian Wearing

She's been a fixture of British contemporary art for decades, but Gillian Wearing—the virtuosic photographer and video artist—has had a lower profile in the United States. That's about to change this fall with Wearing's first retrospective in North America, presented at the Guggenheim Museum and cocurated by Jennifer Blessing and Nat Trotman. Wearing is known for her uncanny self-portraits in the guises of her "spiritual family"—artists such as Diane Arbus, Robert Mapplethorpe, Claude Cahun, and Meret Oppenheim. "She's interested in how photographic images of artists create a kind of iconic identity," Blessing says. The exhibition extends outdoors into Central Park, with a life-size sculpture of Arbus, her Rollei in hand, adding yet another dimension to Wearing's fascination with performance and the theater of everyday interactions.

Gillian Wearing: Wearing Masks at the Solomon R. Guggenheim Museum, New York, November 5, 2021–April 4, 2022

Mimi Cherono Ng'ok

Mimi Cherono Ng'ok's first solo museum exhibition in the United States is an intuitive and tender presentation of twelve works, made across Africa, the Caribbean, and South America, that create quiet juxtapositions between figurative and botanical portraits. Along with a series of photographs, the exhibition includes Ng'ok's first film, which tracks the movements of tree leaves that the artist encountered in La Romana, Dominican Republic, becoming a statement on the raw materials of mourning and memorial. Ng'ok's prints are pinned, unframed, directly to the gallery walls, emphasizing "a sense of vulnerability" in Ng'ok's work, says the Art Institute of Chicago curator Antawan I. Byrd. "I think many will find that the show resonates with our current atmosphere of loss, whether loss of life due to the pandemic or the ongoing climate crisis."

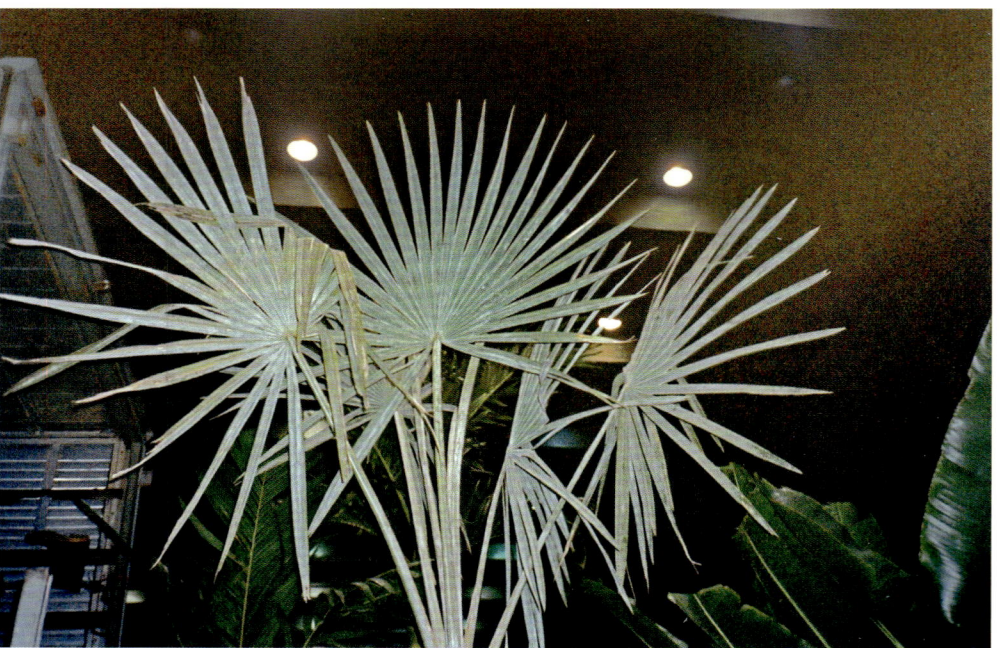

Mimi Cherono Ng'ok, *Untitled*, 2019
© the artist

Mimi Cherono Ng'ok: Closer to the Earth, Closer to My Own Body at the Art Institute of Chicago, June 18, 2021–February 7, 2022

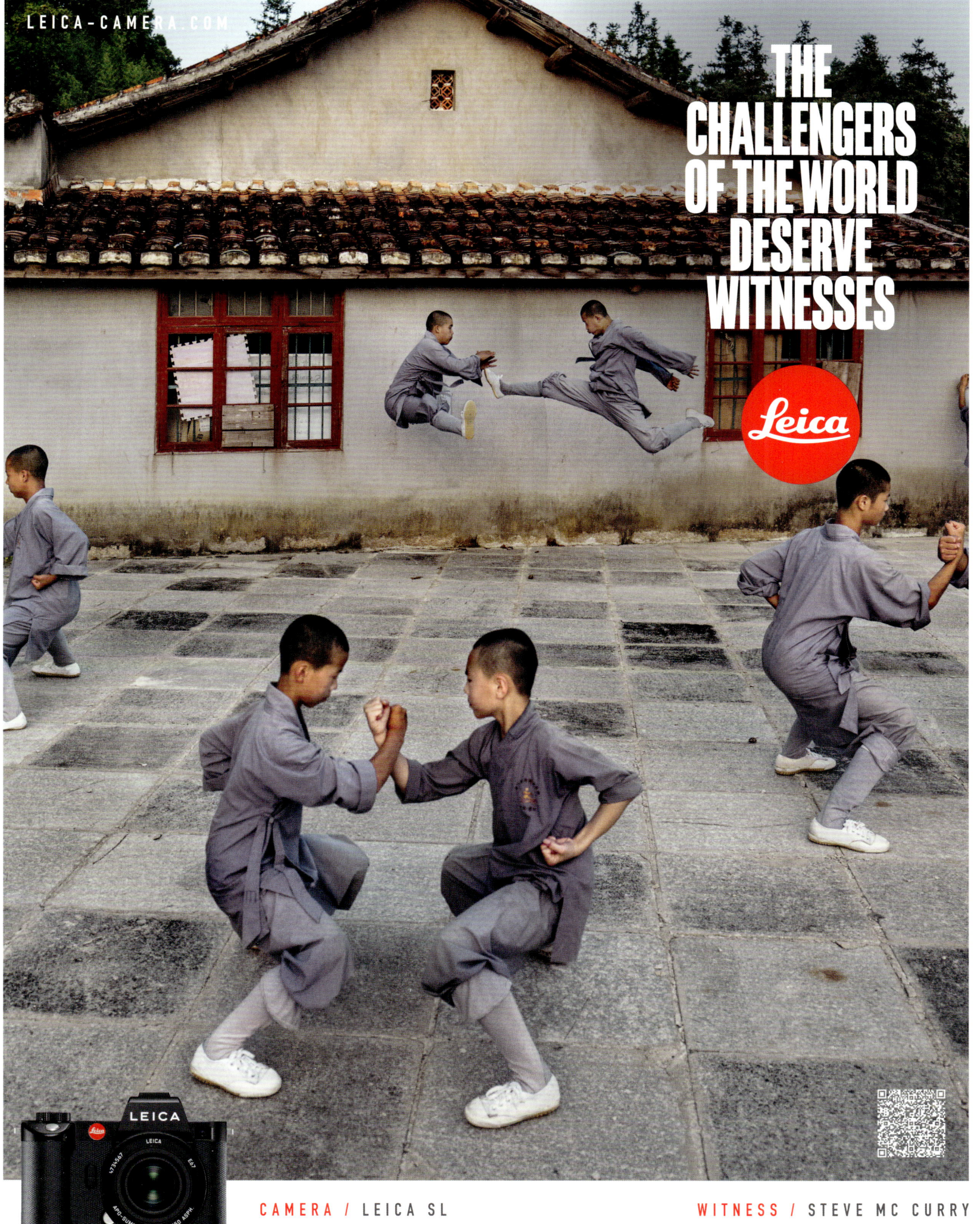

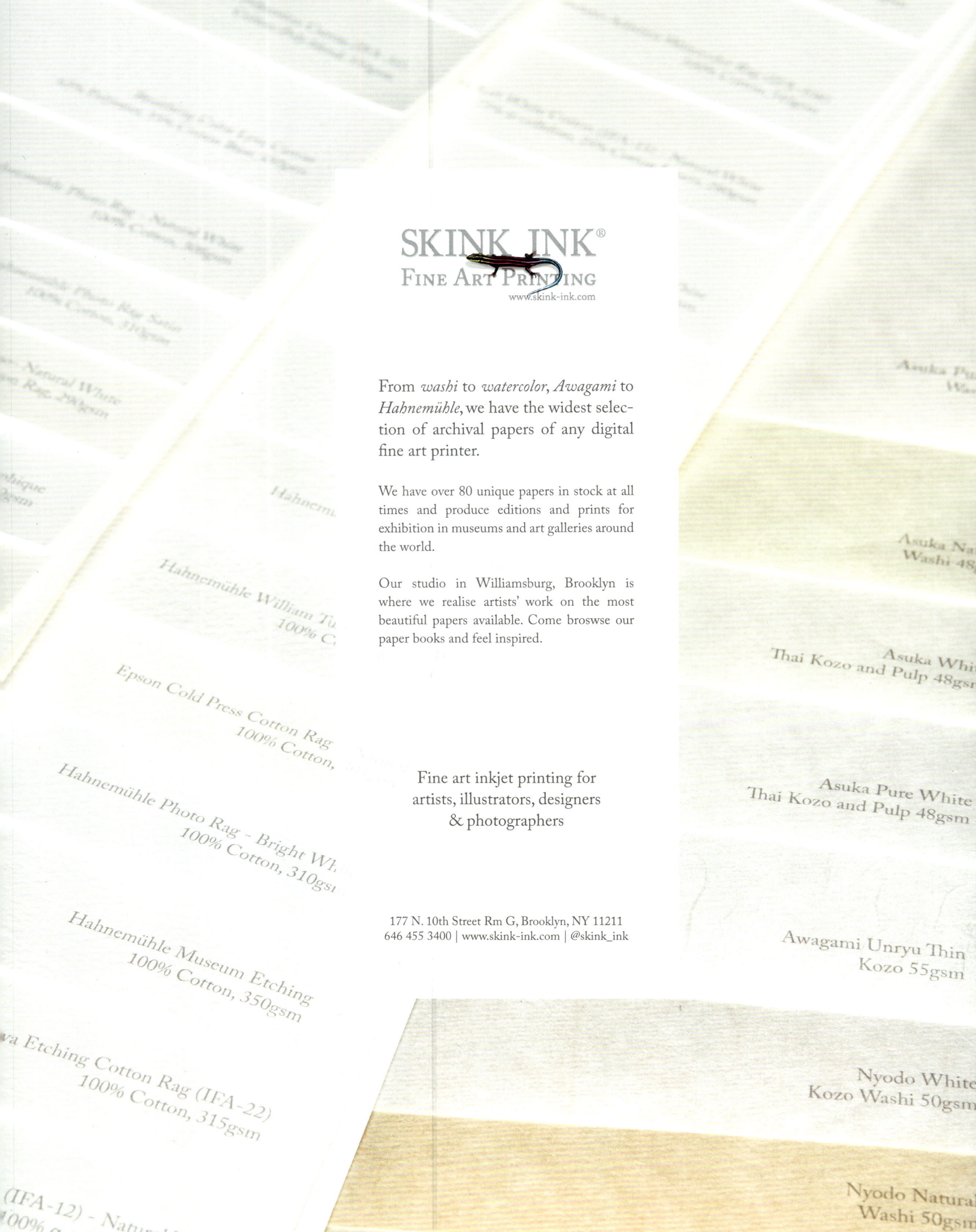

SKINK INK®
FINE ART PRINTING
www.skink-ink.com

From *washi* to *watercolor*, *Awagami* to *Hahnemühle*, we have the widest selection of archival papers of any digital fine art printer.

We have over 80 unique papers in stock at all times and produce editions and prints for exhibition in museums and art galleries around the world.

Our studio in Williamsburg, Brooklyn is where we realise artists' work on the most beautiful papers available. Come broswse our paper books and feel inspired.

Fine art inkjet printing for artists, illustrators, designers & photographers

177 N. 10th Street Rm G, Brooklyn, NY 11211
646 455 3400 | www.skink-ink.com | @skink_ink

Day Jobs

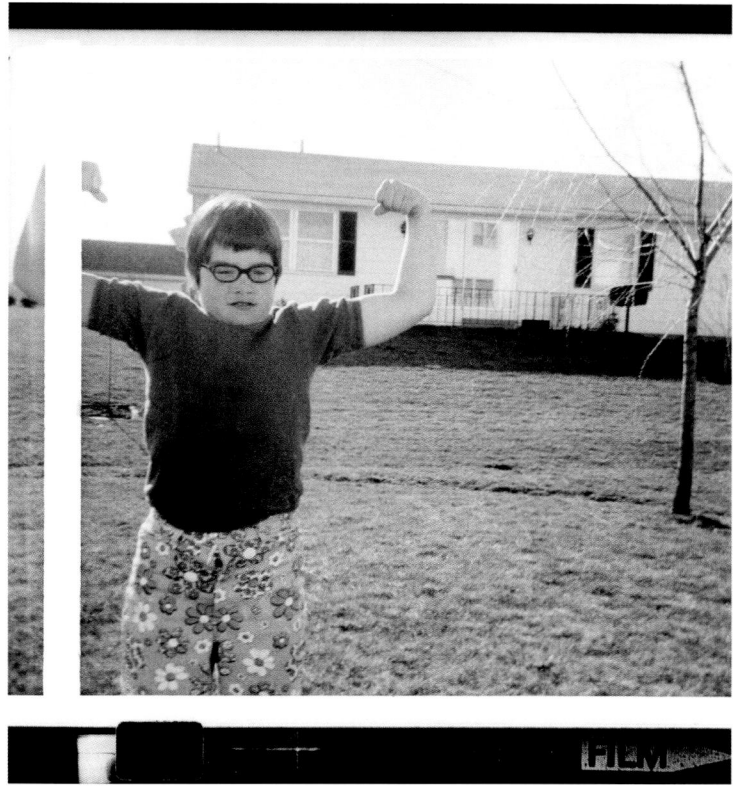

Years before she became a celebrated photographer, Catherine Opie sold greeting cards and loaded trucks.

Kerry Manders

Catherine Opie *loves* to work.

She's been at it since age six, when she began accompanying her dad to the Ohio family business, OP Craft, on weekends, "earning a penny for every cork I put in a salt or pepper shaker, half a cent for every key chain I put together," Opie told me recently. A self-described gearhead, she was enthralled by the factory's machinery, captivated by the process of building things, and enamored of watching her piggy bank grow.

By age eight, Opie had set up her own business. Seeing potential in factory waste, she collected it. "I'd sit on our back patio with my little ax and chop reject pieces of basswood, stuff them into recycled paper bags, then go around the neighborhood in the winter with my wagon selling bags of prime kindling for a dollar," Opie remembers.

Over the years, Opie sold everything from "bad greeting cards" to "Grandpa's garden tomatoes." In her late teens, she worked her "weirdest and least successful" gig, hawking Bibles-cum-photo-albums to Marines. "Picture *this*," she says. "I had to wear a red dress and a feminine straw hat. I was very uncomfortable—scared, even. I lasted a month without selling one unit." Yet door-to-door sales proved an excellent training ground for the future artist; she honed her people skills and learned to handle rejection.

Equally valuable was her first encounter with socially conscious photography. In 1969, Opie wrote a school report on Lewis W. Hine's 1908 photograph of Sadie Pfeifer in a South Carolina cotton mill. Opie was inspired by the idea that photography could "change the laws of this country." She

recounts, "I went home and told my parents that I wanted to be a documentary photographer." They gave her a Kodak Instamatic for her ninth birthday, and she made her first self-portrait—a genre for which she'd later become famous—that same year.

Grades, photographs, money: she always made all three simultaneously. In high school, she did a fast-food stint at Carl's Jr. and documented her school's drama productions, developing the prints in her home darkroom and selling them to the cast. As an undergraduate at the San Francisco Art Institute, Opie worked overnight as a desk clerk at her residence club and picked up an after-school daycare shift at her local YMCA. While pursuing her MFA at the California Institute of the Arts, Opie "loaded trucks on the graveyard shift at a UPS processing plant," quitting only after brutal homophobia and bodily contusions rendered the job untenable.

Opie's parents didn't particularly encourage her artistic pursuits, believing that photography was a fine hobby, not a viable career path. At her dad's insistence, she earned a real estate license after high school and initially attended college in Virginia to become a kindergarten teacher. During her teacher training, Opie showed her dad's then girlfriend, the painter Elinore Schnurr, a box of prints. "You have only ever wanted to do *this*," Opie recalls Schnurr saying. "I don't see you in little chairs for the rest of your life. You need to leave Virginia, move to a major city, and go to art school." Heeding that advice, Opie flourished.

After holding various adjunct positions over the years, Opie landed a teaching position at Yale University in 2000. The move east was brief, though; after just one year, the University of California, Los Angeles, lured her west again with the offer of tenure. She's been teaching there for the past two decades.

Opie is currently enjoying a yearlong sabbatical—the first time in her almost forty-year career that she's focusing exclusively on her art—and promoting the long-awaited and comprehensive survey of her work to date, *Catherine Opie* (2021). "You *always* make your art," Opie says. "This was the reason for all the other jobs I did. *Making my art*. That's the consistent piece of it all."

Kerry Manders is a writer based in Toronto.

Catherine Opie,
Self-Portrait, 1970
Courtesy Regen Projects,
Los Angeles, and Lehmann
Maupin, New York

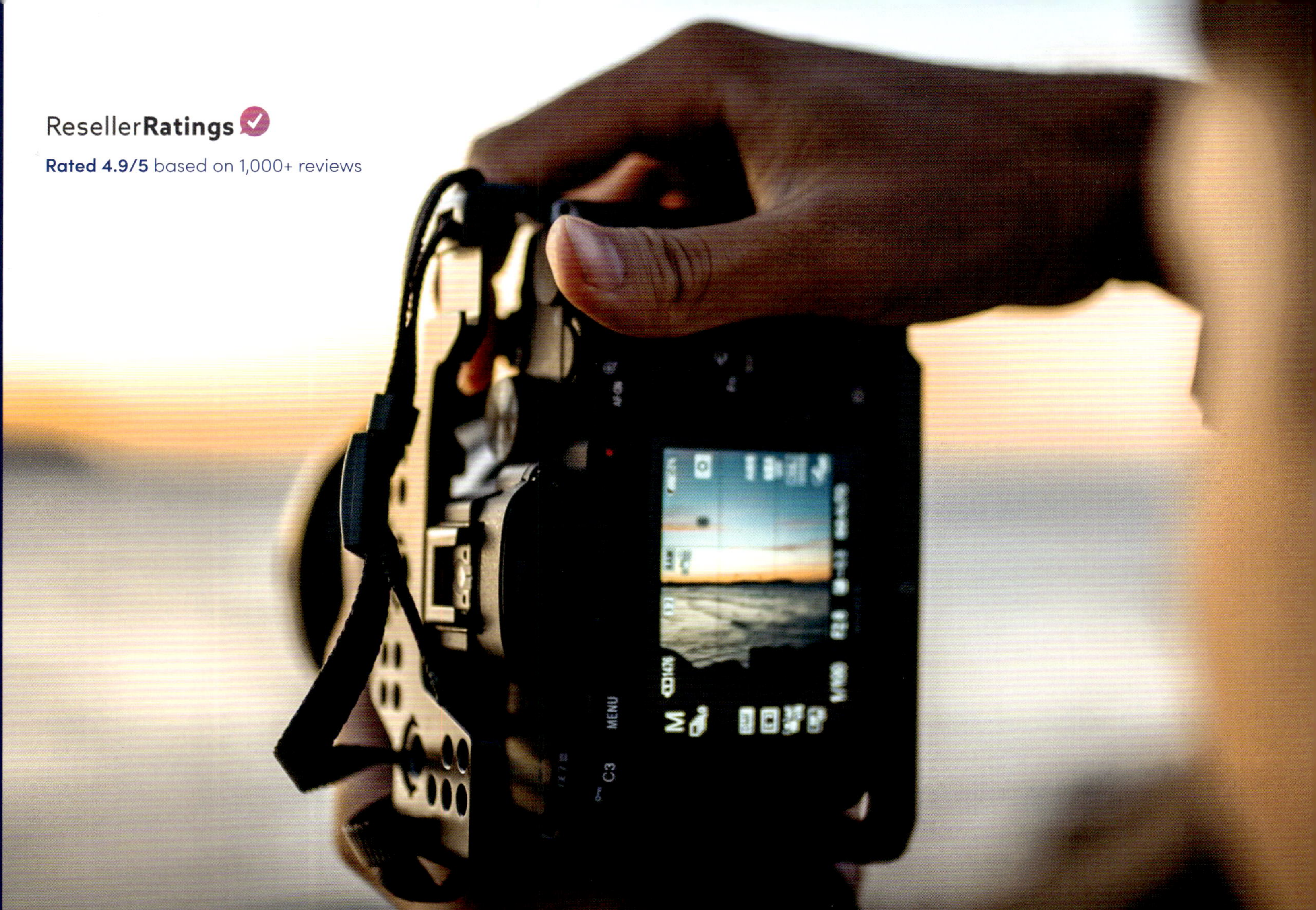

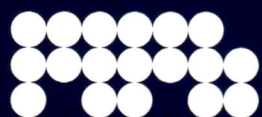

Viewfinder

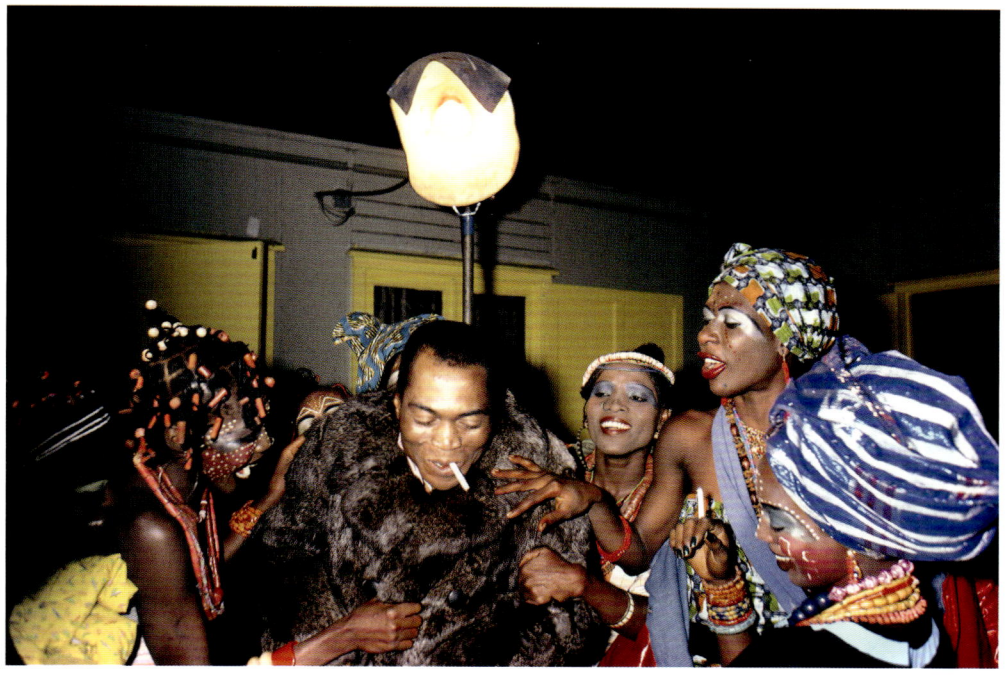

Two recent photobooks offer up nostalgia for nightlife around the world—and offer visions of a post-pandemic future.

Lou Stoppard

To be in a nightclub. Bodies moving in rhythm. The smells—sweat, cigarettes, that sweet tang of a smoke machine. And the beat. The beat, which rewires your movements, your mind. The sway, the ecstasy of release. In that moment, you are saved.

Such memories have been the stuff of lockdown pipe dreams. It is, therefore, both diverting and bittersweet to browse two recently published books on clubbing—one expansive in its broad geography and history, the other contrastingly specific. *Ten Cities: Clubbing in Nairobi, Cairo, Kyiv, Johannesburg, Berlin, Naples, Luanda, Lagos, Bristol, Lisbon 1960–March 2020* (2020) is an ambitious record of these select music scenes. Dave Swindells's *Ibiza '89* (2020) brings together images Swindells made on a short magazine assignment in the summer of 1989, sparked by the influence of the island on the U.K.'s then thriving acid house and rave

scenes, known as the Second Summer of Love.

The books take distinct, even opposing, views. *Ten Cities* tries to push against the idea that clubbing is a frivolous or universal experience, citing, through exhaustive essays from various international figures, the political, economic, geographic, and local particularities of various nightlife scenes. Clubs, the book's editors Johannes Hossfeld Etyang, Joyce Nyairo, and Florian Sievers explain, are "prisms and laboratories of society and the city." *Ten Cities* centers Africa's music and culture, and makes 1960 the narrative starting point because that was when independence swept the continent. "As a general rule, the history of club culture is told without the African musical metropoles," Hossfeld Etyang writes. The authors position Nairobi as their project's home— a vivid picture is painted of the Starlight nightclub where Barack Obama Sr. danced

in the 1960s—before veering off to other cities, chosen in an attempt to disrupt established ideas of certain cities as clubbing meccas and others as backwaters or slums.

Amusingly, *Ibiza '89* does everything *Ten Cities* tries to avoid; it is Eurocentric and fawning (Ibiza, we learn, is "Europe's best party island," according to the music producer Terry Farley), and it paints clubbing as hedonistic and vaguely manic, focusing on the young, the beautiful. Still, the photographs are lovely to look at.

In the 1930s, the South African musician and author Todd Matshikiza, then a young boy, attended a party thrown by the musician Boet Gashe, an event he recalled in 1957, in *Drum* magazine: "You saw the delirious effect of perpetual motion. . . . Perpetual motion in a musty hold where man makes friends without restraint." The line, which captures the heady feel of clubbing, the existential epiphanies found in ephemeral places,

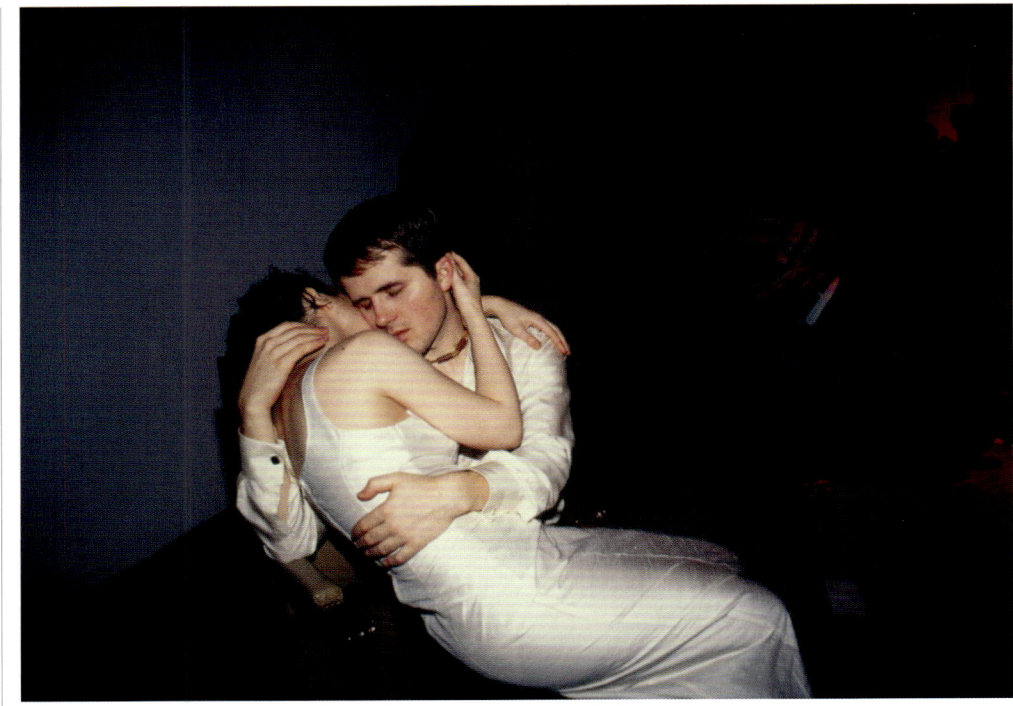

Clubs are shaped not just by dancing bodies and good DJs but also by transport links and governments.

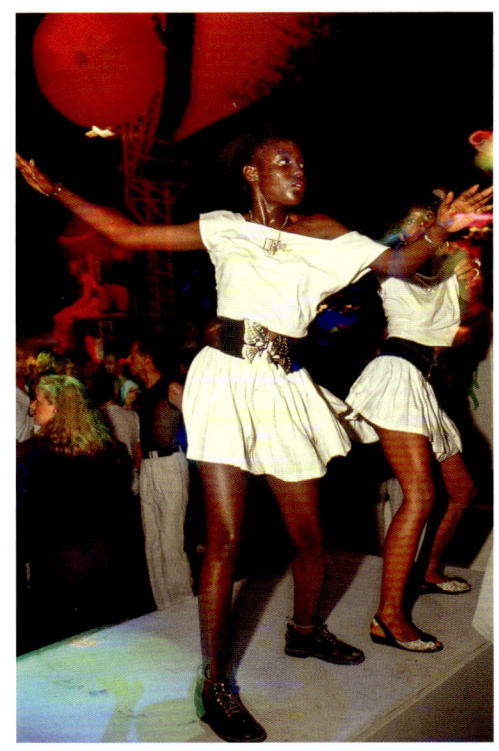

could be a description of any one of the photographs of gyrating revelers in *Ibiza '89*, but it is quoted in *Ten Cities*. Its inclusion there highlights the challenge of analyzing, or indeed photographing, club culture. How does one balance a focus on the shared and at the same time on the specific, the local, the "scene"?

It is notable that so many astounding clubbing photography projects exist— for example, Tod Papageorge's *Studio 54* or Tom Wood's *Looking for Love*. Yet nearly all work around familiar themes: beauty, sex, and glamour, peppered with moments of sexual rejection and flashes of exhaustion. *Ten Cities* is smart in not scrupling to celebrate these familiar elements, while simultaneously homing in on the unexplored, the theoretical, the minutiae. We are reminded that clubs are shaped not just by dancing bodies and good DJs but also by transport links, alcohol taxes, parking spaces, coups, elections, and governments. Yet gems by Jürgen Schadeberg and Tobias Zielony lend a "God, to have been there" air and offset some of the more intensive academic positing.

For those convinced that COVID-19 has decimated nightclubs, it will be uplifting to remember that they have survived big trouble in the past, be it a monthlong, dusk-to-dawn curfew in Nairobi in 1982, regulations that banned amateur bands in Kyiv in the early 1970s, or ad hoc surveillance, such as that of Fela Kuti, whose growing popularity with Lagos crowds briefly irked the Nigerian government, which, ironically, raided him right ahead of FESTAC '77, a landmark international festival celebrating African culture.

If *Ten Cities* encourages reflection, *Ibiza '89* thrills to escapism, embracing the cliché of sun, sea, sand, and sex—the gaze on a thong-clad bottom, the close crops on beautiful youths, the sweat on an entangled couple. It is a fascinating lesson in how myths are made, how rose-tinted glasses are applied. In the book's introduction, Swindells recalls how clubbers on the island would tell him that 1989 was too late, he should have come earlier: "You'd have loved it here in 1987!"

And yet, despite Swindells's mocking tone, his book is driven by the same nostalgia, proffering the idea that those were the glory years, that later, in Farley's estimation, the scene "lost its character." The beauty of the pictures and the hazy memories tussle with the reality briefly alluded to in Alix Sharkey's 1989 essay, produced on the same commission as the images, with its smattered references to burnout, addiction, and local distress. But today's zeitgeist is nostalgic too. Just weeks after its publication, *Ibiza '89* sold out, trading for triple the price on fashion resale sites—evidence of the current thirst for the retro in fashion, photography, and, most visibly, on Instagram. Still, how appropriate. As both *Ten Cities* and *Ibiza '89* show us, great clubs cannot exist without some nostalgia, without the sense of time slipping away, without FOMO, without the intoxicating promise of unrepeatable experiences, all bolstered by fables and hearsay.

Lou Stoppard is a writer and curator based in London.

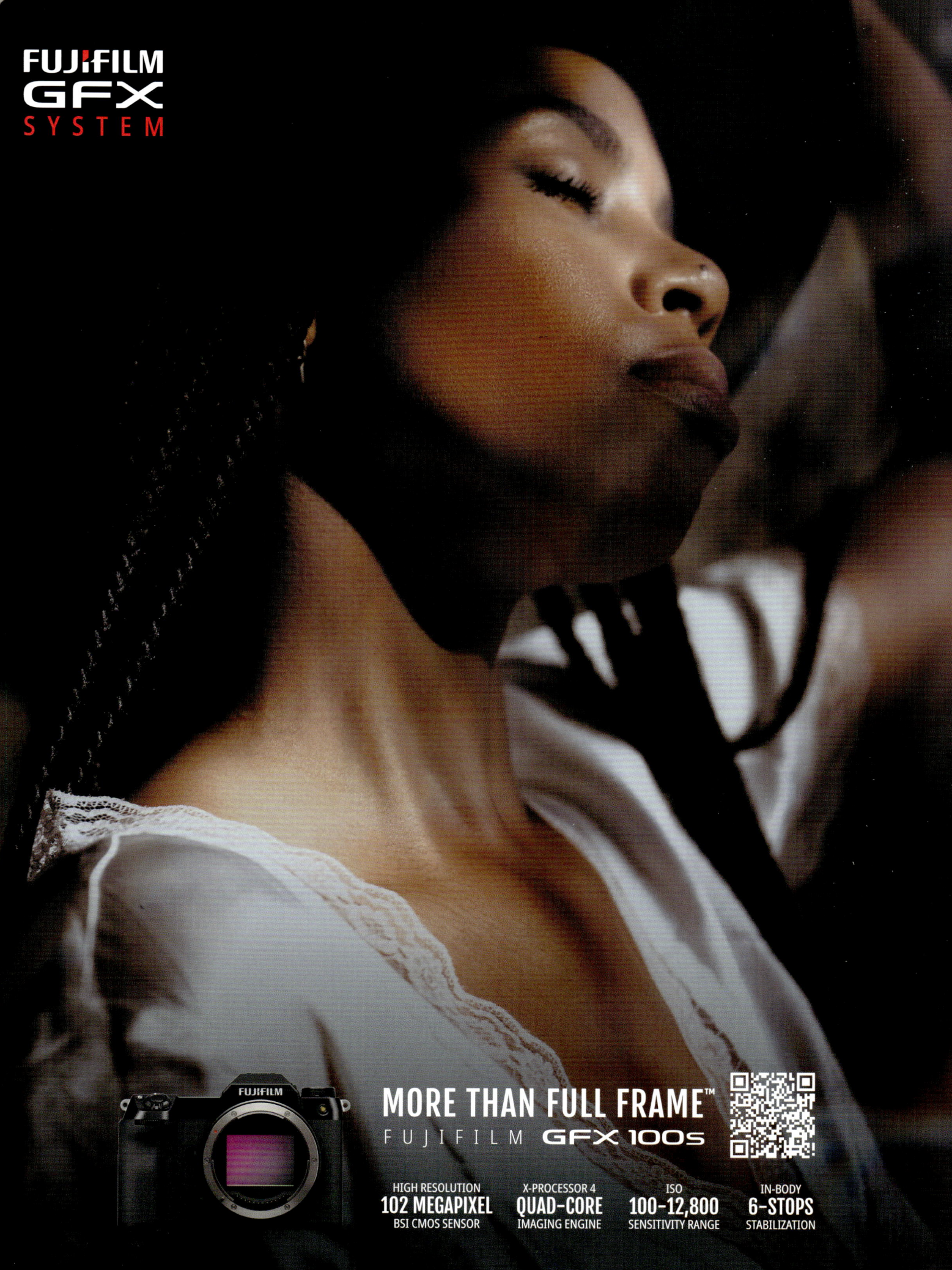

Curriculum
By Geoff Dyer

In the introduction to his latest book, *See/Saw: Looking at Photographs* (2021), Geoff Dyer reflects that writing on pictures has been a "pleasurable sideline for the past couple of decades." He admits that he hasn't really ever had a main line, only a "multitude of sidelines." Dyer's extensive, and eclectic, bibliography suggests as much: he has penned titles on everything from D. H. Lawrence to Andrei Tarkovsky to life aboard an aircraft carrier. His writing on photography is associative, humorous, and sometimes idiosyncratic, while remaining indebted to a background in literature and figures like John Berger. This realm of study can be seen in Dyer's reflections on Eugène Atget, Roy DeCarava, Dayanita Singh, and others, where close reading becomes close looking.

L. Subramaniam, *Le Violon de L'Inde du Sud*, 1980

This was the first piece of South Indian classical music that I really fell for, while living in Paris in the early 1990s: a performance of gorgeous inventiveness and immense rhythmic and spiritual power. Having spent hours trancing out to its intricate, fathomless beauty, I was curious, when I met a young Swiss violinist with ambitions to play in an orchestra, to know what he thought. I lent him the CD but, steeped as he was in the Western classical tradition, he didn't like it at all. "Then you're an idiot," I said. "You'll never be a decent musician. And if you had your violin with you now, I'd shove it up your arse." The memory of his shocked expression at this eruption of doughty English sophistication is as enduring a source of delight as the music itself.

George Eliot, *Middlemarch*, 1871

Reread *Middlemarch* this year, forty-five years after I first read it as a reluctant eighteen-year-old. A masterpiece, obviously, but I'd forgotten what fun it is, how happy you are, after taking a couple of hours off, to pick it up again and find yourself instantly reimmersed in George Eliot's world. Far wittier than I'd remembered too.

Raymond Williams, *Culture and Society 1780–1950*, 1958

Books first read in my early twenties mean more and more to me as I get older, and no book from this time means more to me than Williams's reappraisal and expansion of what constitutes the English literary tradition. In a famous postscript to *The Making of the English Working Class*, Williams's friend E. P. Thompson writes that class is an *experience*. And so, too, is reading. I date my slow emergence from a student mindset to some kind of adult intellectual consciousness from the time I experienced Williams's work.

Fred Eaglesmith and Tif Ginn, 2020

The last gig I went to pre-lockdown—and, at the time of writing, still the last gig I went to—was at McCabe's Guitar Shop, in Los Angeles, to hear Fred Eaglesmith and Tif Ginn. Coincidentally, this was just weeks after I'd started listening to Eaglesmith's dark, moving, very funny, brilliant storytelling in songs. I don't think I've listened so consistently to anyone's songs (as opposed to pieces of instrumental music) except Bob Dylan's. Eaglesmith has been hard at it for a good while, so there are a lot of albums of varying quality. *6 Volts*, from 2012, before he teamed up with (and married) Tif, is the best place to start on a long and wonderful trip.

John Szarkowski, *Atget*, 2004

"Latent in every act of complete reading," writes the literary critic George Steiner, "is the compulsion to write a book in reply." But there's no telling how long it might take to act on this compulsion. In the case of John Szarkowski's *Atget*, there was a delay of almost a decade and a half before I was able to publish my response. Szarkowski reproduces a hundred pictures by Eugène Atget, each accompanied by a little essay on the facing page. I badly wanted to do my own version of a book like this, but the compulsion gradually became a source not of inspiration but torment. And then, after the urge might have been expected to atrophy, the perfect subject fell into my lap— Garry Winogrand!

Friedrich Nietzsche, *Ecce Homo*, 1908

I love Nietzsche and—possibly because I am no kind of scholar myself—I love scholarly editions full of notes and bustling with editorial support. Stanford University Press's epic project of retranslating all of his work has been underway for a while now, often with extended pauses between publication. This newest installment is a volume of six short works— including *Ecce Homo* and *The Case of Wagner*— written late in the day when there were signs that poor Nietzsche's marbles were starting to roll.

Peter Mitchell, *Early Sunday Morning*, 2020

Peter Mitchell's latest book, *Early Sunday Morning*, takes its title from Edward Hopper's painting, and there are faint echoes of the Hopperesque mood of lyrical vacancy in these images of the north of England in the 1970s and '80s. That was a grim time, but there's a promise of a new dawn. One photograph shows a derelict terraced house on which someone has sprayed "Rave On!" next to the gaping hole of a bedroom window. The picture was taken in 1983, so it's like the archaeological discovery of some kind of prophecy—a Rosetta Stone—the meaning of which would only become fully clear years later, when rave culture lit up and transformed the battered nation.

Dayanita Singh, N. Rajam, late 1980s

There's a double pleasure when a photographer one loves takes a picture of someone whose work one loves, as in my friend Dayanita Singh's photograph of the great Indian violinist N. Rajam. I like the way the soloist and her instrument are hemmed in by all of the attendant clutter, especially the gigantic *tampuras* that will form the sonic backdrop to the cosmic intricacy of her playing. It's like Hamlet when he says, "I could be bounded in a nutshell and count myself a king of infinite space, were it not that I have bad dreams." The difference is that Rajam's musical dreams are of a transcendent loveliness.

Opposite, clockwise from top left: Peter Mitchell, *Rave On, Elford Place, Leeds*, 1983; Eugène Atget, *Versailles, Park*, 1901; Cover of Raymond Williams, *Culture and Society, 1780–1950*, 1971; Cover of L. Subrâmaniam, *Le Violon de l'Inde du Sud*, 1980; Cover of Fred Eaglesmith, *Cha Cha Cha*, 2010; Dayanita Singh, N. Rajam, late 1980s

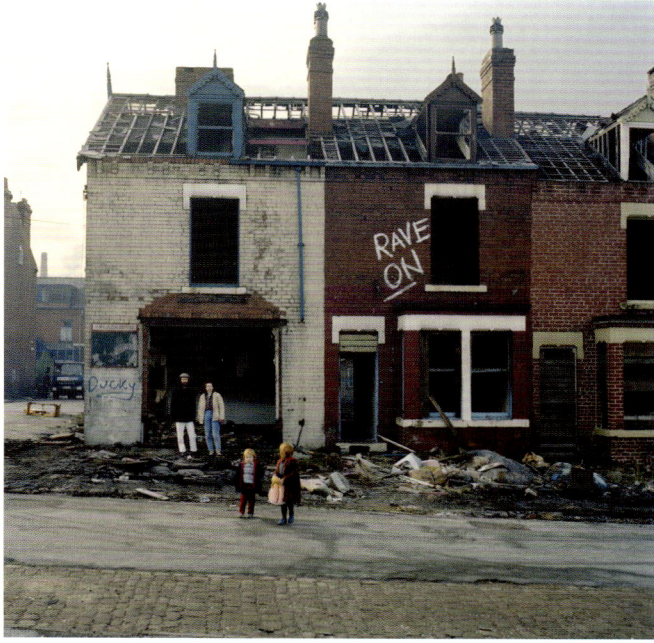
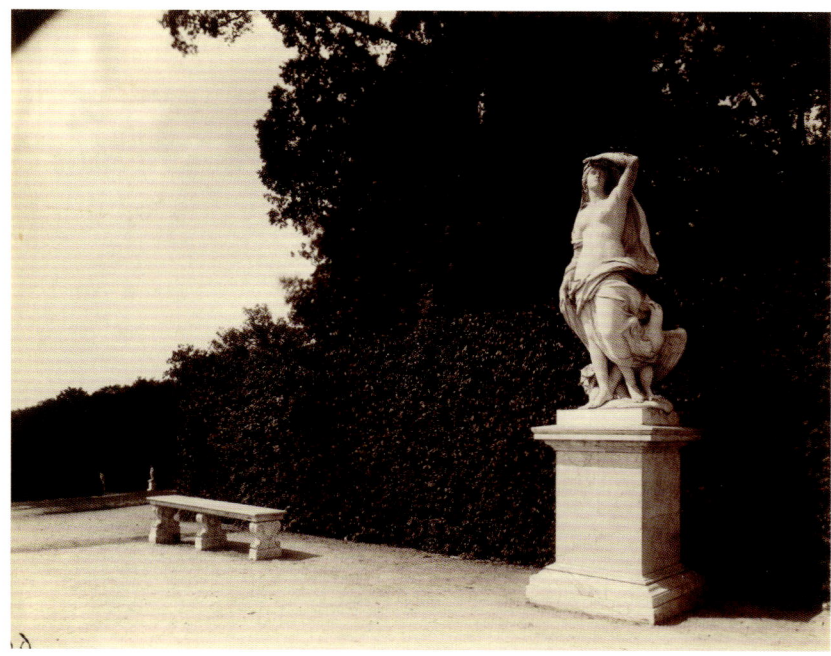
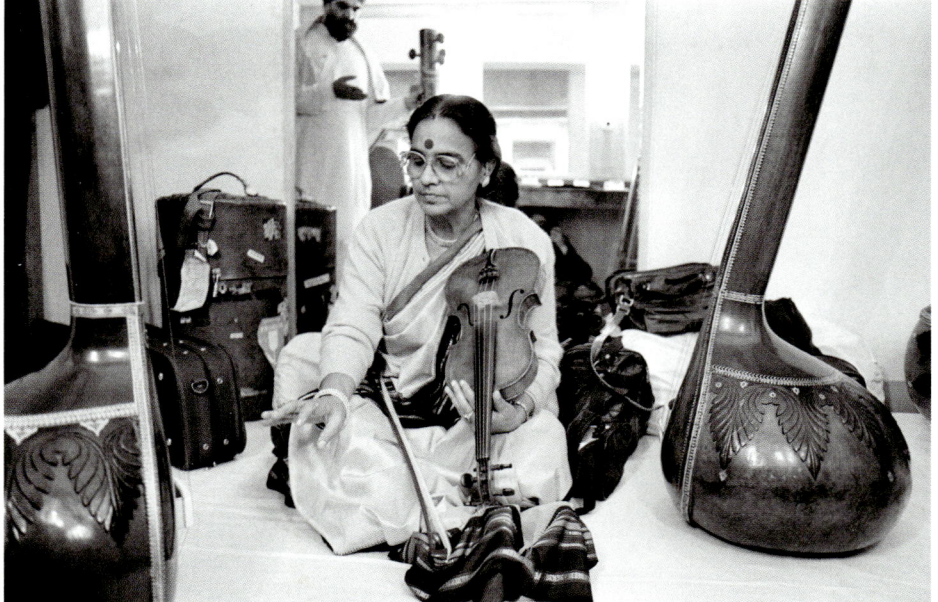
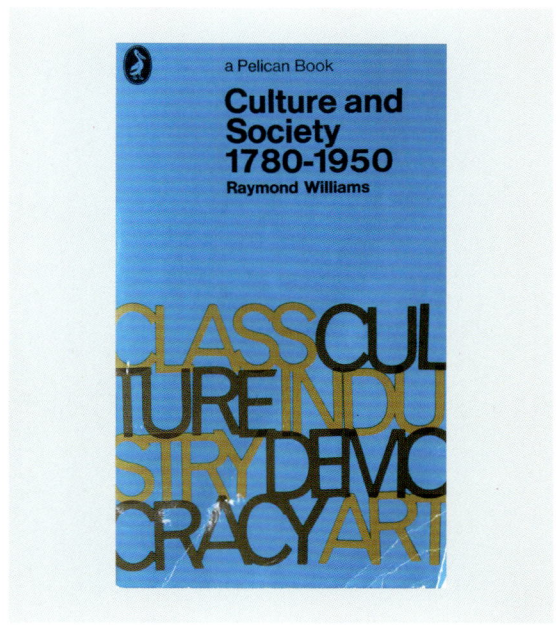
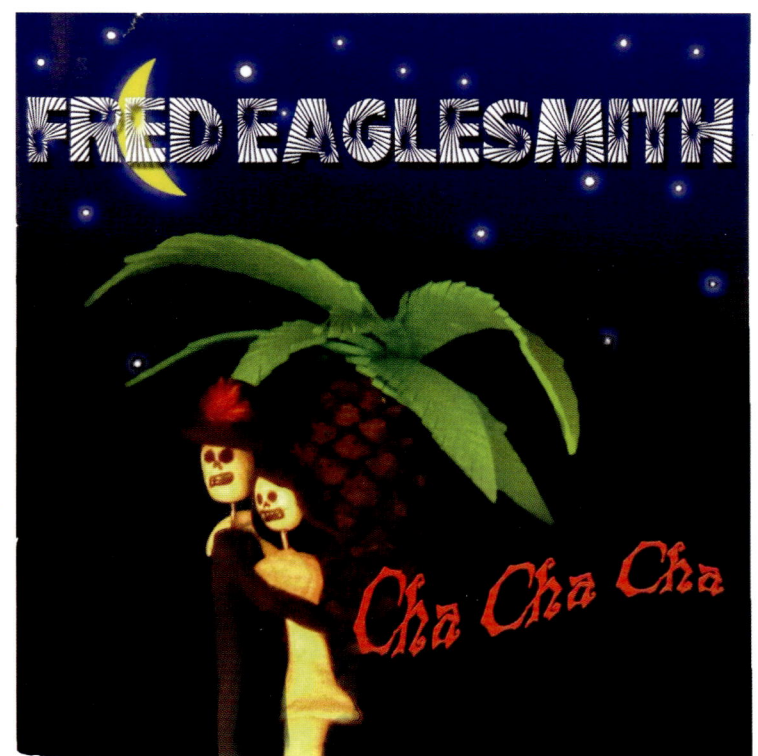
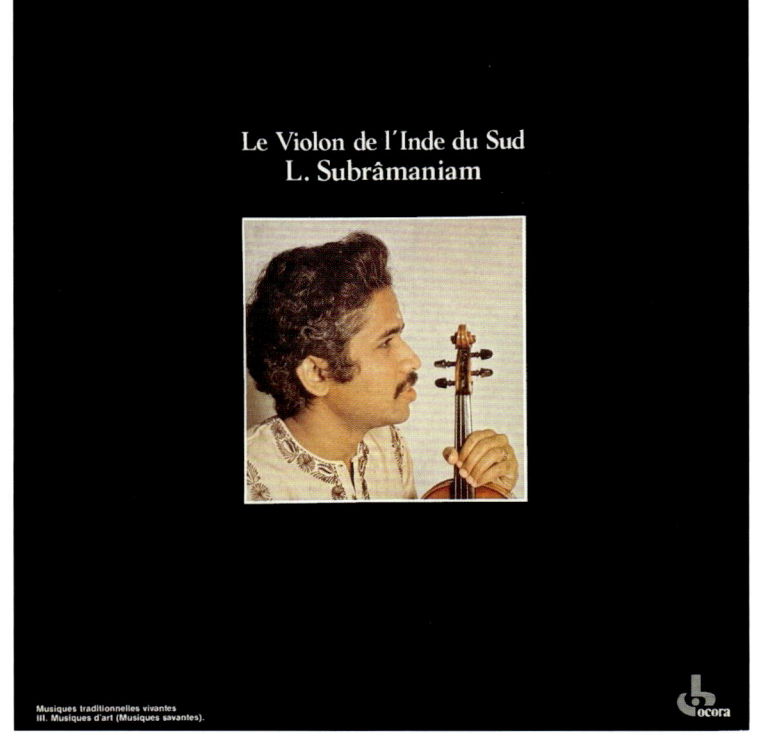

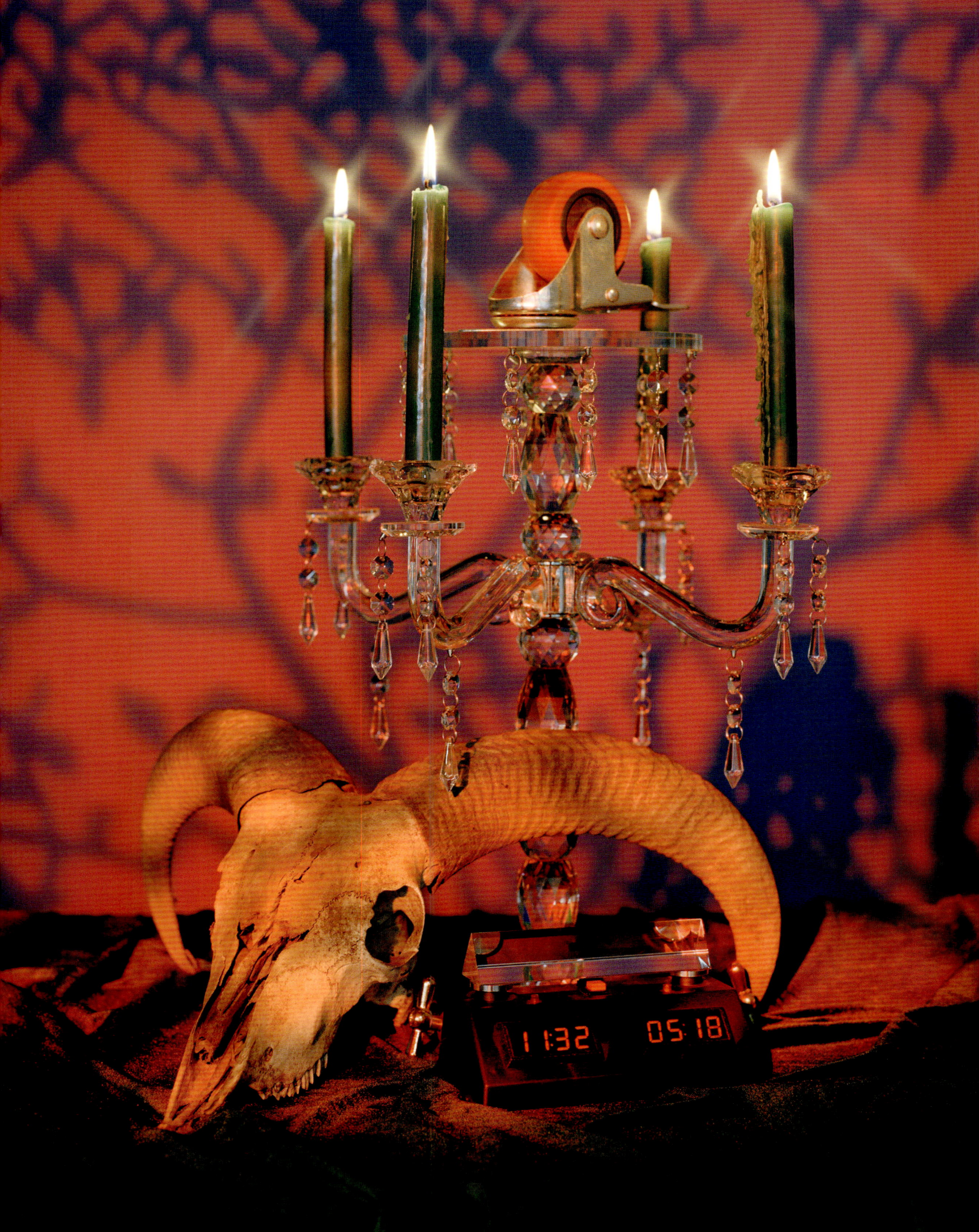

Awol Erizku, *Dada Flex (Slight Drip)*, 2020
Courtesy the artist and
Ben Brown Fine Arts, London
(See page 60)

Cosmologies

In the introduction to his popular 1980 television series *Cosmos*, the astronomer Carl Sagan walks along a rocky headland, illuminated by a magic-hour glow, and ruminates on human fascination with the infinite vastness of the universe. The size and age of the cosmos may be beyond our comprehension, he reflects, but we are driven, nonetheless, to contemplate the mystery of existence. Sagan notes that this allure is not just about the awesome and the unknowable—it is also a story about us, a story about people.

This isn't an issue about astronomy, but rather one that explores the desire to better understand the textures of our local universes, the worlds that artists themselves create—from Deana Lawson's monumental staged portraits tracing cosmologies of the African diaspora to Michael Schmidt's acute observations on the realms within realms of a once divided Berlin. We see how a constellation of strangers in the United States can be brought together through Judith Joy Ross's precise, empathic vision. Across portfolios, we find surreal experiences in the depths of the River Thames, inside a photographer's studio, or among the unexpected oddities of everyday life. In "Cosmologies," artists cast their attention on the great mysteries of personal origins. Tracking their locations in space, time, and history, they remind us of the elegant enigmas that can be unraveled close to home.

—**The Editors**

Deana Lawson

A Conversation with Greg Tate

The Conjurer

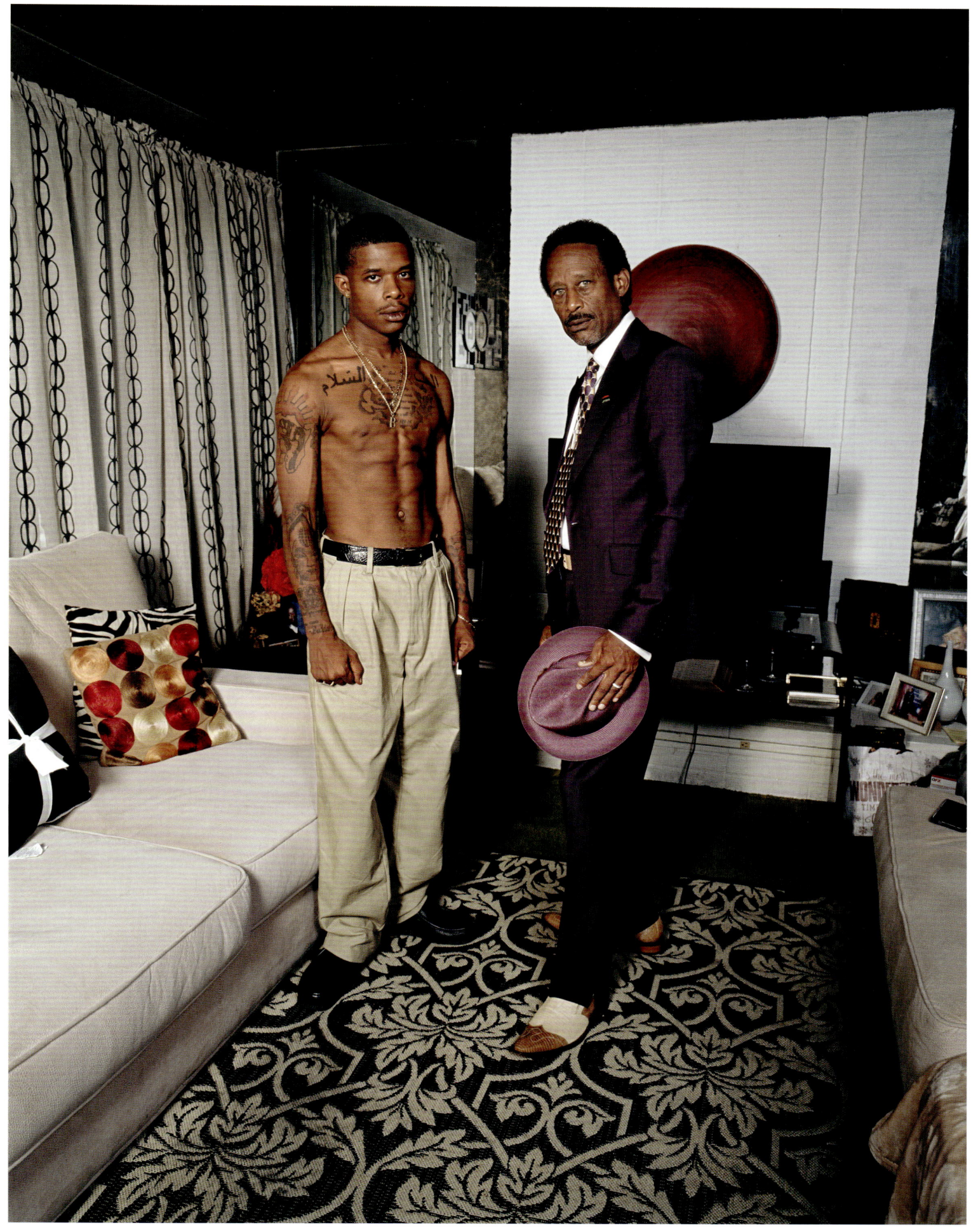

Barrington and Father,
2021

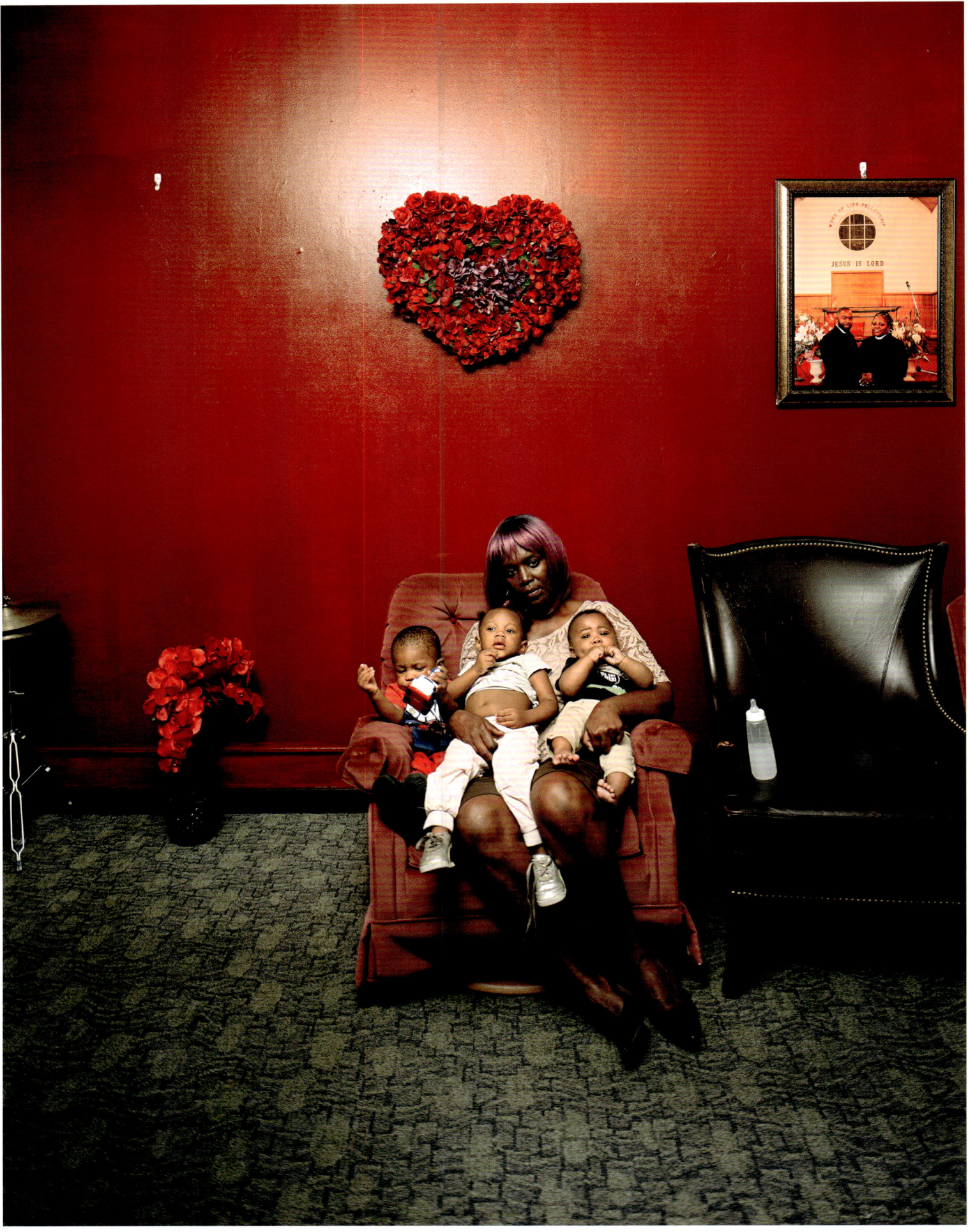

Young Grandmother, 2019

As this is written in early spring, Deana Lawson has two exhibitions up in Manhattan, one at the Guggenheim Museum, where she is presenting her show *Centropy* as the 2020 Hugo Boss Prize winner, and another at Sikkema Jenkins, her gallery in Chelsea. A third major show is upcoming this fall at the Institute of Contemporary Art, Boston.

Lawson's recognition as a profound orchestrator of convulsively charismatic images of Black subjects was inevitable—not least because of her unique depictions of Black folk in domestic spaces in a time of Black pictorial hypervisibility. She has stated that her work "negotiates a knowledge of selfhood through a profoundly corporeal dimension; the photographs speaking to the ways that sexuality, violence, family, and social status may be written, sometimes literally, upon the body."

On another occasion, Lawson revealed to an interviewer some of her primary inspirations: "vintage nudes, Sun Ra, Nostrand Ave., sexy mothers, juke joints, cousins, leather-bound family albums, gnarled wigs, Dana Lawson, purple, the Grizzly Man, M.J., oval portraits, Arthur Jafa, thrift shops, *Breakfast at Tiffany's*, acrylic nails, weaves on pavement, Aaron Gilbert, the A train, *Tell My Horse*, typewriters, Notorious B.I.G., fried fish, and lace curtains." Our brief chat on Zoom revisited a few of these madeleines and sifted in a few more epiphanic treats (and treatises) for good measure.　　　　**—Greg Tate**

Greg Tate: **I want to start off by asking you about your journey to becoming an artist who makes photographs—someone who's pursuing a singular vision through the medium.**

Deana Lawson: Well, one of my earliest memories as a child is trying to build a flying car with my twin sister, Dana. I remember pulling all these things out of the back room from my toy box, and I was so excited that we were going to rig up something that could elevate us off the ground and have us float off into the sky. I had a lunch box for a seat, and some rope, and some other gadgets, but the more we started to work on it, the more I became overwhelmed that what we were trying to make wasn't going to happen. A slow seeping disappointment settled in that we didn't have the knowledge to use the materials we had in our bedroom to make us levitate. So one of my earliest impulses was to make something happen.

I come from a family that wasn't into the learned arts, but art was everywhere, through the way my parents cooked, through language, through the way my cousins could tell a story. My cousin Shannon had a knack for telling these stories that are always strange and unusual about local people in the family. Her laser-like observations about things going on throughout the family are drawn from the way everybody confides in her. And for good reason, because she's the one who takes care of everybody when they get older. I've never met anybody since who can captivate me with their storytelling the way Shannon can.

GT: **She sounds like a combination of a detective, a nurse, and a priest.**

When did you learn that photographs are a medium that could possibly provide you with that degree of storytelling detail and intimacy?

DL: I don't know how much a picture can tell a story, but definitely the first time I saw Diane Arbus's photographs, when I was in college, and something in the subjects' faces and their postures . . . I felt like I was looking at them and at the photographer at the same time, and that was when I knew it was possible. Though I would get a similar impact looking at my father's pictures in our family albums. Except those were people I knew.

GT: **Your father was pretty consistent about taking pictures?**

DL: *Very* consistent. Always had his camera when we traveled, whenever we had an event, birthdays, Christmases.

GT: **When did you start taking pictures of the family?**

DL: My first year in grad school at RISD. I wasn't plugged into a Black community in Rhode Island, and I didn't want to take pictures of myself. So, I figured I should go back home to Rochester, to what I knew. I asked my mom to put on a wedding dress in our living room. And when I brought that picture back to a critique at RISD with Sarah Charlesworth—who was lukewarm at the time about my work—she said, "Here is something that you need to revisit." So I continued returning to Rochester to photograph my cousins and my aunts. I showed a picture of my aunt at Rush Arts, around 2000, where I had her wear a sequined dress. Her living room is ivory leather, and a there's a little menagerie of objects, and she always has long acrylic nails and is poised and beautiful. That was another sign—photographing my family in spaces they inhabit. There was a transformation that was beginning to happen. I realized that I didn't need to bring them to a studio. That was when I began to recognize the power of the

What I'm doing integrates mythology, religion, empirical data, dreams. It's about Blackness, but it's about something else too.

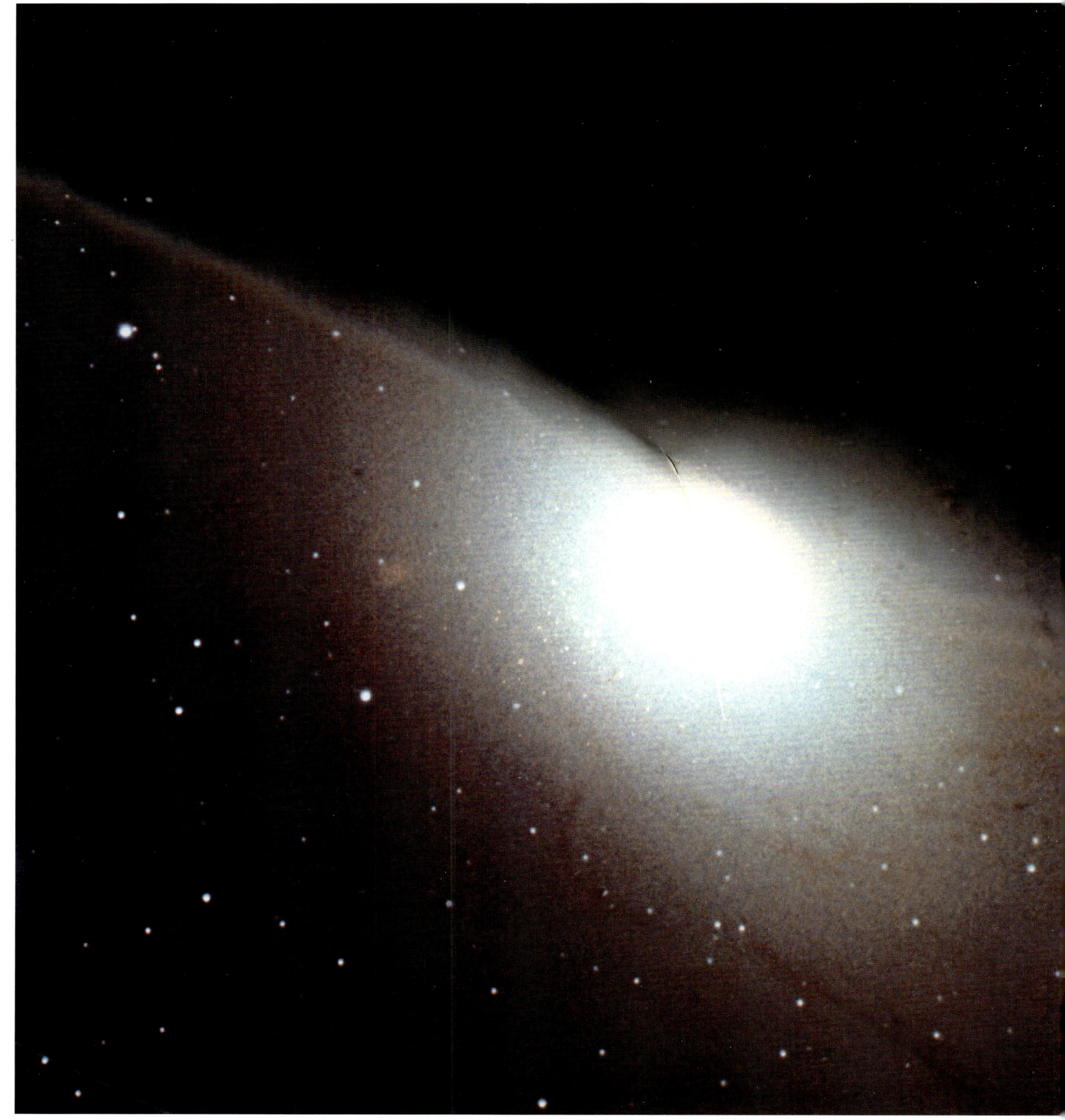

Black Horizons, 2020

interior space and the power of the figure coming together.

GT: **After a time, you moved outside of the family circle in pursuit of the strange and familiar.**

DL: Eventually, I felt like I'd exhausted something working with family and realized that what I was looking for wasn't only found in blood kin. I started to go to church in Rhode Island because I didn't know how else to find Black people there. I remember one woman named Hazel, who I photographed at the church in front of a curtain. It looked like it was in a private space because churches have this feel that's private but not domestic. I was looking for community besides my party-crowd grad-school friends. And a yearning for home.

GT: **Let's go back. What compelled you to pursue art with a capital A for your initial university education? Still quite the leap for some Black middle-class families.**

DL: Yes. Well, when I went to undergrad, I went for business. Dana and I were dressing alike because we always envisioned working as a team. We had gone to a high school that promoted STEM and that was what success was to us. So at Penn State, we went into international business. It was a beautiful year to be in college, that freshman year between 1997–98. The years *The Miseducation of Lauryn Hill*, *Mos Def and Talib Kweli Are Black Star*, and Erykah Badu's *Baduizm* were in the ether, and during the same time we attended the Million Woman March. Things started to crack open in terms of these existential questions: Who am I? What am I here for? Dana decided to leave business school and switch over to African American studies and English. A good friend of ours became deeply involved in poetry, and I realized spoken word wasn't for me, and that I'd always wanted to do fashion design. I applied to Parsons, but they denied me, and I'm so happy they did or I might not be talking to you today. I was moping until I read Iyanla Vanzant, and she was saying, "Whatever is in you must come out, or it'll kill you." That's when I decided to transfer to Penn State's art school, where the students were a bit stranger. Of course, my parents didn't know what was going on with their daughters. We'd left home for college with perms and shoulder-length hair and came back with dreadlocks.

GT: **Y'all got turned out by Lauryn Hill! That bohemian intervention is so necessary for so many of us who were raised properly. Discovering that, Oh, you can be Black and walk round in the world looking like that. In terms of art school, did you take drawing, painting, and sculpture classes?**

DL: Yes. I remember my sculpture teacher introduced me to the work of Kara Walker. I went to the library and looked at her silhouettes. I saw fantasy and nightmare and circus and speaking to history. I knew I was definitely in the right area. The next semester, I enrolled in photography and discovered Arbus. That sealed the deal.

GT: **At a certain point, you start to unabashedly render nakedness and Black flesh and Black folk exposing themselves to your camera in domestic spaces. I'm curious whether you see your work as some kind of statement about Blackness and photography.**

DL: I don't think I ever meant to make a statement about Blackness directly, but I remember looking at many nudes, and not being impressed, and saying, "If I had done this, I would've . . ."

GT: **Upped the game, ha!**

DL: [*laughs*] I always knew that I had a certain vantage point as a woman—most of the nudes I saw were by men, and I had a whole other idea of what the erotic and desire looked like. But it was a slow process. I recall looking at some of Katy Grannan's pictures in grad school—her project *The Poughkeepsie Journal*, where she put ads in newspapers and went to the houses of people who responded to her ads. I was interested in how she was working. I began looking closer at the power of melanated skin in color, not black and white, and how, if you captured it in color with the right sort of lighting, with the pose, and the space, that it could be transcendent. So, I just kept at it without trying to make a statement about Blackness. And I still don't know if I am. But there was curiosity and a strong conviction about putting certain elements together and what could happen.

GT: **At a certain point, you became more emboldened and audacious in terms of your verbal interaction and your directorial demands on people. What occasioned those breakthroughs? What got you to break your own fourth wall and go beyond what your subjects were, maybe, comfortable with?**

DL: Part of it was figuring out what I was willing to do in order to make something happen. There was a woman in Harlem I met online when I was living in New Haven, and I decided to drive to Harlem and make this photograph. Distant travel started to open up. That woman, Berette Macauley, and I ended up becoming lifelong friends, and she and another subject helped me go to Jamaica. That led to me traveling to other places that I wasn't familiar with.

GT: **I know that you've dealt with resistance from subjects in sometimes contentious negotiations, which required another level of being emboldened and audacious. At what point did you decide that you were going to be more like a film director, like, I'm going to get this shot no matter what?**

DL: It takes a lot of psychic energy when you get rejected. It still hurts me. It's like a punch in my stomach. It takes a lot to go up to a stranger sometimes and not know what's going to happen. I haven't done it in a while, but I've seen people on the train I want to go up to and realized that I'm not ready yet. I'm never super confident about that.

GT: **Are you saying you have no spidery-sense, or that you've been known to ignore it?**

DL: Both. I do have a spidery-sense, but sometimes I'll ignore it when I feel

If I can put pictures out there that represent truth as I see it, it's like being a news reporter and a great philosopher.

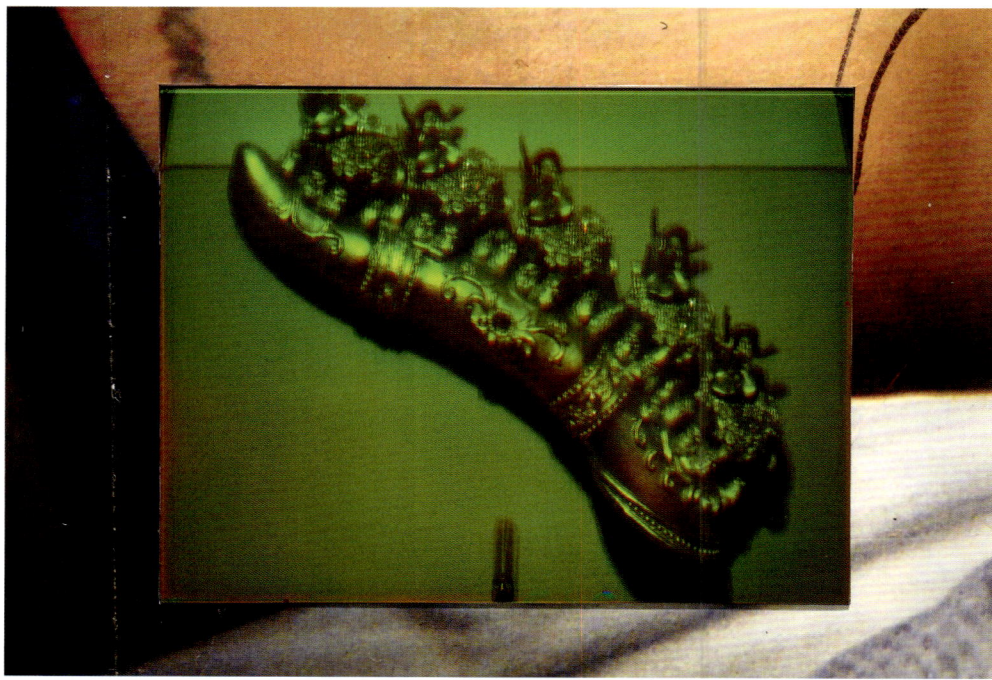

Installation view of *Deleon? Unknown*, 2020, with hologram detail, in *Deana Lawson: Centropy*, Solomon R. Guggenheim Museum, New York, 2021
Photograph by Thomas Müller

compelled enough. Luckily, knock on wood, I've gotten some amazing results from situations that could've been not good. But there's a part of me that is bold and believes that the picture must prevail *at all costs*.

GT: **Photography brings its own level of power and seduction: What are the ethics of making art with real people? Then the whole situation arises that whatever you put in a gallery is a representation of Black folks, and you're setting yourself up as middle ground between Blackness and the white gaze. There's the ethics of that too.**

DL: I think photography is a slippery slope especially when you're dealing with somebody's likeness, somebody's body. This is the one technological medium in the arts that's seen as a record of the creative, autographic arts, meaning "made with the hand," same as painting and sculpture. Yet people will take a photograph as the truth more than any other medium. In that sense, there is a certain power to it. And if I can put pictures out there that represent truth as I see it, it's like being a news reporter and a great philosopher.

At the same time, I know that I'm showing at predominantly white spaces. My goal was to become so big that eventually the name becomes so popular that it becomes a household name, and more Black folks would have access to the work without having the fine-art knowledge of white spaces. For me, my heroes were artists like Basquiat. I want to be big like Basquiat, except I'm using a camera where he was using paints. I hope to make work that speaks two tongues so that the community I am making the work of would know what I am talking about.

GT: **Toni Morrison was once asked if she expected the people she was writing about to read her books. She said, "No, but if they did read them, they would recognize themselves in them."**

DL: Exactly, because not only would that community know what I'm talking about, but they would know it better than curators who have the art language. And I've had proof of this—I've had friends and strangers who aren't in the art world look at the work and pick up on subtle shit and have a complex language to talk about it more so than curators who default to me out of fear of not knowing how to talk about the work. I'm not afraid of the white gaze or exploitation because I know my intentions. My goal is to raise consciousness about Blackness in a certain proximity and

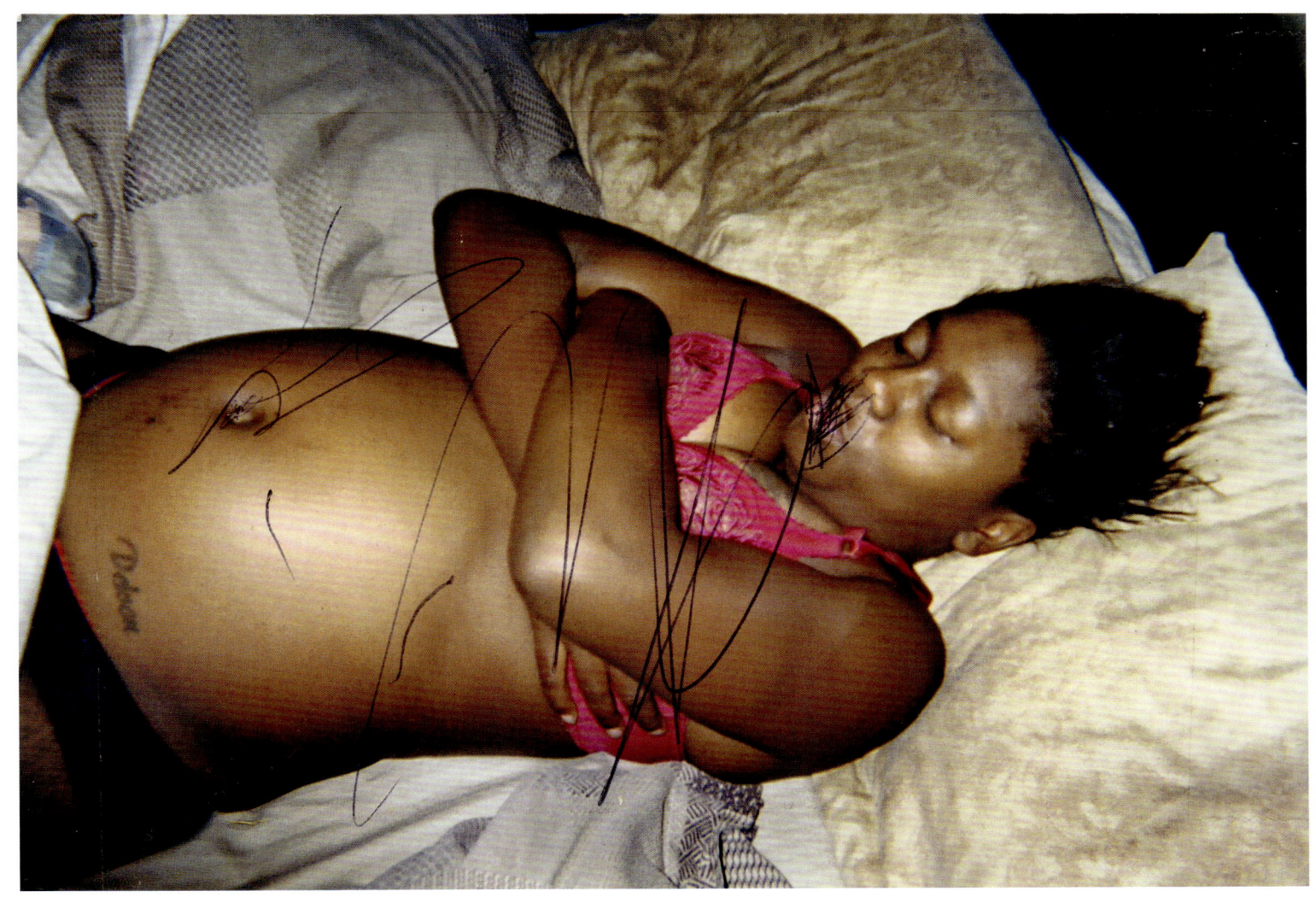

Deleon? Unknown, 2020

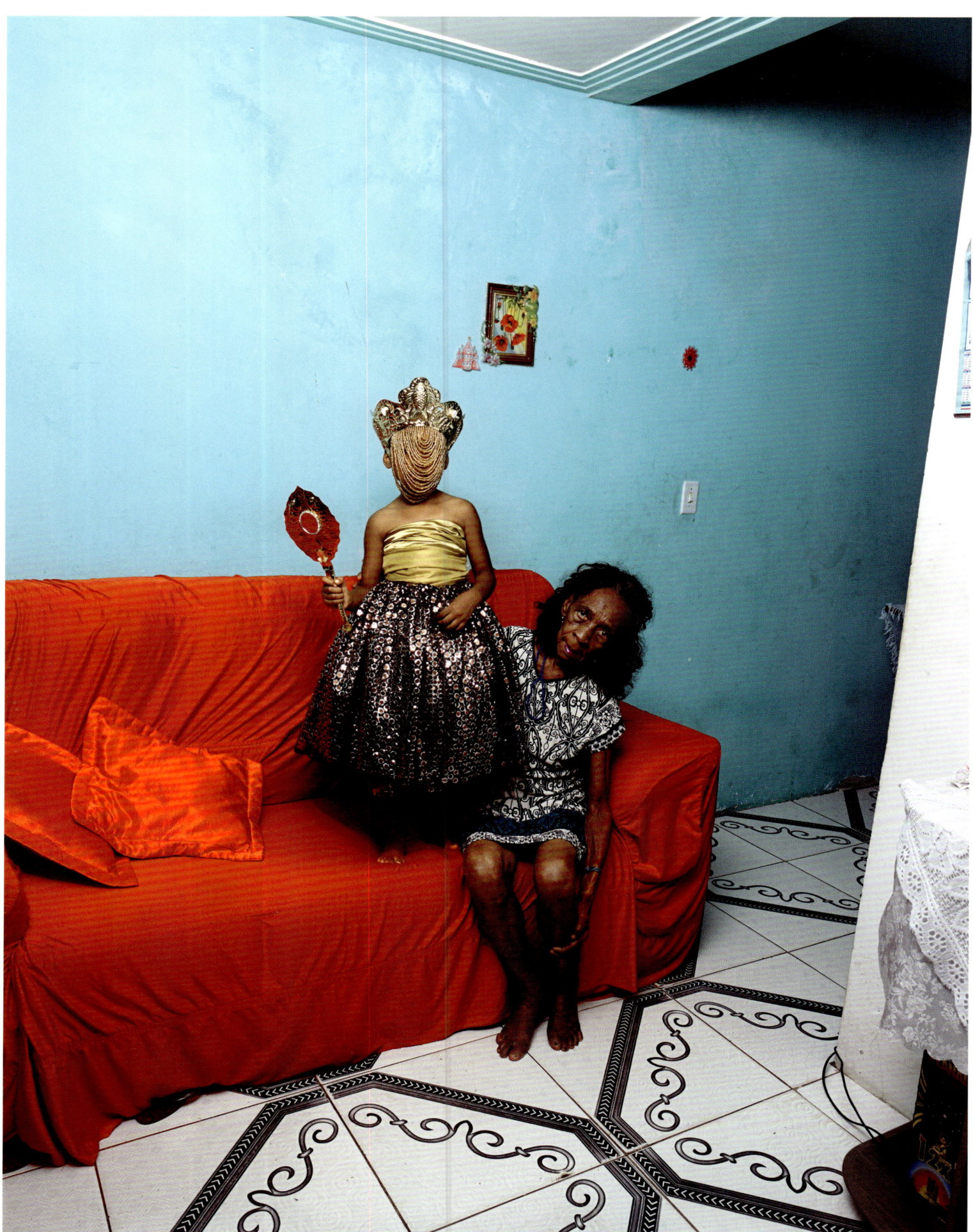

An Ode to Yemaya, 2019
All photographs © the artist and courtesy Sikkema Jenkins & Co., New York, and David Kordansky Gallery, Los Angeles

framework that's about transforming power and ideas of value.

I don't know if people truly understand—or maybe because I haven't vocalized it yet—the scope of the work. That it's trying to push other ways of knowing, in other fields. If, say, I was born in other lifetimes, in Haiti, I would probably be the woman selling jewelry on the side of the road with a creative force that has to come out. Or, if I was born in 800 BCE would I have been a priestess? Or doing some alchemy? The tools I've chosen for this lifetime are modern technology, but the spirit behind them . . .

GT: **Conjure! Voodoo! Hard to get across in conversation but very present in the work.**

DL: Yeah! What I'm doing integrates mythology, religion, empirical data, dreams. People try to position me as just taking pictures of Black bodies, but if we were taking Blackness as a norm, what else would we be paying attention to in the pictures? It's about Blackness, but it's about something else too.

GT: **You shot in Jamaica, and you shot in the DRC [Democratic Republic of the Congo], and in Haiti twice; you level those worlds of Black difference because of your intimate approach. We may not know where the pictures were taken, we just know it's always with Black folk at home, with themselves, and there's no sense of any gaze around that's outside of that tribe. Once you go into another culture as an American with a camera, all kinds of anthropological baggage follows you there. How do you think of yourself in those places as opposed to more familiar African American spaces?**

DL: I'm highly aware of myself as an outsider in those spaces because I don't speak the language often, but I embrace that outsider position. I think of other projects in photographic history where the photographer wasn't American, and it's almost like they have an edge . . . a clarity because of their position as a foreigner. The most obvious would be Robert Frank's *The Americans* or Jacob Holdt's *American Pictures*. Or Bertien van Manen, a Dutch woman photographing in Appalachia, resulting in her work *Moonshine*—her work is insane. So even though we know the role of the outsider historically has contained gaps of misinterpretation, implied ethnographic viewpoints, and racism, there are these outliers, examples where that removed vantage point (or

bird's-eye view) delivered something that rings with clarity and beauty. Also keep in mind, I am an artist, not a documentarian. I am continually destabilizing the image as a record or document, since my directorial hand is so strong. The final composition that the figure and I arrive at may or may not have anything to do with the person(s) I am depicting.

GT: **I want to go back to conjuring and religious imagery and talk about the presence of holograms and cosmologies in your new work.**

DL: Holography, at its best, is truly enigmatic, no other process that I know activates my psyche in this way. For me, holograms are a means to push consciousness through visuality. A way to imagine a possible field, invisible to the human eye, but one that could potentially become visible through holography. The first full holographic/photographic piece I made was *Deleon? Unknown* (2020). In this image, an anonymous figure lies on her back, her eyes are closed, her arms are unusually crossed, almost like an Egyptian mummified figure. Her pose oscillates between rest and death, and yet her body, particularly her stomach, seems full of life . . . Is she five months pregnant? The pen scribble made by my child Grace is concentrated around the mouth and looser by the arms and belly. The hologram near her stomach depicts an elephant tusk–like object, which may be difficult to decipher. The hologram glows an alien greenish yellow. Perhaps I was drawn to this tusk because it conjured childhood memories of my mother's elephant collection . . . or maybe I was channeling the Kingdom of the Edo people in Benin City, where real carved elephant tusks served as spiritual points of contact and were placed on elaborate shrines dedicated to divine kings. The sum of all parts here—the found picture, a child's mark, the hologram of the tusk, the mirror frame—creates a vibrating unnameable thing. The inlaid glass hologram inside a traditional photographic print amplifies the supra-sensible within the real, which is a metaphor for how lived experiences could operate.

GT: **You've figured out a way to augment the sense of mystery. You've told me that your holographer initially told you that it would be difficult to insert a holograph into a regular picture. I thought, Never tell a sister there's no way to do something she wants to do. MLK said that we were the veterans of creative suffering, but we're also the veterans of creative speculation.**

DL: That's the truth. The holograms are so sensitive to light that the laser hitting the picture has to be relatively at a 45-degree angle to be perceivable. I had to figure out how to have this piece of glass in the picture be placed like a jewel and be flush to the picture. In his essay "The Work of Art in the Age of Mechanical Reproduction," Walter Benjamin compares the painter to the magician and the photographer to the surgeon. The painter is doing tricks like a magician, but the photographer is like a surgeon using a knife to cut into the body, slicing into the real world, into reality, making that incision. Like you're taking this frozen moment from real time, that's fixed and will never move, and seeing what kind of alchemy *can occur*.

Greg Tate is a Harlem-based writer and musician. He is the author of several books, including *Flyboy 2: The Greg Tate Reader* (2016).

Anne Hardy
Return of the Light

Lena Fritsch

Soft color fields, obscure chemical compositions, hazy space photographs—Anne Hardy's recent work presents us with evocative photograms that oscillate between the concrete and abstract, between the real and the fantastical. The hard-to-define images move gradually from an inky black to bright hues. Their color palette ranges from cool blue and turquoise tones to warm reds and orange tints, conveying an alternation between coolness and heat, or—as the title of one image suggests—the "rising of heat."

The photograms are based on encounters with light and small objects that Hardy gathered from the foreshore of the River Thames while she was working on her 2019 commission for Tate Britain, *The Depth of Darkness, the Return of the Light*. The large-scale, dystopian installation transformed the museum's neoclassical façade into an abandoned building decorated with fairy lights, ripped banners, and a rhythmical cascade of objects. The dark, mystical aesthetic was accompanied by a soundscape that used elements recorded at the river.

Hardy's first photograms came into existence in 2015, when she was working on an exhibition at Modern Art Oxford. Using leftover materials and dusty debris swept up from the studio floor, she made a series titled *Process Photograms* that is comparable to the photograms of *The Depth of Darkness, the Return of the Light* in its atmospheric aesthetic. Through intuitive as well as highly controlled alchemical darkroom processes, Hardy composed her recent photograms during lockdown. London, usually bustling and busy, showed its vulnerability and was forced to stand still. Against this background, the link of the photograms to Hardy's immersive Tate work seems particularly fitting, as the installation was essentially, according to Hardy, "about a point of collapse and fragility and what might spring from that as a result." The Thames debris can be viewed as a sad representation of the extreme threat we humans cause the planet, which is gradually heating up. It symbolizes countless untraceable people and their long-lasting impacts on the earth, linking different times and spaces.

However, *The Depth of Darkness, the Return of the Light* is a multilayered photogram series that references the micro as much as the macro, the tangible outside as much as the intimate inside, physical space as much as perception, the conscious as much as the unconscious. The fragments from the river convey an infinite planetary aesthetic, and real objects suggest fantastical images. Asked about these relationships and transformations, Hardy has stated: "I'm interested in the 'gap' between what you call the concrete and the abstract as a productive space of reencounter and imagination, in which knowledge or certainty becomes more tenuous. . . . The micro and infinite seem interchangeable to me. It's all about your perception and what scale of measurement you decide to apply—the same systems and energies are at work."

Whether the atmospheric photograms are viewed as depictions of tiny river objects or as fantastical space images, the series draws attention to time and its endless cycles of transformation, as reflected in titles such as *Rising Heat* or *Into Darkness*. Hardy herself stresses the potential of change. In the soft forms and bright colors of her photograms, there is a sense of postapocalyptic magic that turns old waste into new, beautiful art.

Lena Fritsch is a writer on photography and curator of modern and contemporary art at the Ashmolean Museum, University of Oxford.

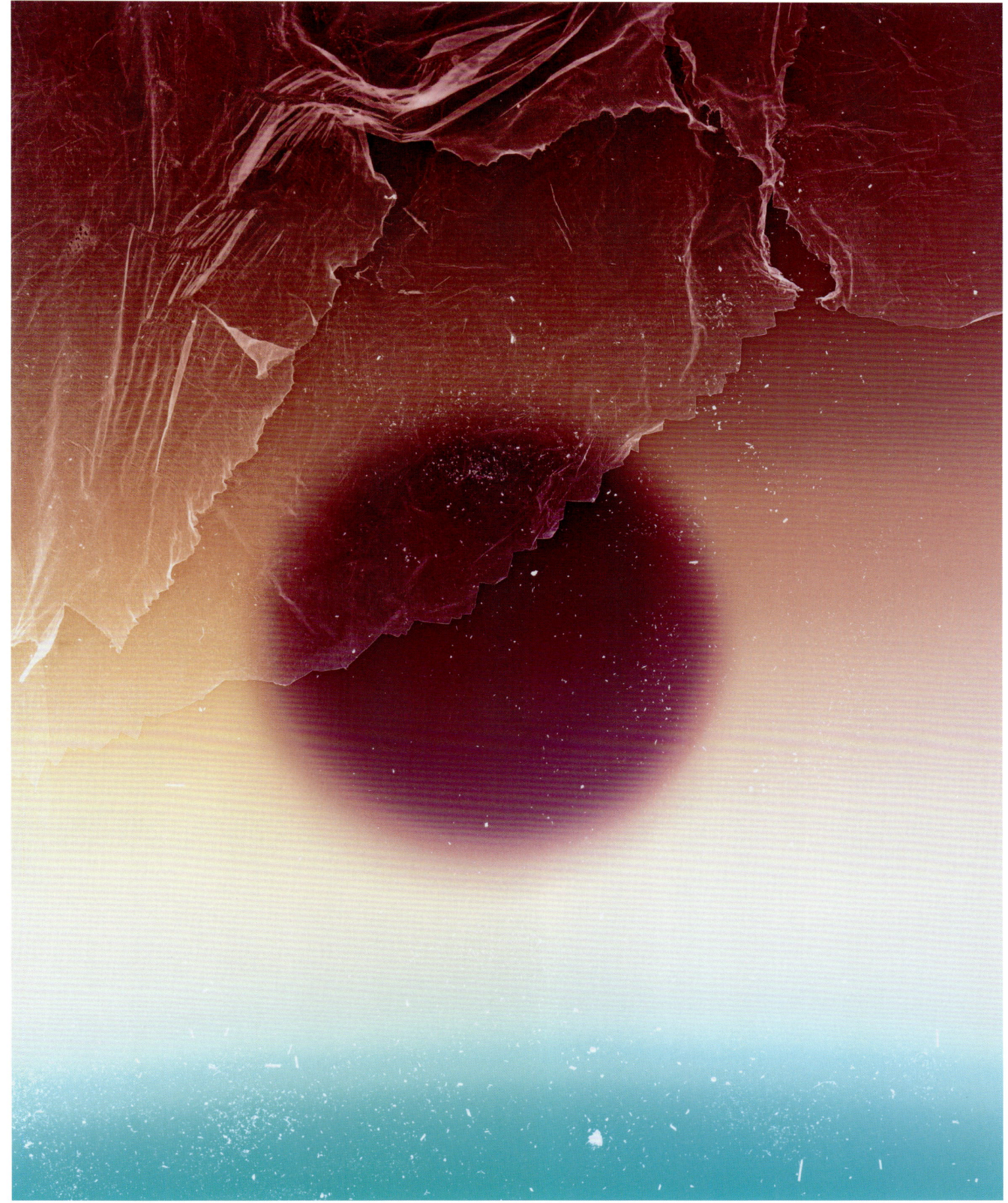

Equilibrium, 2020

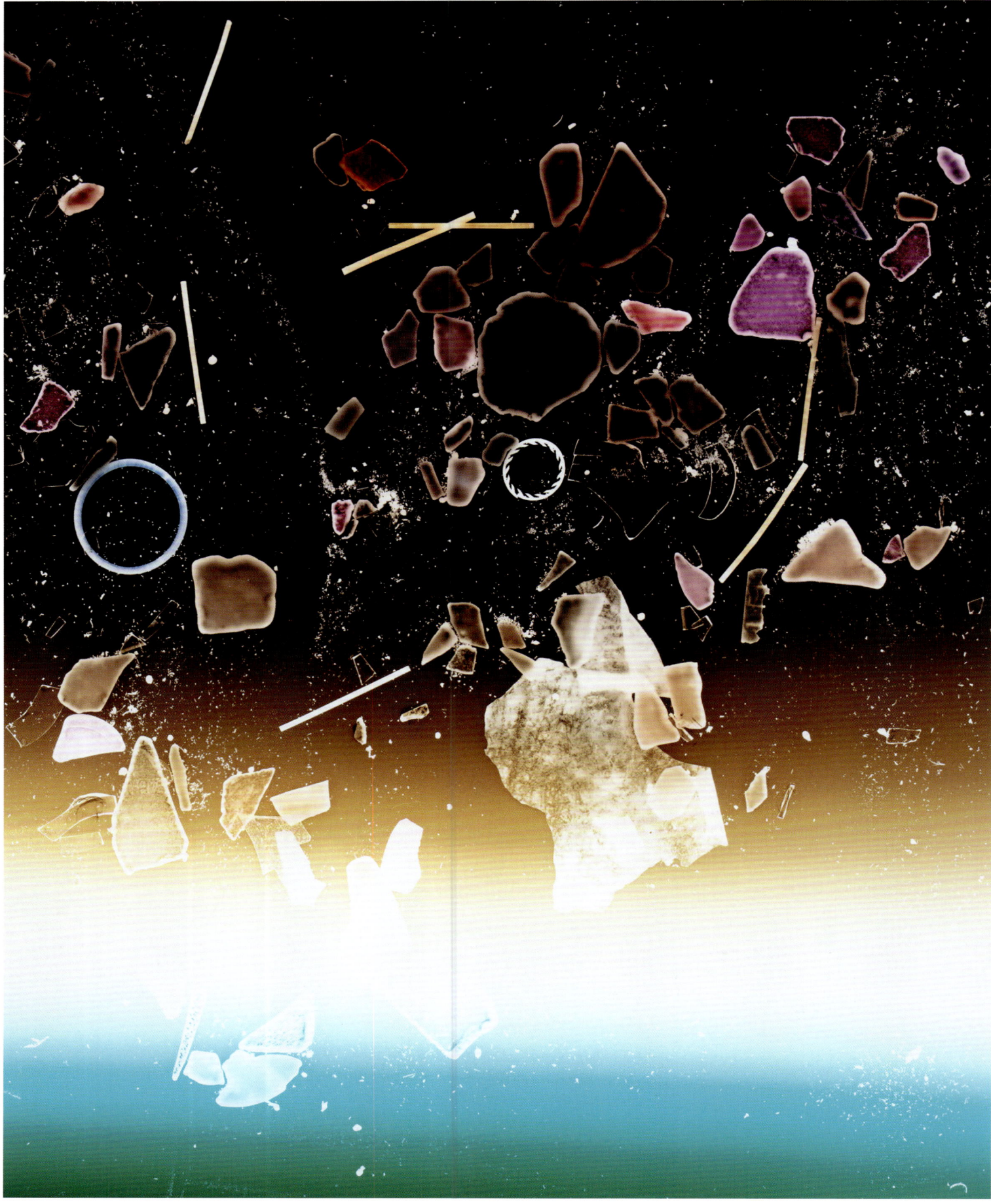

Descent, 2020

Call Sign, 2020

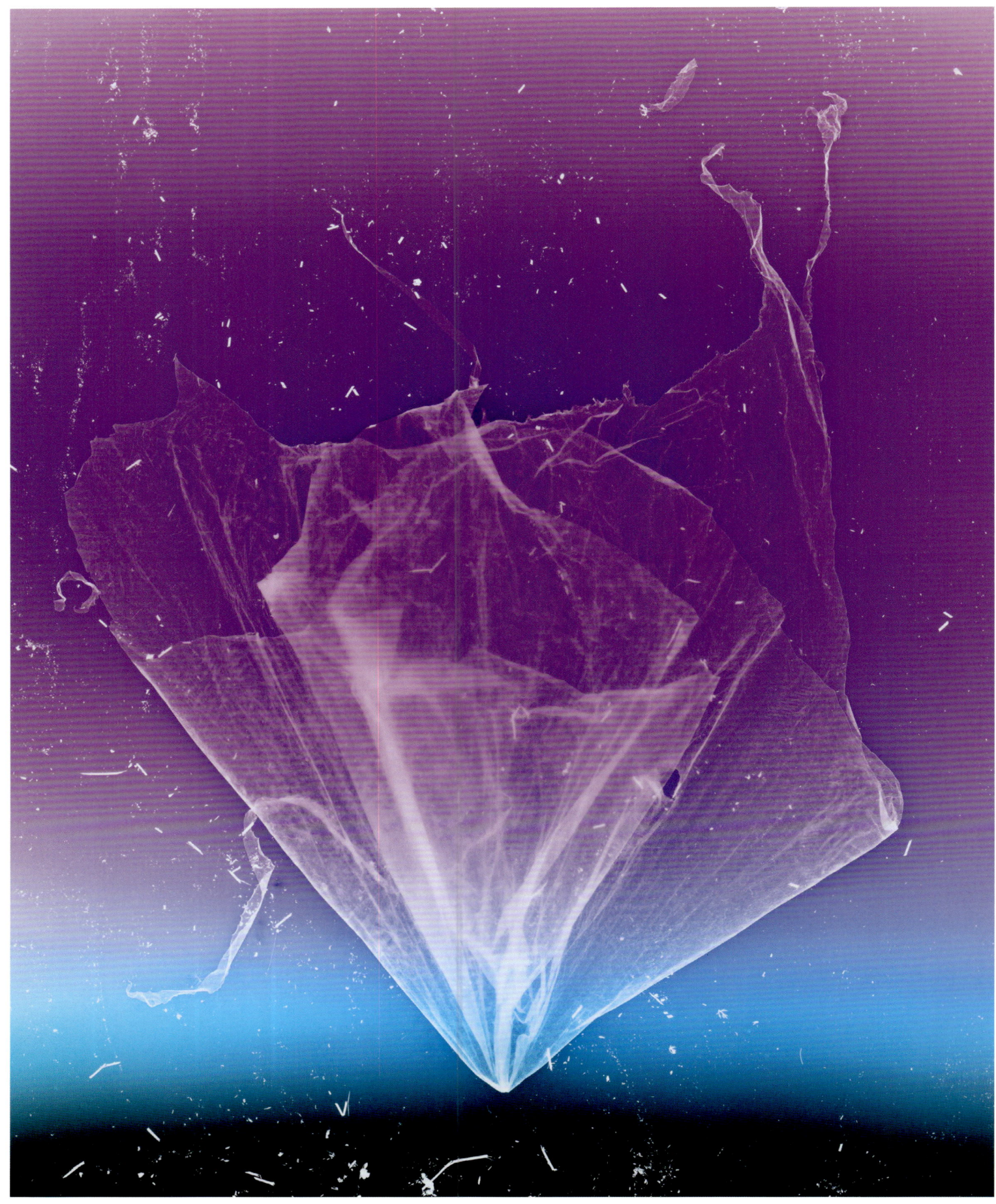

Simultaneous Reality,
2020

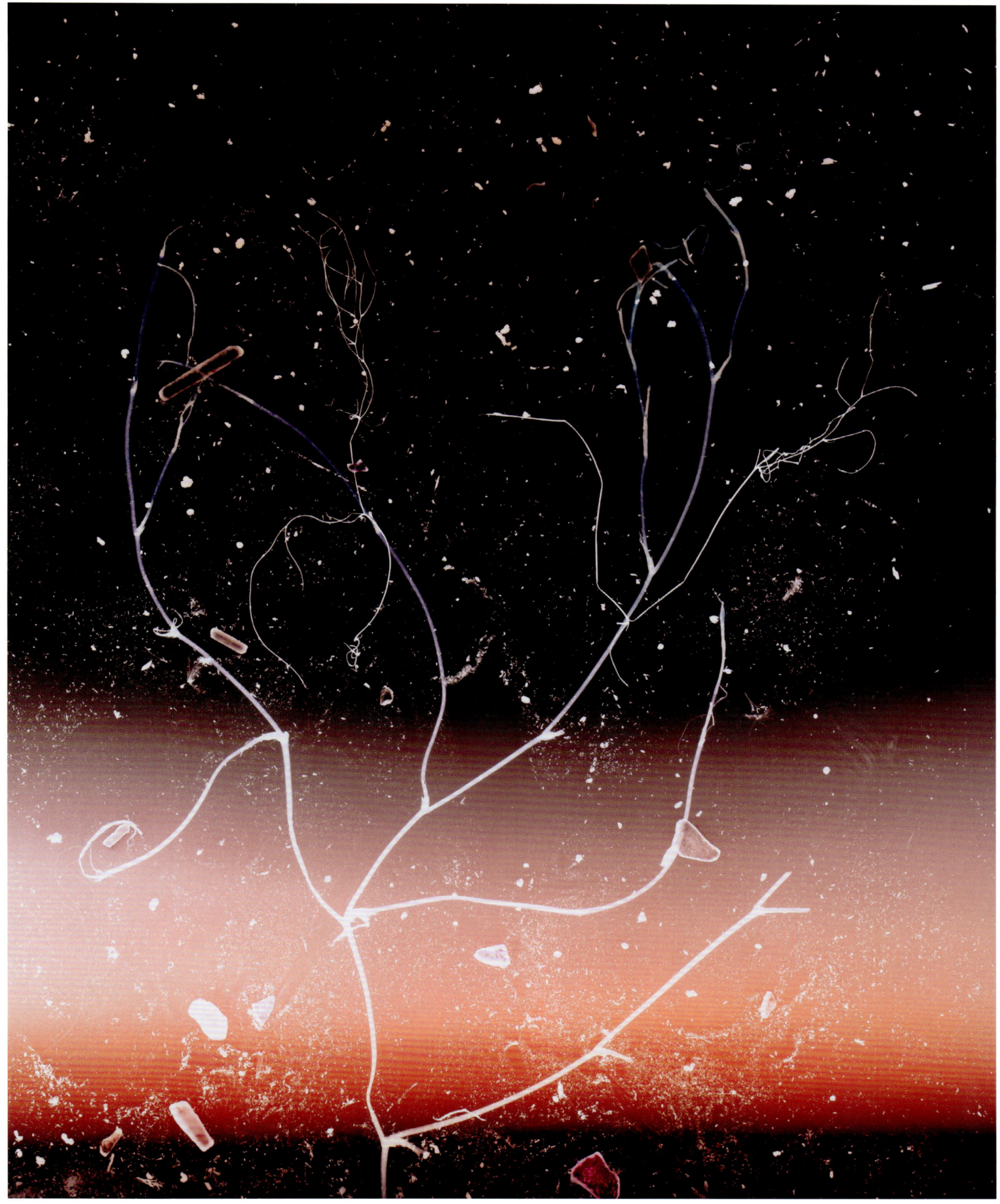

Rising Heat, **2020**

All images from the series
The Depth of Darkness,
the Return of the Light
© the artist and courtesy
Maureen Paley, London

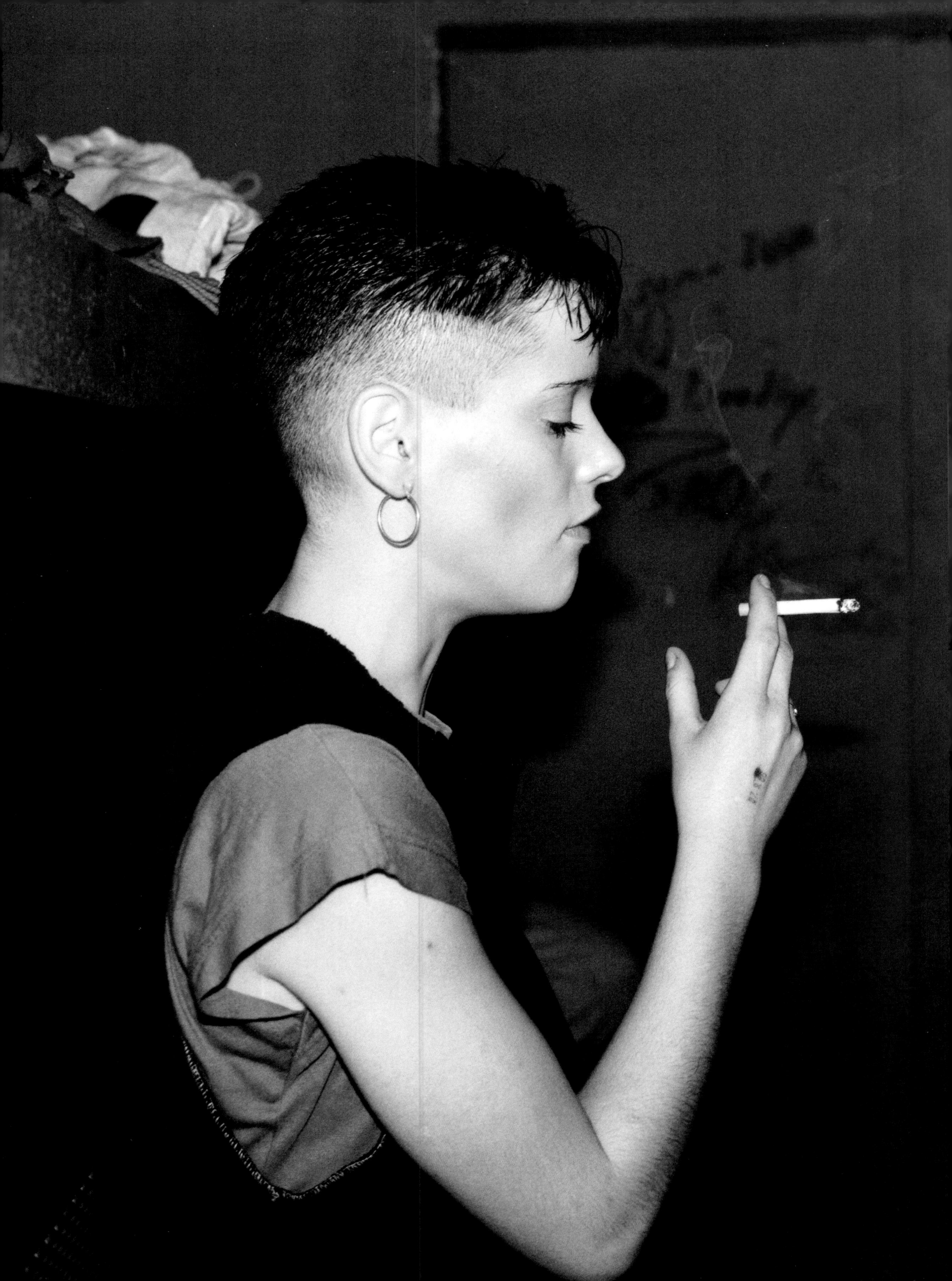

For Michael Schmidt, the divided German capital formed the subject of his life's work—and the impact of his austere vision continues to be fully discovered.

Berlin Stories

Gesine Borcherdt

An ostensibly endless front of gray fire walls lines up against a leaden sky. Here and there, crooked antennae stick out from rooftops as if trying to establish some type of contact. The mud of the wasteland in front of them is scored with tire tracks. In the foreground, there's a street: asphalt skirted by a sidewalk. Yet however stringently these lines divide the picture, there's little to see. The photograph is part of *Berlin nach 45* (Berlin after 45), a series showing West Berlin exactly as empty and dreary as it was when the Berlin-born photographer Michael Schmidt made the body of work between 1978 and 1980. The war was still everywhere—both the Cold one and the war before it, with Nazi Germany against the Allied world. Though every picture he took in his hometown from the mid-1960s until the fall of the Berlin Wall, in 1989, is intrinsically silent, this is no peaceful silence. Schmidt, born in October 1945, five months after the end of the war in Europe, shows West Berlin as a kind of wound—not picturesquely scarred, nor spectacularly gaping, but quietly festering like an infected sore.

After 1961, Berlin was a walled city, a concrete island divided into East and West, stuck amid the sealed-off GDR (the former German Democratic Republic) ruled by a socialist dictatorship.

Both sides were full of vacant lots, piles of rubble, prefab housing developments, and scrub: a war-damaged, lethargic, dystopian, and isolated city where every view was blocked, every street a dead end. In the 1980s, my parents often drove us down the bumpy transit corridor as we traveled from our home in West Germany through parts of the GDR to reach West Berlin, running the prescribed route's gauntlet of border-control bullies. Had you told me then that a few years later I would live in a reunited, *open* Berlin, I'd have thought you were joking. Back then, the atmosphere was a mixture of menace and apathy, constriction and gigantism, nonchalance and sadness. The wall sent shivers down my spine: sometimes stoically concrete, sometimes bursting with graffiti, it was a physically oppressive symbol of violence. For me, it represented not only my own parents fleeing the marauding Red Army at the end of World War II when they were kids but also my relatives stuck on the East side—traumas that the country still hasn't processed. This city, I felt, was just craters and concrete. And yet, or perhaps *because* of this, Berlin exerted a tremendous pull. Schmidt must have felt it too. The divided city was his life's subject, the essence of everything he wanted his art to express.

Schmidt was born and mainly grew up in Kreuzberg, a Berlin district of crumbling buildings and questionable social housing, of workers and Turkish migrants, and later of punks. Until Schmidt's death in 2014, Kreuzberg remained his terroir—only Wedding, a district of industrial buildings and tower blocks, was of similar interest to him. An assignment from the local authorities early in his career sent Schmidt to photograph seniors, foreign citizens, and women at work. Schmidt had actually trained to be a police officer and, as he once said, "only changed sides" because, ultimately, "it was all about justice." And since Schmidt was known to be disarmingly frank, with a Berliner's gruff wit or, as they call it here, "a bark as big as his heart," his art was free from voyeurism or

romanticization. After learning the basics at the Association for Amateur Photography in 1965, he quickly set out on his own, explaining: "When they photographed rain, it looked like glass beads. When I photographed rain, it looked like rain."

It's clear that Schmidt didn't like to curry favor, and his career as a photojournalist failed, possibly because he thought sending the popular weekly *Der Spiegel* a roll of film would suffice. And anyway, the student demonstrations of the 1960s, the drug scene of the '70s, people with champagne bottles dancing atop the wall on November 9, 1989—none of that interested him as a photographer. While Berlin was writing postwar history, Schmidt wandered through empty backyards, playgrounds, and vacant lots. He declared garbage, grass, cars, puddles, and parking garages worthy subjects at a time when that sort of thing could only be justified, if at all, as documentary photography. But Schmidt was concerned with more than objectivity. Working with a large-format camera in diffuse light, he developed a unique visual language that combined documentation and abstraction, and the results were just as raw and empathetic as he was. For him, gray not only symbolized Berlin's hopelessness, it became a personal stance of sorts—a stance against the harshness and certainty of black and white, against good or bad, right or left. In all of his series, which often only appeared in books and exhibitions decades later, Schmidt constantly reinvented himself without giving up the resistance that characterized his work from the start. For him, photography wasn't a window to the world but a kind of curb that slowed down the view.

His first photobook, *Berlin Kreuzberg*, from 1973, for which Schmidt photographed dirty children, broken façades, and men rummaging through garbage cans, is an early testimony to this approach. Its images resemble the reportages of Paul Strand, Schmidt's role model when he first took up the camera. In the

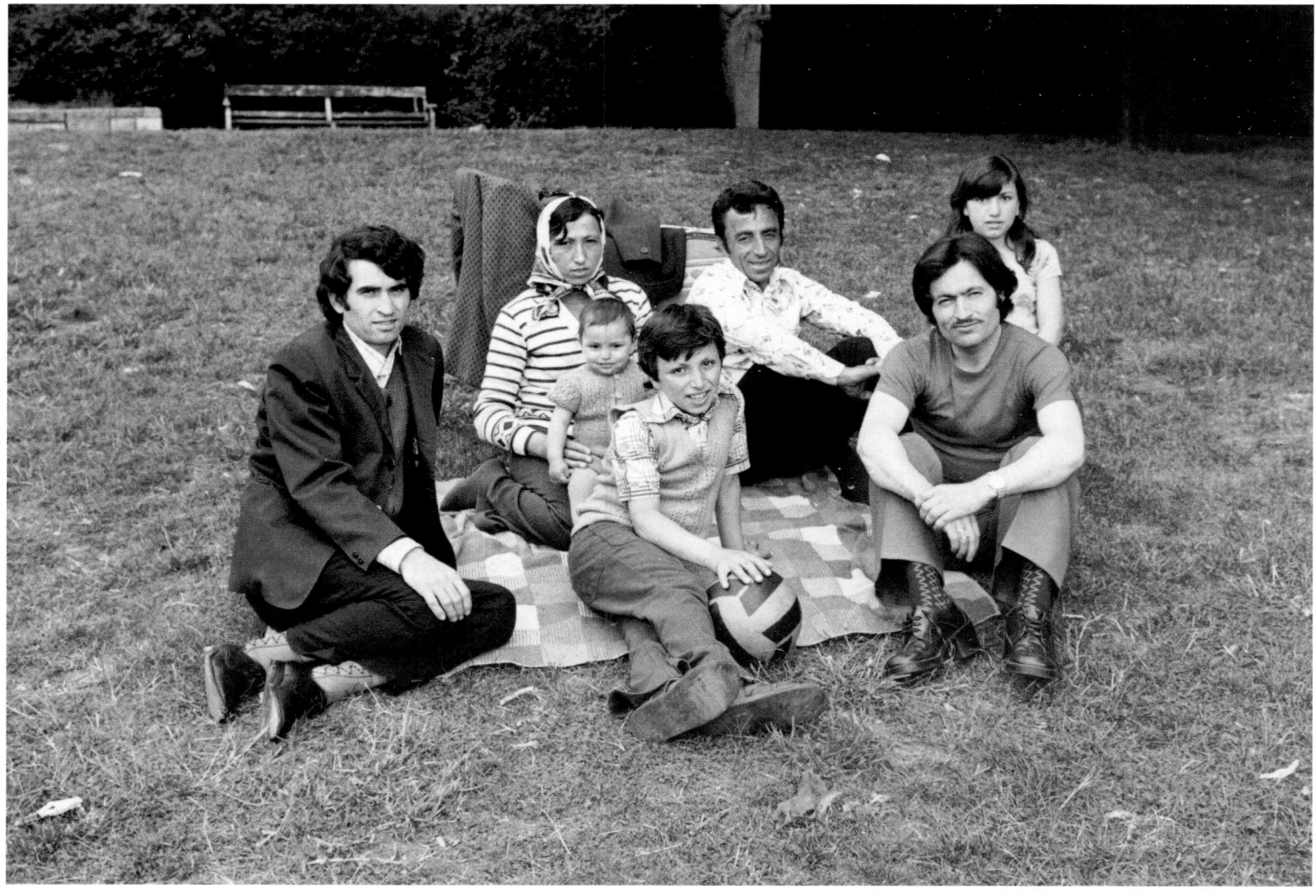

Berlin: Stadtlandschaft und Menschen (Berlin: Urban Landscape and People, 1972–76) series, Schmidt separated architecture from people: tower blocks, backyards, and train stations look utterly deserted, while the adults and children sitting on a scruffy lawn in *Türkische Familie auf dem Kreuzberg* (Turkish Family on the Kreuzberg, 1972–76) appear friendly but tired. In the series *Berlin-Wedding* (1976–78), he went a step further. These are severe, uneventful images of an empty, modern, and damaged urban space. Portrayed within the oppressive architecture of their offices or apartments, the people look like props—all of which now reads like conceptual commentary about being locked up. Playground climbing frames and concrete seating areas echo the monotony of the tower blocks. Again and again, images are cut through by fences, and one phone booth appears four times in a row from different angles.

This modus operandi is reminiscent of the work of Bernd and Hilla Becher, who at that same time were documenting the empty industrial architecture of the Ruhr area in westernmost Germany, elevating typologies and series to basic principles of the medium. But unlike those famous colleagues, who paved the way for a new generation of photographers at Düsseldorf's academy of art, Schmidt was denied international recognition. In 1979, he came to the Ruhr area as a guest lecturer at the renowned Folkwang school in Essen, where there was an opening in the faculty after the photographer Otto Steinert died. One of Schmidt's pupils was the Bechers' future student Andreas Gursky. "Michael Schmidt was intense from the first," Gursky told me recently. "He immediately established an intimacy, always looked you in the eye. We'd also spend time together in the evenings. He catapulted me out of my comfort zone, never mincing his words. He was a hardcore

Opposite: *Landwehrkanal (Fraenkelufer)* from the series *Berlin-Kreuzberg,* 1969–73; this page: *Untitled,* from the series *Berlin nach 45* (Berlin after 45), 1980

Visual barriers and obstructions make this series a masterpiece of the unspectacular, a metaphor for the hopelessness of youth.

Berliner: he'd only seen gray all his life. It was challenging, but he literally woke me up. It's a shame that he didn't get a professorship, if only as a counterpoint to the Bechers."

It's quite possible that Schmidt is so under the radar now because he went back home. In 1976, Schmidt founded the Werkstatt für Photographie (Workshop for Photography) at the adult-education center in Berlin-Kreuzberg, which would run for ten years. It was there, with Schmidt, not someplace such as the city's Neue Nationalgalerie, that the American photographers William Eggleston and John Gossage first lectured, taught, and showed their work in Germany. Aside from Essen and Düsseldorf, West Berlin was the country's third big photography hub, though hardly anyone remembers this now.

Schmidt may never completely step out of the shadow of the wall, but his reputation is growing. With the intimate pictures from the *Waffenruhe* (Ceasefire, 1985–87) series, which the curator Peter Galassi showed at the Museum of Modern Art, New York, in 1988, Schmidt first received international attention. These are images that are diametrically opposed to any objectivity, though without becoming dramatic either. Schmidt doesn't give up this position when he shows a speck of dirt on a pane of glass, punks gazing vacantly into the black picture space, the graffitied wall and bridge railing in close-up. Those perennial weeds hog the lens as if to prove that something still thrives in this city of Einstürzende Neubauten's experimental music and *Christiane F.*'s teenage drugs and sex, even if it's just scrub. Sometimes the background is blurred,

In the end, Schmidt's importance in the history of photography should also be measured by the generations after him.

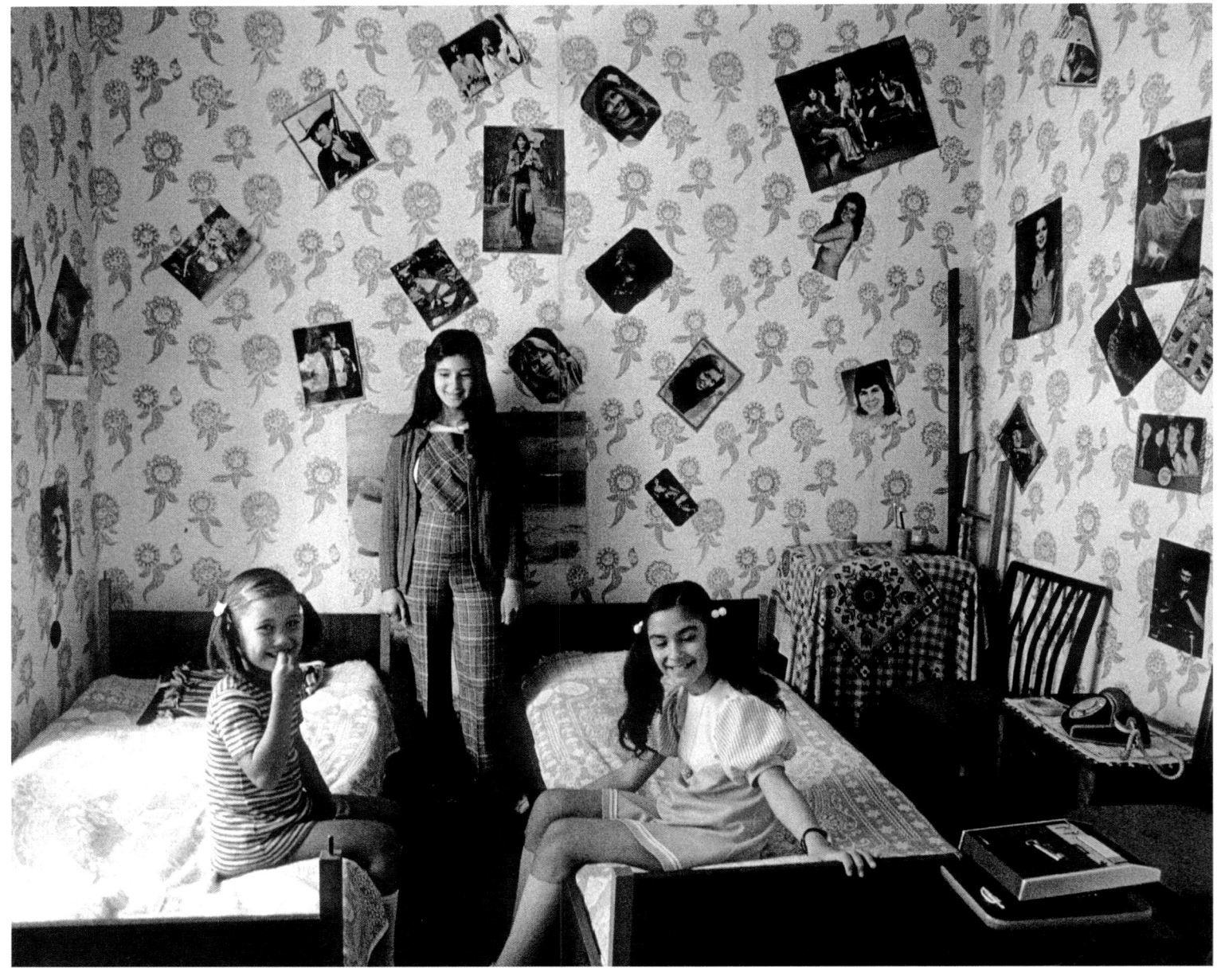

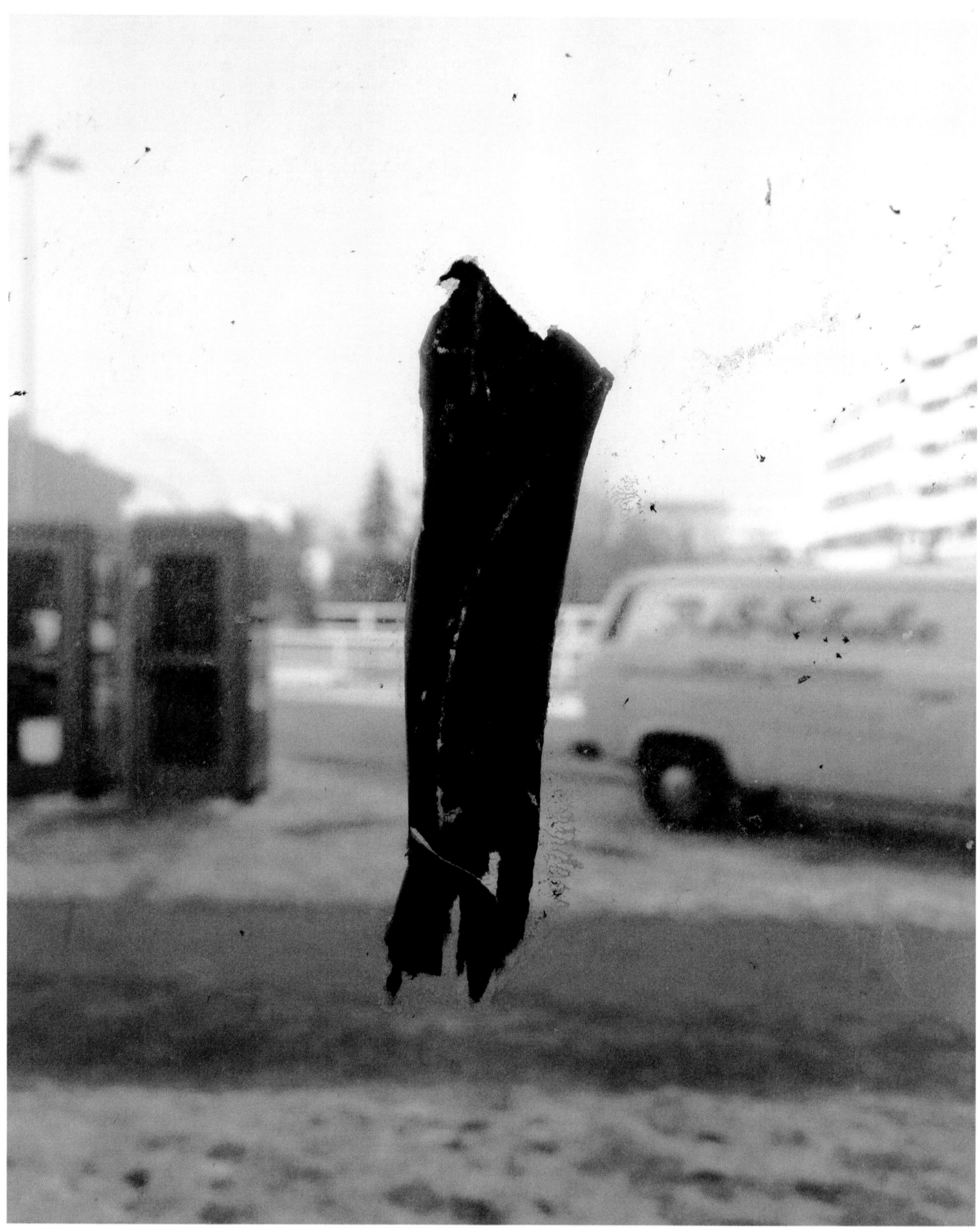

Untitled, from the series
Waffenruhe (Ceasefire),
1985–87

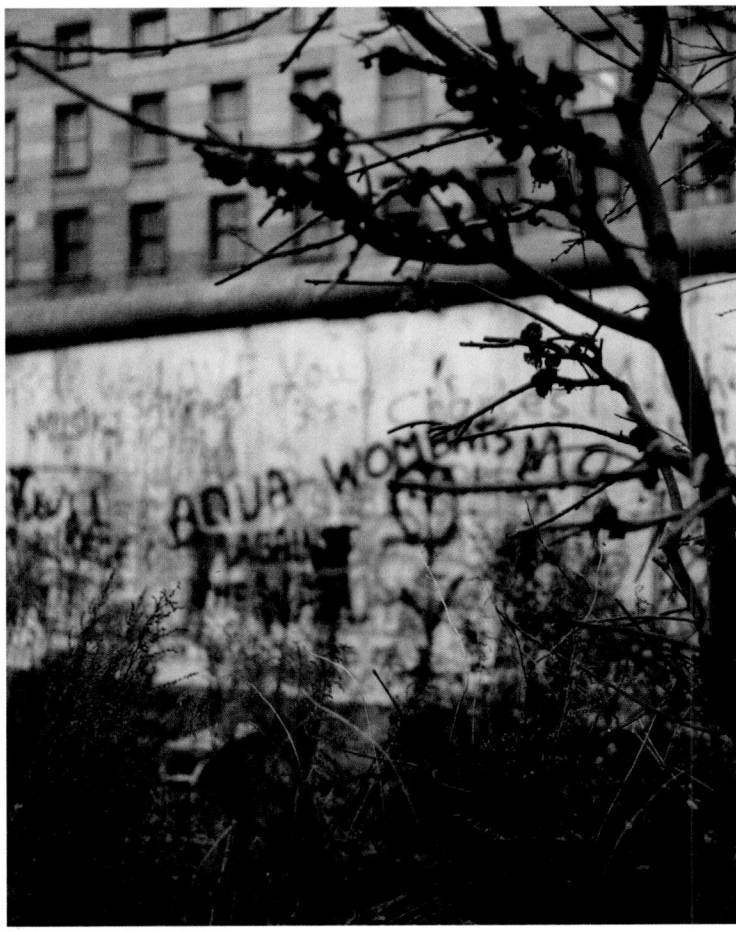

Untitled, from the series
Waffenruhe (Ceasefire),
1985–87

sometimes what's in front is out of focus, as if Schmidt were hiding from something, only to then photograph a pile of dirt in front of a concrete wall. It is these visual barriers, obstructions, and obscurations that make this series a masterpiece of the unspectacular, a metaphor for the hopelessness of youth, a psychogram of the divided city.

Schmidt could not have suspected that the wall would fall just two years after he made *Waffenruhe*. What he did notice, while others lapsed into euphoria, was the friction that the two Germanys' reunion entailed. With *89/90* (1989–90), Schmidt photographed his first series in East *and* West Berlin: prefab apartment blocks, a hollowed-out Trabant car, broken guardhouses, an East German police jacket on a tree, the wall, concrete balustrades, an open garbage can (the same one twice), and dilapidated façades that cannot immediately be placed in either part of town. Everything is brutal and pragmatic; there's no trace of any magical historical turning point. Instead, there's Schmidt's crouched gaze, peeking through holes, passages, fences.

In many people's minds, the wall is somehow still standing. Schmidt must have suspected this would happen when he devoted *one* more series to Berlin: *Ein-heit* (*U-ni-ty*, 1991–94), the title itself suggesting that reunification wasn't going very smoothly. Though also designed as a book, it was shown at MoMA, in 1996, and at the New Museum, New York, in 2011, but neither presentation worked as well as the one at Haus der Kunst, Munich, in 2010. Hung in one long row at the monumental museum Hitler commissioned as his personal art temple in 1933, Schmidt's work looks doubly fragile, vulnerable, and lost. The images use the semiotic languages of the different political systems that Germany has lived through: the Nazis' National Socialism, the GDR's Socialism, and, now, this freshly reunited democracy. Some images, such as those of people in uniform, are photographs of photographs; others are Schmidt's own images of burned-out people or partiers with blank faces— a bottle of Valium, a street corner with a hydrant and a plastic bag, and, of course, the wall. Nobody better communicated this divided nation's scattered life and its citizens' existential ambient noise than Schmidt.

In the end, Schmidt's importance in the history of photography should also be measured by the generations after him. With their digitally edited and large-scale color photographs, the so-called Becher students—Gursky, Candida Höfer, Thomas Struth, and Thomas Ruff—might be antipodes of sorts. In contrast, younger Berlin artists such as Wolfgang Tillmans and Tobias Zielony direct their lenses toward the precarious and diffuse as Schmidt did before them. For many of them, he has become a role model, an artist's artist whose sympathy for the marginalized and whose fondness for the book form more closely correspond to the ephemeral feel of our fragile times than overwhelming formats bursting with color. In fact, in the last few years before his death, Schmidt was more and more associated with the contemporary. The presentation of his work at three biennials—Berlin in 2006 and 2010, Venice in 2013—is proof of how unsettled and relevant his work still is, and of how much its potential remains undiscovered.

Schmidt's first retrospective, late and more than deserved, originated last year in Berlin and travels to Paris, Madrid, and Vienna. It's regrettable that the exhibition won't appear stateside. After all, Schmidt learned a lot from the great American photographers. Especially now that we've all learned what isolation means, now that we've felt the walls inside our heads shoot up faster than the weeds he loved to photograph, this West Berliner can open us up to entirely new perspectives.

Gesine Borcherdt is an art journalist and curator based in Berlin. Translated from the German by Florian Duijsens.

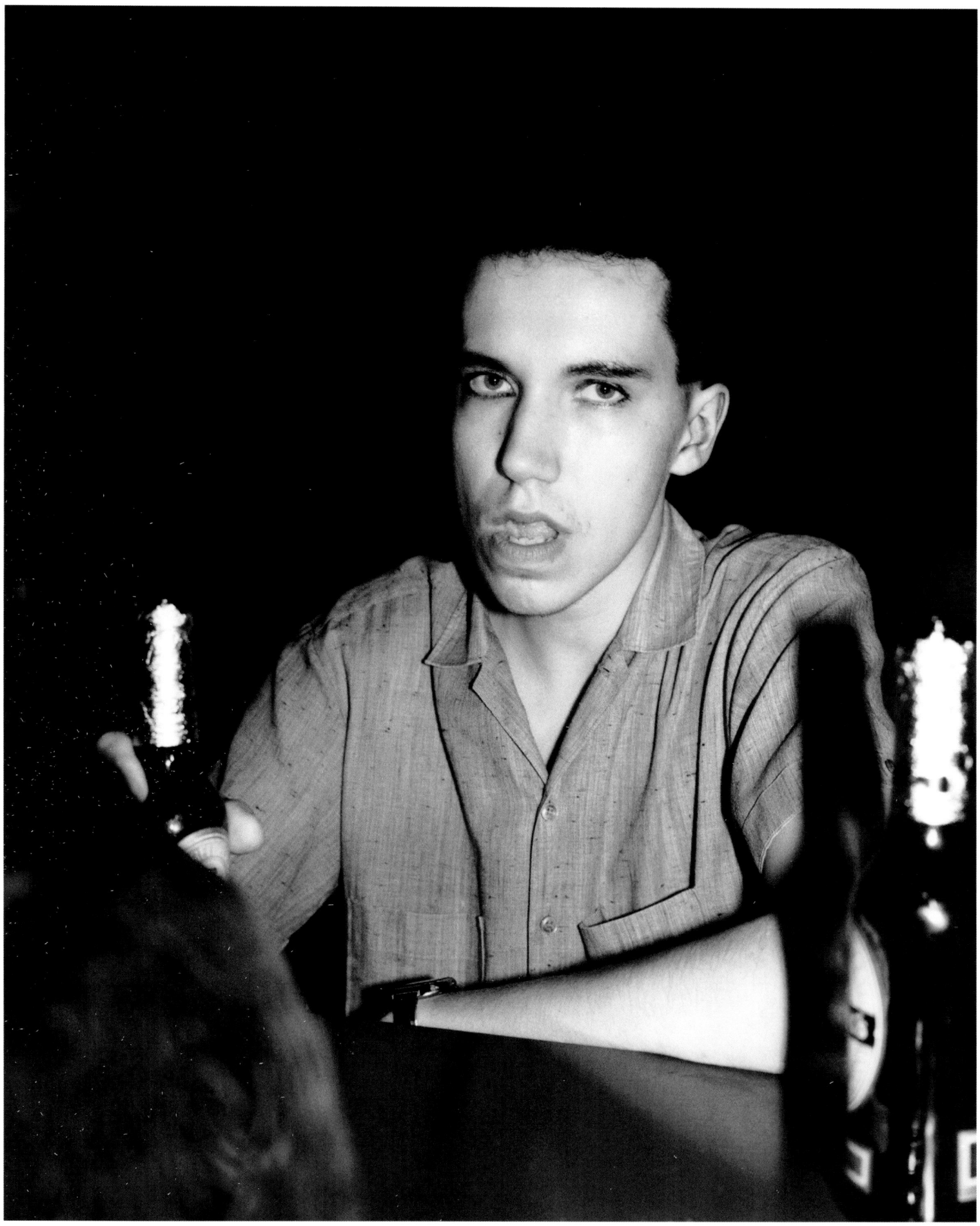

Untitled, from the series
***Waffenruhe* (Ceasefire),**
1985–87
All photographs ©
Foundation for Photography
and Media Art with the
Michael Schmidt Archive

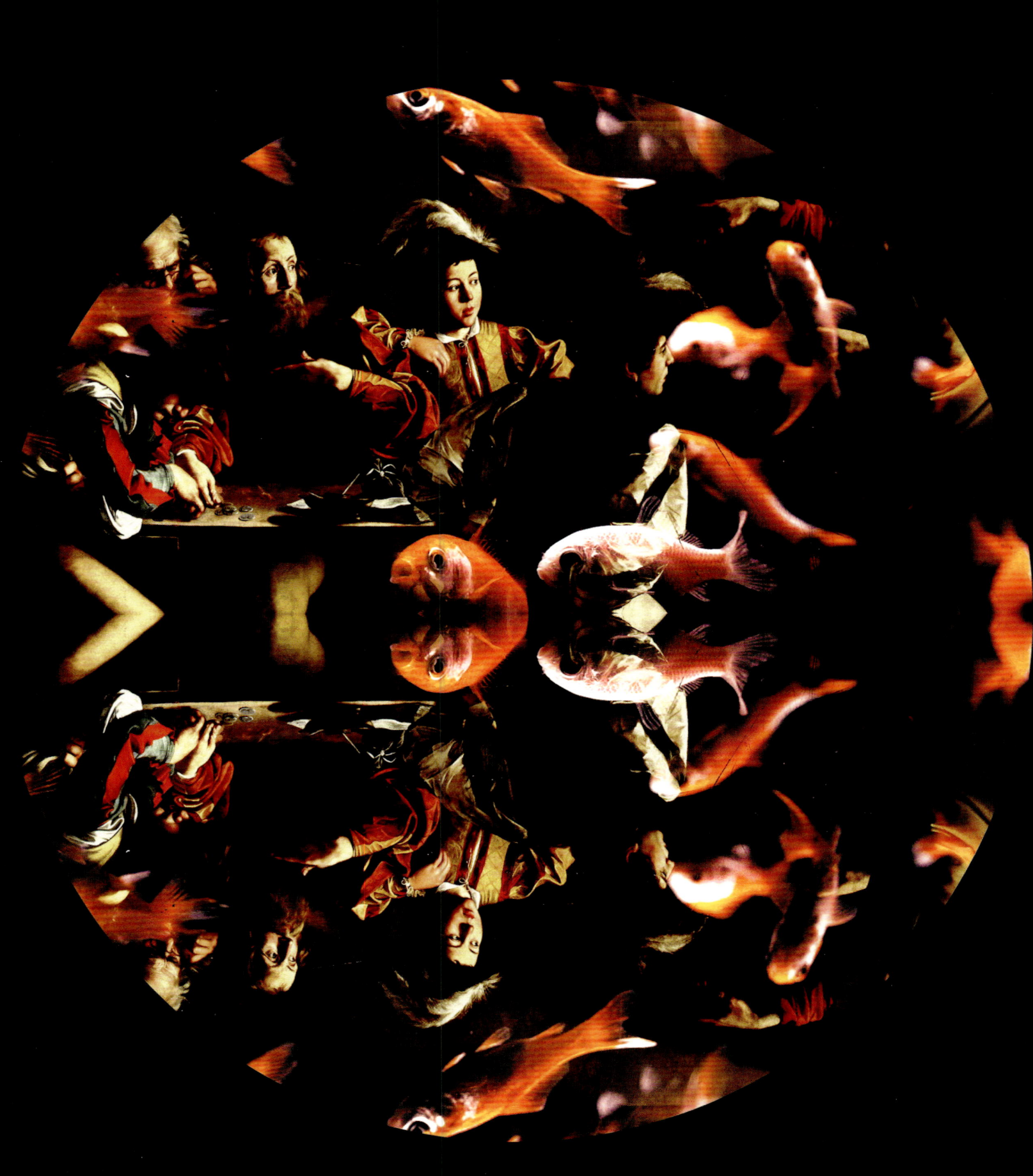

Theo Eshetu

Infinite Screens

Raised in Africa and Europe, the prolific artist
makes kaleidoscopic videos that reflect the dilemmas
of biography and belonging.
Emmanuel Iduma

*The Slave Ship (The Law
of the Sea),* **2015. HD video
installation**

The opening to the mirror box is a gilded frame through which
viewers can watch a kaleidoscopic film. Titled *Brave New World*
(1999)—versions of which have been installed in exhibitions in
Washington, D.C., Rome, and New York—the film is "a very simple
idea but very effective," as one viewer says to Theo Eshetu, its
creator. You poke your head into the mirror box where the film is
playing, and where, given the continuous loop of bisymmetrical
clips, you get the illusion of being surrounded by seemingly
endless reflections of yourself as you watch. Filmed with a Super 8
camera, the footage is looped together from a thrilling array of
sources, including a ceremony of the Ethiopian Orthodox Church,
a commercial for an Italian insurance company, and enchanting
images of dancers in Bali. "The idea is that it sort of creates an image
of the world, no?" Eshetu asks a mesmerized viewer as they both
stand in front of the mirror box, observing its fantastical twists.
He is proposing an image of the world tripled or quadrupled many

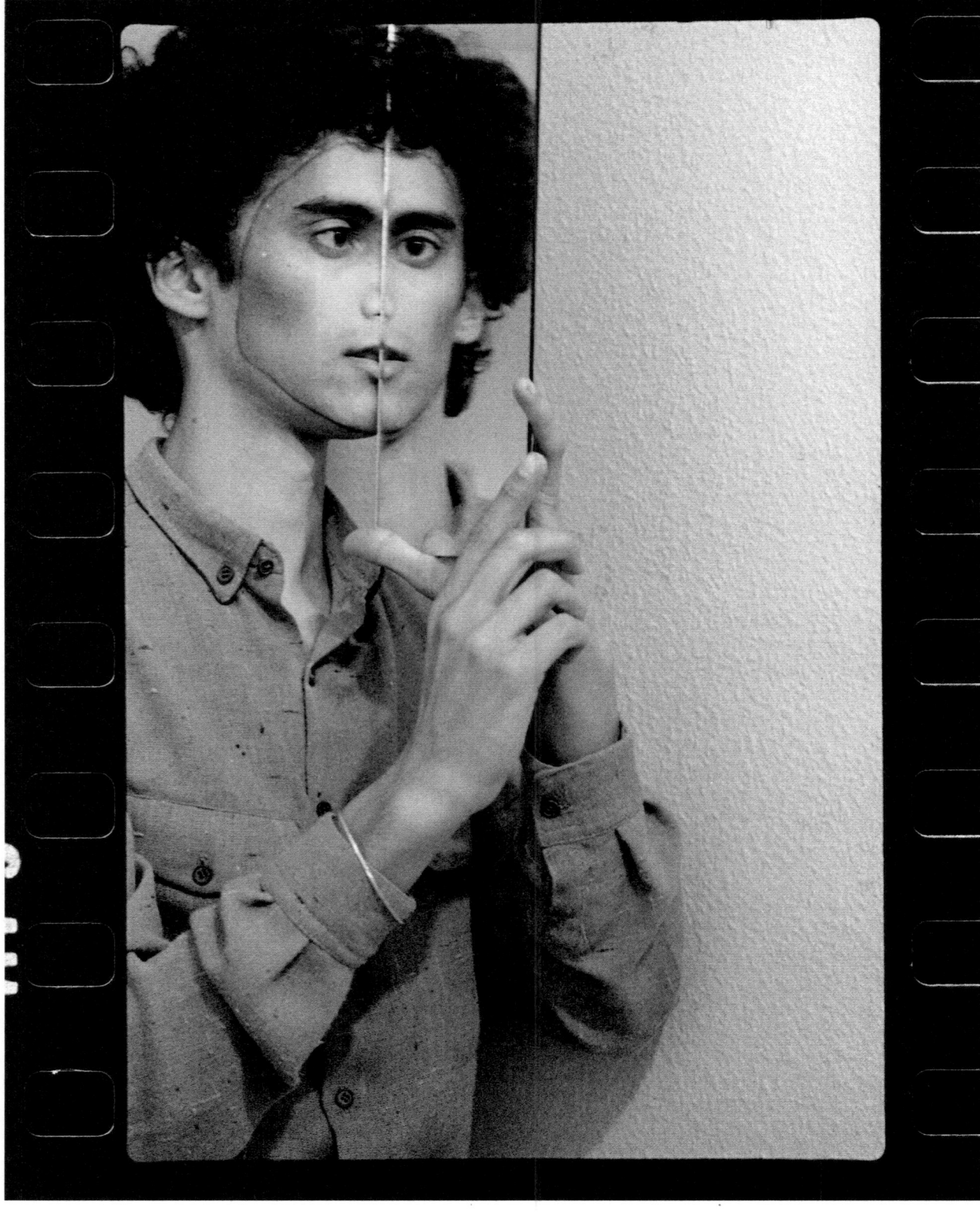

Self-Portrait with Mirror,
1979

times over, so that what is seen is not simply illusory but infinite and indeterminate, as though gathering the entirety of the world's faces into a single orb.

Brave New World is a quintessential primer for Eshetu's four-decade career; the artist's video work—for cinema, television, and exhibitions—is often an assemblage of images or clips from a range of histories and worldviews. His biography gives a clue as to what informed his nonprovincial outlook. Born in London in 1958 to an Ethiopian father and a Dutch mother, Eshetu spent his childhood between Ethiopia, Senegal, Yugoslavia, the Netherlands, and Italy, due, for the most part, to the peripatetic nature of his parents' work. When he was ten, he spent time with Ato Tekle-Tsadik Mekouria, his grandfather, a diplomat and perhaps Ethiopia's most renowned historian. Eshetu was out of school and somewhat bored. During a trip to Pompeii, his grandfather gave him an Instamatic camera, effectively launching his fascination with photography and his career—a recurring origin tale for many artists. "I recognize it's a cliché story," says Eshetu.

More than twenty years later, perhaps to make something of that cliché, he returned to Ethiopia to create *Blood Is Not Fresh Water*, a 1997 film dedicated to the life of his grandfather, whom he had seen only twice in the years since. The film explores the cultural and spiritual history of Ethiopia, drawing a cyclic line from the Queen of Sheba to the pomp of the Ethiopian Orthodox Church to Lucy, the oldest known human skeleton at its discovery. By making *Blood Is Not Fresh Water*, Eshetu recently told me, he could delve into the contrast between "the TV image of famine in Ethiopia" and his "childhood memory of a bright, wonderful place." And he could connect with his Ethiopian self. The experience of being biracial causes a split, in a sense, of identity. "I create dialogues between these two perspectives," he says, connecting his European and African selves. In a statement about the video, he explained, "I don't have a photographic memory of the places where I lived as a child, but often photographs remind me of a past existence I don't recall having seen."

In Eshetu's videos, biography—what he calls "lived experience"—is never the end in itself. It enables him "to merge two cultures into giving an outlook on something." Some of his earliest photographs are conceptual touchstones for such a world-blending approach. One double-exposure image, *Self-Portrait* (1975), taken when he was sixteen, shows a quarter of his face juxtaposed with more than half of a mask, depicting a convincing image of a humanoid figure; in *Self-Portrait with Mirror* (1979),

Till Death Us Do Part, 1982–86. Multimedia installation. Installation view in *Monitors*, 1987, Galleria MR, Rome

Eshetu's earliest photographs are conceptual touchstones for a world-blending approach.

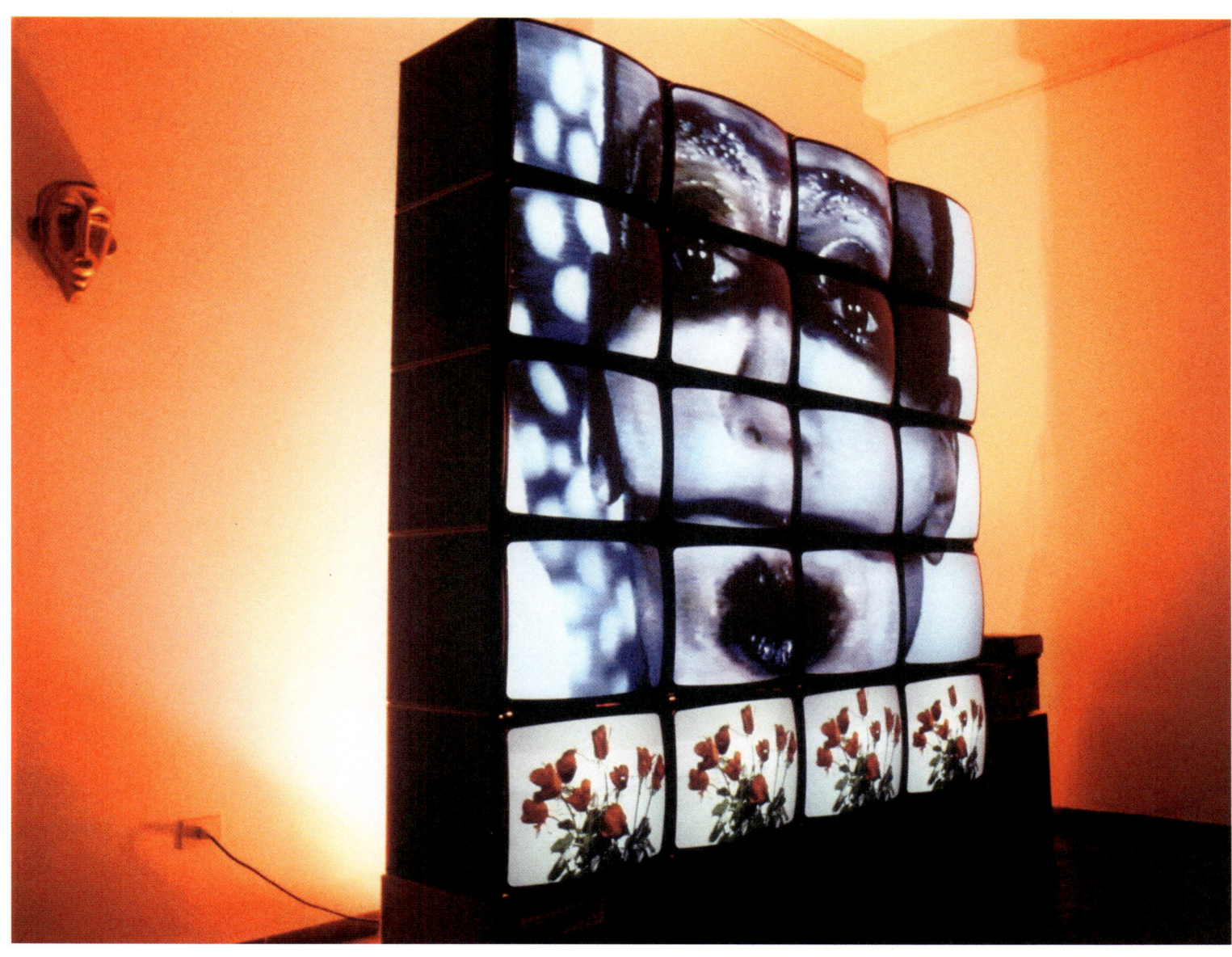

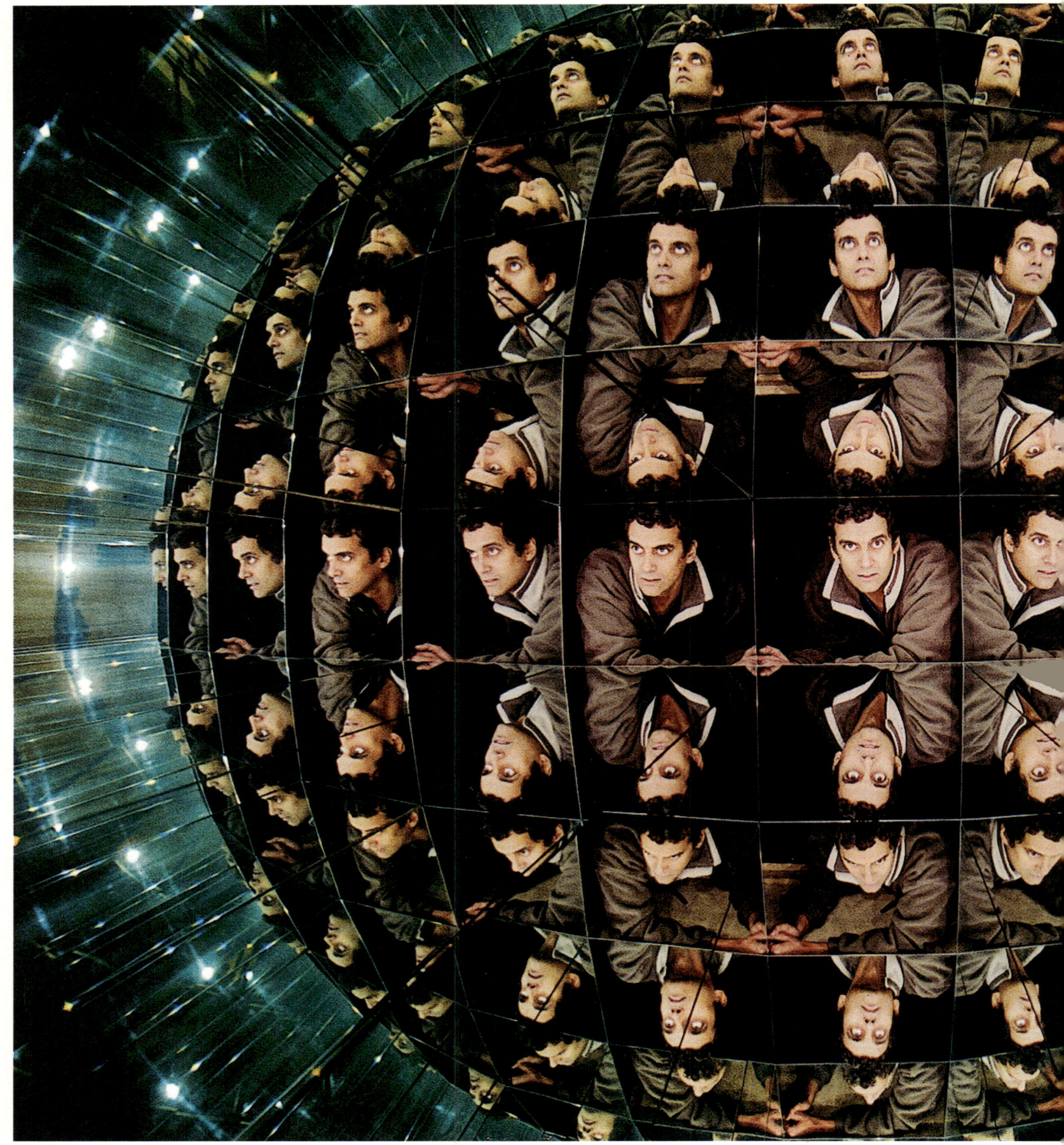

Brave New World, 1999.
Multimedia installation.
Installation view in *Lavori in Corso*, 1999, Museo d'Arte, Contemporanea di Roma, Rome

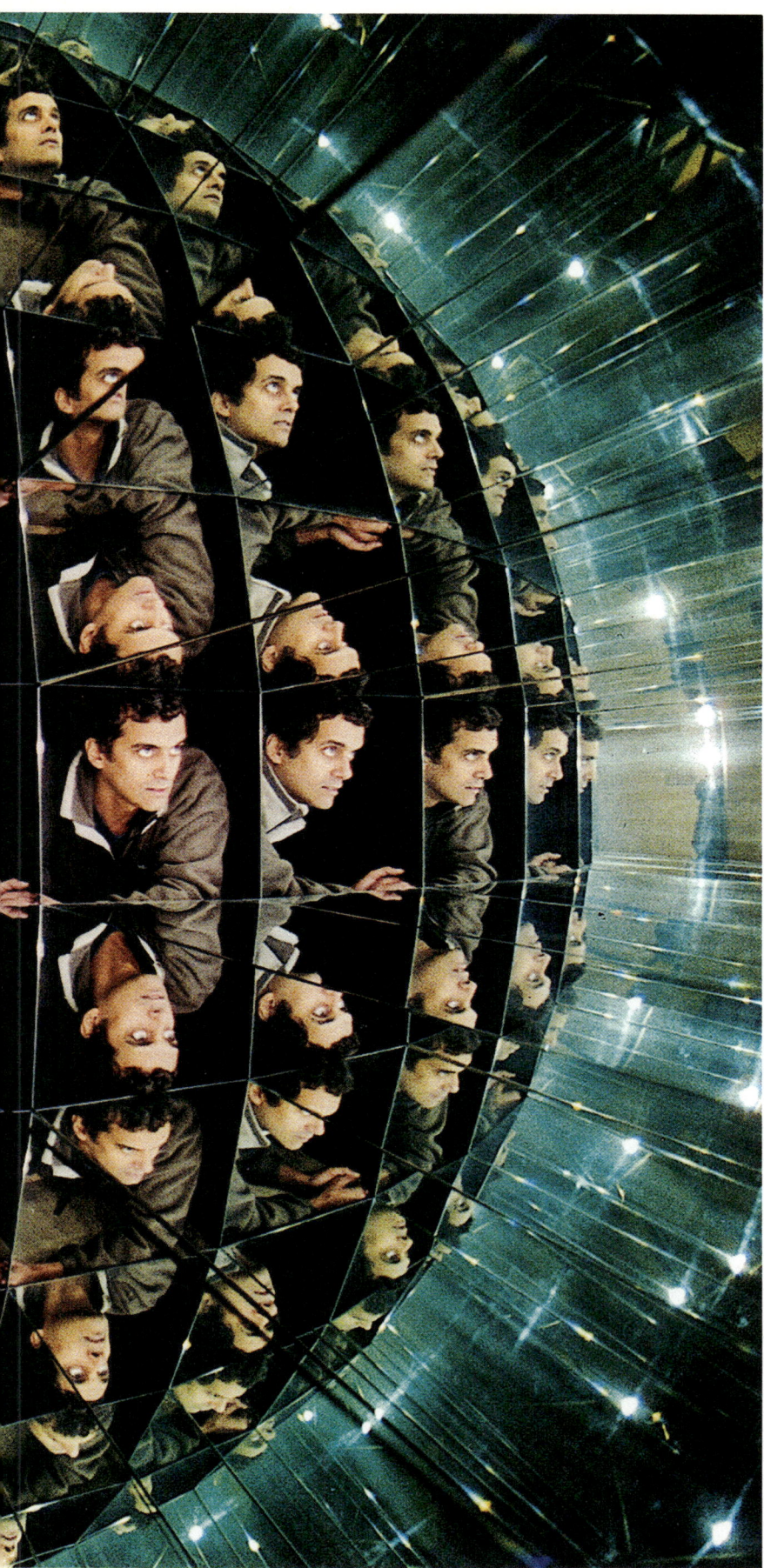

his face is bifurcated with a mirror, giving the illusion of a two-faced figure. Masks became a leitmotif in his early photographs, mostly black-and-white images taken in the years leading up to his studies in London, where he obtained a degree in communication design from North East London Polytechnic in 1981, and just before he took up video art full time. For Eshetu, these early photographs point to "the beginning of an artistic process, where aesthetic and conceptual considerations merge."

Before he started making videos, Eshetu took photographs of musicians, including Bob Marley and Marvin Gaye. This was how, as a shy teenager, he could come close to his musical heroes. "I learned about photography by photographing musicians live on stage. The performative element was instantly the first material that I was drawn to," he says. Yet he understood that he was also engaging with the relationship between reality and representation. Thinking about that relationship remains at the core of what Eshetu does; his affinity for music continues to influence his sensibilities. The videos Eshetu makes are notable for their soundtracks, with affecting crescendos and decrescendos indicating emotional charge.

Identity and belonging, as complex propositions in a world of pluralistic knowledge, are underlying dilemmas in Eshetu's work: the relationship between the self and the non-self. "The non-self," he says, "is a recognition that you have your self and others have their selves." He is searching for a non-totalizing worldview. In *The Slave Ship (The Law of the Sea)* (2015), a video installation evoking the history of slavery, bilaterally symmetrical moving images are shown in a circular frame, as though to indicate the limits of thinking about cataclysmic histories in a linear, straightforward fashion. Other videos by Eshetu achieve a similar destabilizing of the singular view: *The Return of the Axum Obelisk* (2010) presents a documentation of the restitution of a cultural artifact to Ethiopia by Italy in fifteen screens and *Till Death Us Do Part* (1982–86), recently presented at the Museum of Modern Art, New York, considers the exponential growth of 1980s media culture in twenty screens.

In a conversation with the late curator Okwui Enwezor, published in *The Body Electric* (2017), the first comprehensive monograph of Eshetu's work, the artist notes that he was part of a larger movement by Black filmmakers and video artists in Europe who were questioning regimes of representation. "We were driven by the need to define our identity because we saw that it wasn't represented on TV or in cinema," he said. "We had to create it ourselves." But he was faced with a formal dilemma. How could he identify with the medium? Cinema has a well-documented history, and, by the 1980s, independent filmmaking had also taken off. "I created a bond with the medium itself," he told Enwezor. "I created an artificial distinction between film and video, as a device, which gave me a path. What started as the malaise of not knowing my identity became what I have somehow tried to solve, and transforming that to making videos has helped me do that." He was an artist who came of age when television was the central medium to produce videos for, or rebel against, and, in the early 2000s, the Internet was taking over as the central platform for the dissemination of images. By 2002, Eshetu moved away from making videos within the context of television—his work began to be shown mainly in art installations or film festival screenings.

Perhaps his videos are best suited to be shown in art contexts where, at the very least, Eshetu can break "out of the single-monitor mold," to quote Wulf Herzogenrath, who writes in *The Body Electric* of Eshetu as one of the pioneers of video art. Eshetu, Herzogenrath says, was part of a generation of artists who "extended televisual monocultures and their linear narrative structure by applying new collage techniques and exploring possibilities by which to disrupt the chronological narratives of the single living-room TV." Eshetu had studied communication,

Making work for television or exhibitions, Eshetu is attentive to video as a nomadic form.

which, he says, produced a different relationship to film and video making than if he had studied fine arts. With a fine arts perspective, one is concerned with self-expression, while coming from a communication background, "you somehow have the tools of this expression, so you explore those tools."

Eshetu's exploration has widened in range and expression, such as in *Atlas Fractured* (2017), a film produced in two versions for the Kassel and Athens editions of Documenta 14, where he continued to work with masks. The Athens version, projected on a cave wall, shows a slow pan of faces filmed against masks, paintings, and photographs, until, in most cases, they are transmogrified. The film is mesmeric. *Atlas Fractured* is accompanied by the intermittent voices of a range of thinkers—Carl Jung, James Baldwin, Langston Hughes, Toni Morrison, and Maya Angelou, among others—whose views emphasize the value of knowledge that is receptive to what is unknowable. In the Kassel version of *Atlas Fractured*, the filmed portraits and footages of historical incidents were projected onto a giant banner that had previously hung at the entrance to Berlin's ethnological museum. The banner, which showcased masks from each of the museum's departments, had been cut into sections to be discarded when Eshetu recovered them.

If the arc of Eshetu's career indicates anything—in his transition from photography to video, from making work for television to installing exhibitions—it is that he is most attentive to video as a nomadic form, one that is able to take shape under any rubric. In his conversation with Enwezor, he states: "I think there's an almost comical interplay in my works, through which rules are constantly being set up and broken: a certain liquid quality that makes them fit into various spaces."

Nearly every year since 1982, Eshetu has premiered or exhibited his videos in and outside Europe, in the major global

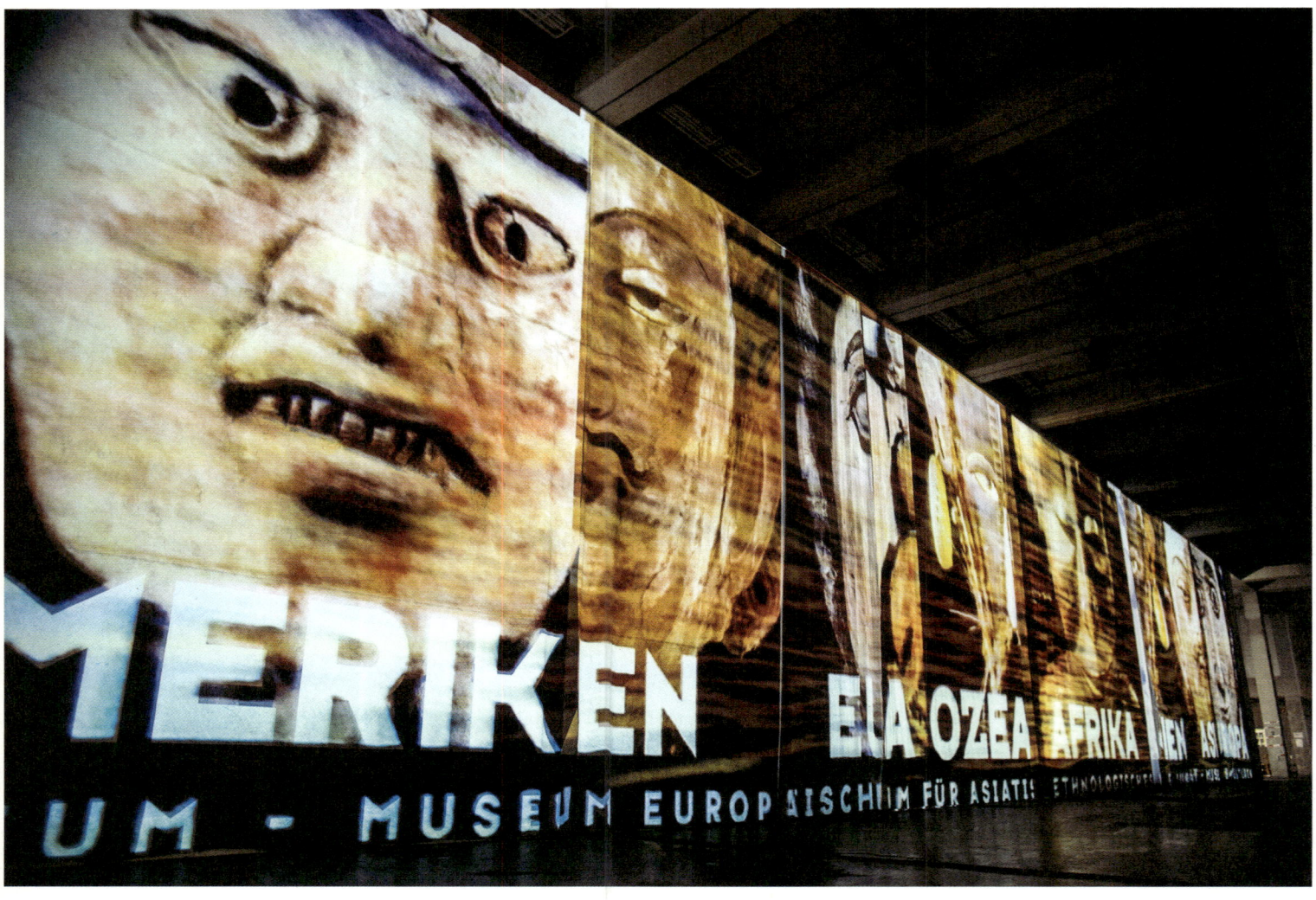

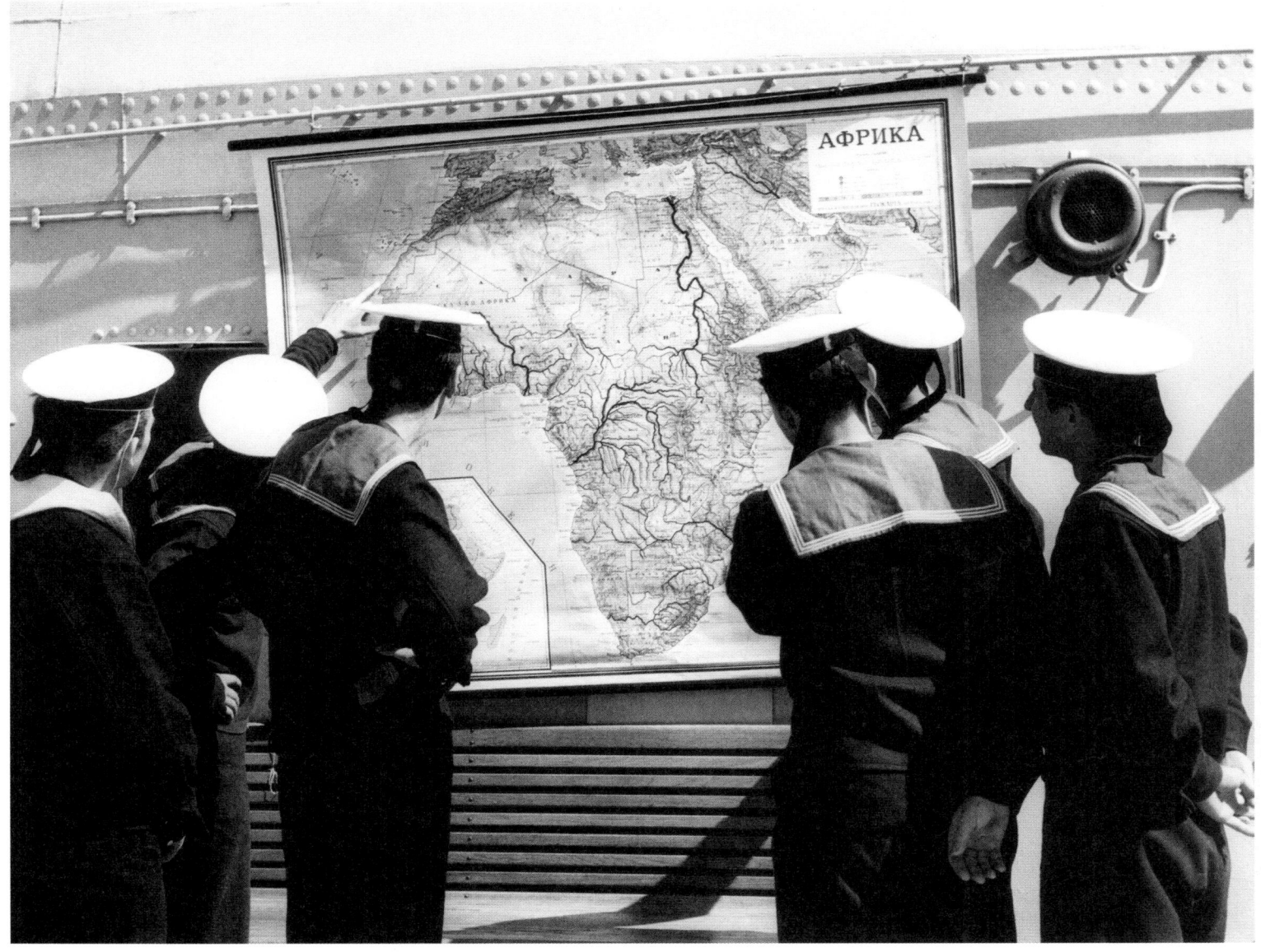

video art festivals as well as in notable museums and galleries. Alongside artists such as John Akomfrah and Isaac Julien, and members of the Black Audio Film Collective and Sankofa Film and Video Collective, Eshetu is a pioneer—a diasporic African artist who has shown the inexhaustible potential of video art as a primer for the politics and aesthetics of belonging. Yet, he is only beginning to receive broader attention, at least in the United States—in addition to a recent screening at MoMA, Eshetu's work was included in *The Sorcerer's Burden*, a 2019 group exhibition at the Contemporary Austin. Perhaps his significance is most telling in his 2010 work *The Return of the Axum Obelisk*, which predates the current, widespread cause célèbre of restitution of African artifacts in European institutions as a cultural necessity. He is currently making an essayistic film about the move of the ethnographic collection from Berlin's Museum of Asian Art to the Humboldt Forum. This controversial new museum in Berlin has served as a kind of laboratory for several of Eshetu's recent works, including *Ghostdance* (2020), a video installation for the Gwangju Biennale, filmed, in part, at the Forum.

Eshetu is elusive on the question about the influence of biography. In 2015, when he was commissioned to produce work on the Non-Aligned Movement, he recalled that he had lived in Yugoslavia, where his grandfather had been Ethiopia's ambassador in Belgrade. He went to the Museum of Yugoslav History, delving into the extensive photography archive of the former Yugoslav leader Josip Broz Tito, in search, as he put it later, of "oblique traces of biography, tangential associative thoughts, fragments of forgotten memories, and unwritten personal histories."

The result is *The Mystery of History and His Story in My Story* (2015), an essay of forty-four photographs. One of the most intriguing images shows six sailors facing a map of the African continent. Their stance seems like a synecdoche for Europe as it observes Africa. It equally reflects the fusion of Eshetu's bicontinental family history with a grander one, a confluence from which he sprung as an artist. "This idea of biography," he says, "is not anything really to do with me. It's to do with a hypothesis of a world vision."

Emmanuel Iduma is a writer based in New York and Lagos and is the author of *A Stranger's Pose* (2018).

Batia Suter
Galaxies

Brian Sholis

For many people, the late twentieth century marked the end of an era of master narratives. We could no longer take the nightly television newscast as a summary of the day. We realized that the *Encyclopedia Britannica* excluded as much information as it enclosed between hard covers. Burgeoning Internet access revealed to us people, both across town and across the planet, whose attitudes and actions contradicted our beliefs. After a century and a half of mass media placating viewers, it was once again our responsibility to knit together, from myriad disparate fragments, a coherent story of the world.

The Swiss artist Batia Suter, who lives in Amsterdam, has made such efforts a running theme of her expansive and lyrical assemblages of printed pictures for more than twenty years. What was once an idiosyncratic catalog of enthusiasms—"very often, I buy a book for one image," she once said in an interview— became, in time, an attempt to grapple with how a universal emerges from the particular.

It all began innocently enough: Suter scanned pictures from secondhand books and magazines that she bought in stores and flea markets, then placed those images side by side on-screen in a kind of private database. When visitors to her studio reacted to the collections in similar and surprising ways, she began refining the collections more purposefully. In the early 2000s, as she was gathering the materials that would become her 2007 book *Parallel Encyclopedia*, Suter also presented her found pictures, alone or in small groups, at mural size on gallery and museum walls. Those presentations emphasized disorientation or confusion: not only was she inserting into a room visual material that recalled other eras, but often she also chose subject matter that toyed with viewers' ability to comprehend the space around them.

The photobook, however, is Suter's natural métier. *Parallel Encyclopedia #2* arrived in 2016, replicating its predecessor's aleatory structure and bringing together more than a thousand images, mostly of the natural world. *Radial Grammar* (2018) concurrently brought some formal coherence, with its focus on circular shapes and concepts, and, by superimposing some images, a new narrative complexity. Her most recent book, *Hexamiles (Mont-Voisin)* (2019), furthers this overprinting technique, drawing together landscape pictures in an ecstatic vision of the natural merging with the technological.

For her recent exhibitions, Suter enlarged some pictures to mural size. But she more often mimics the palimpsest structure of her books by covering large walls with grids or overlapping collages of poster-size prints. Seeing her work at this scale emphasizes the mechanical production, the sheer materiality, of her source materials. Halftone dots, scratches, and other "imperfections" testify to the lives they lived prior to arriving in Suter's collection, locating them in a temporal arc just as she recombines them into something timeless.

Here, in a sequence created specifically for this issue, we have a car, some citrus, and a "camera" as well as the sea and the stars. They come from such sources as a 1940s-era agricultural manual, a 1965 encyclopedia with three volumes dedicated to children, and Carl Sagan's epochal 1980 book *Cosmos*. "If you have just one historical image, like you'd see in . . . an old book in a flea market, it's far away, it's a bit dusty and old," Suter has said. But once you "place it next to another time, another grid, another structure, you can get it awake."

Brave Light Series, 2021
Courtesy the artist

Brian Sholis is a writer and editor based in Toronto.

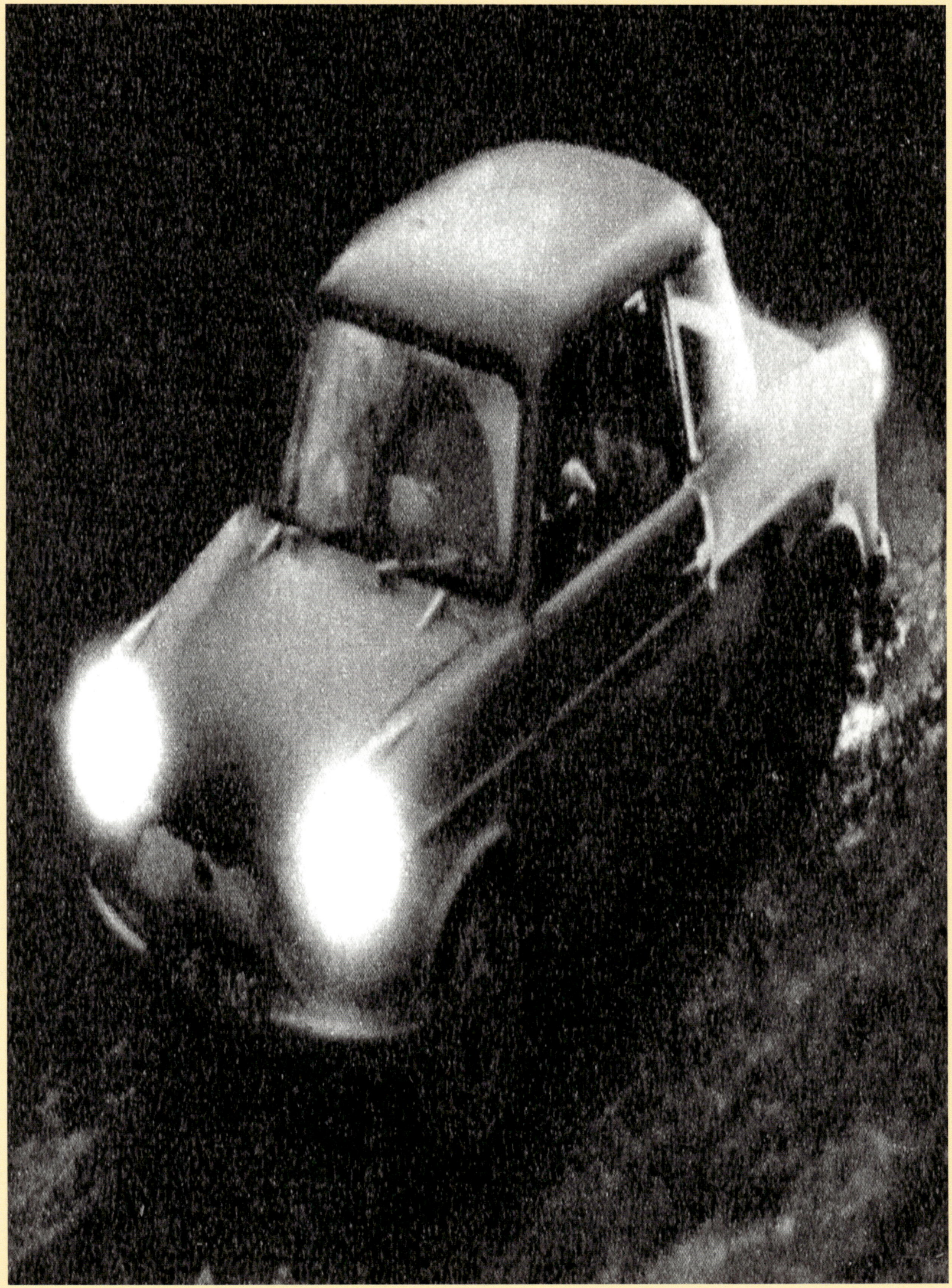

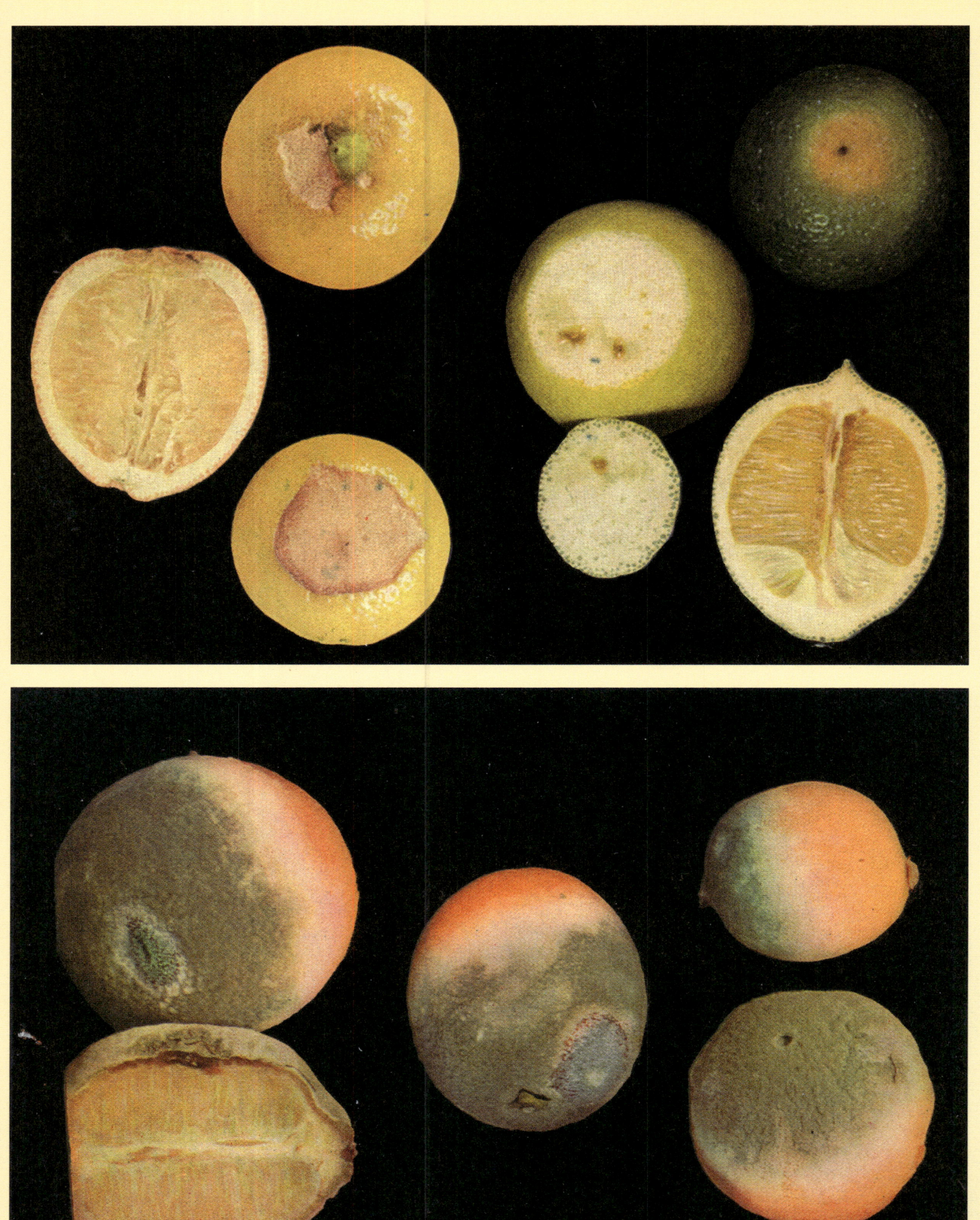

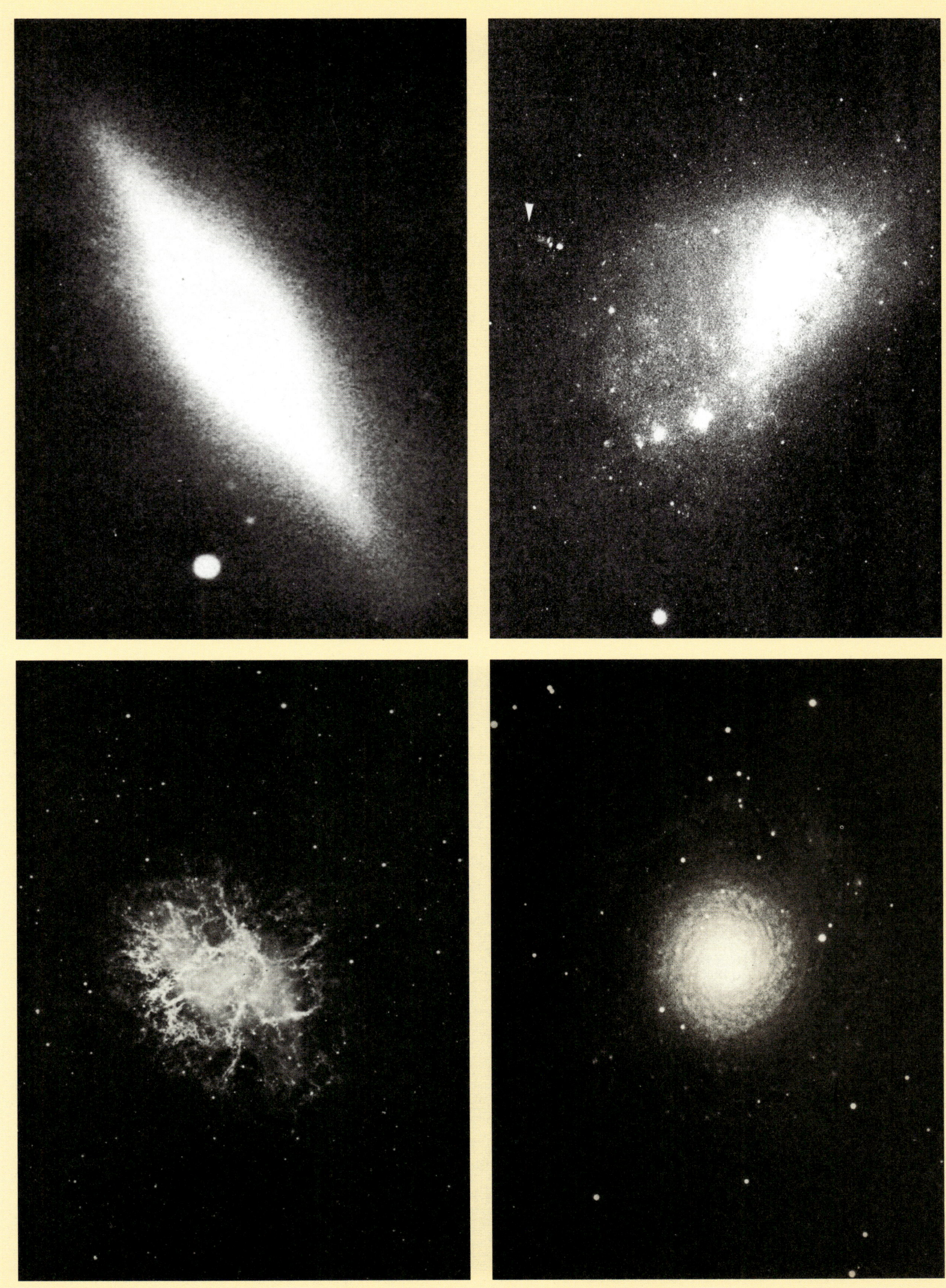

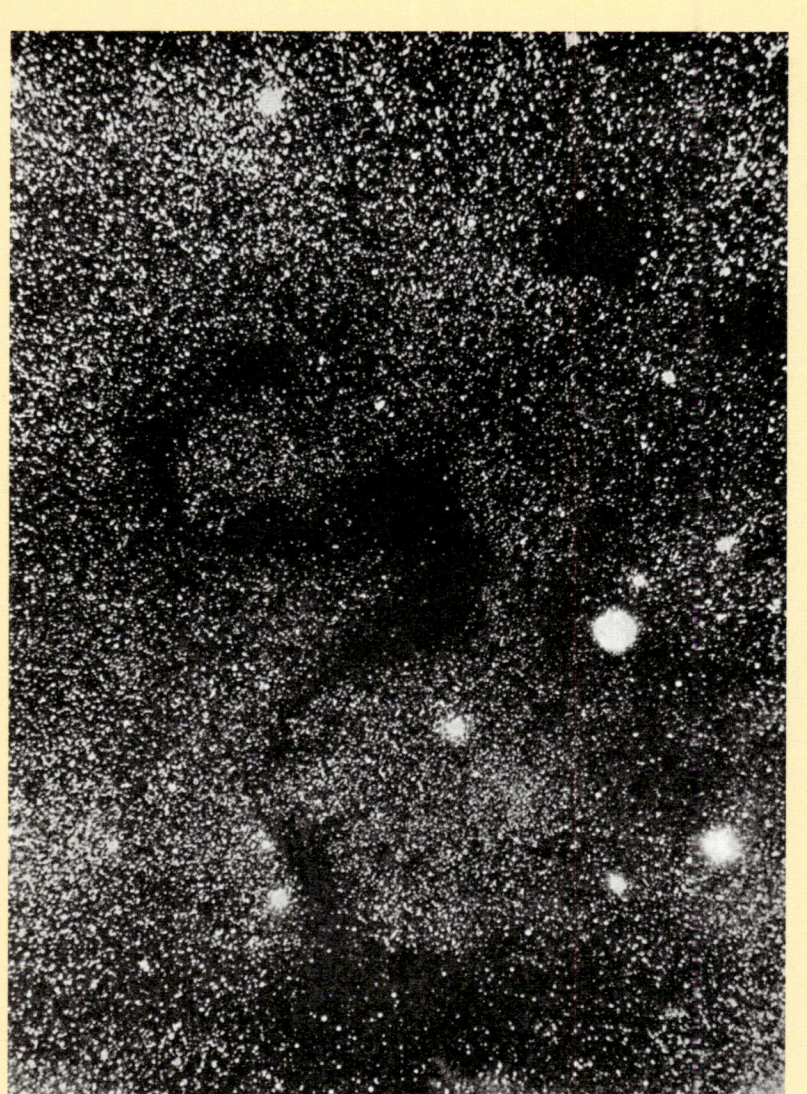
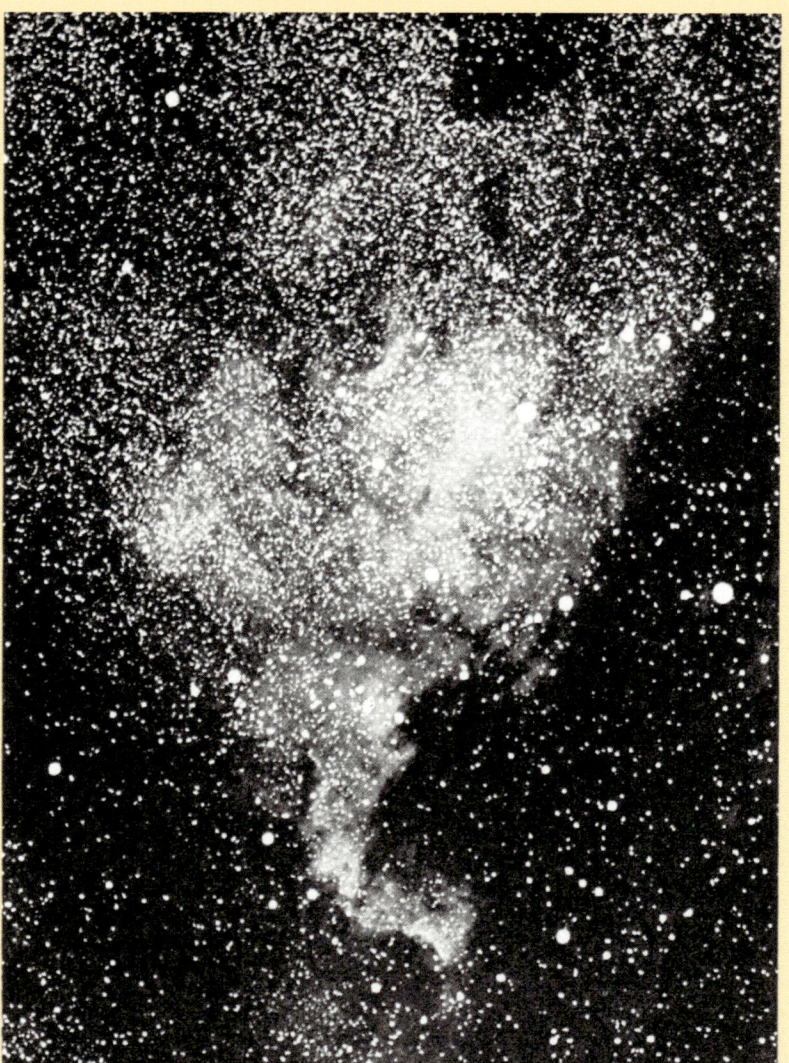

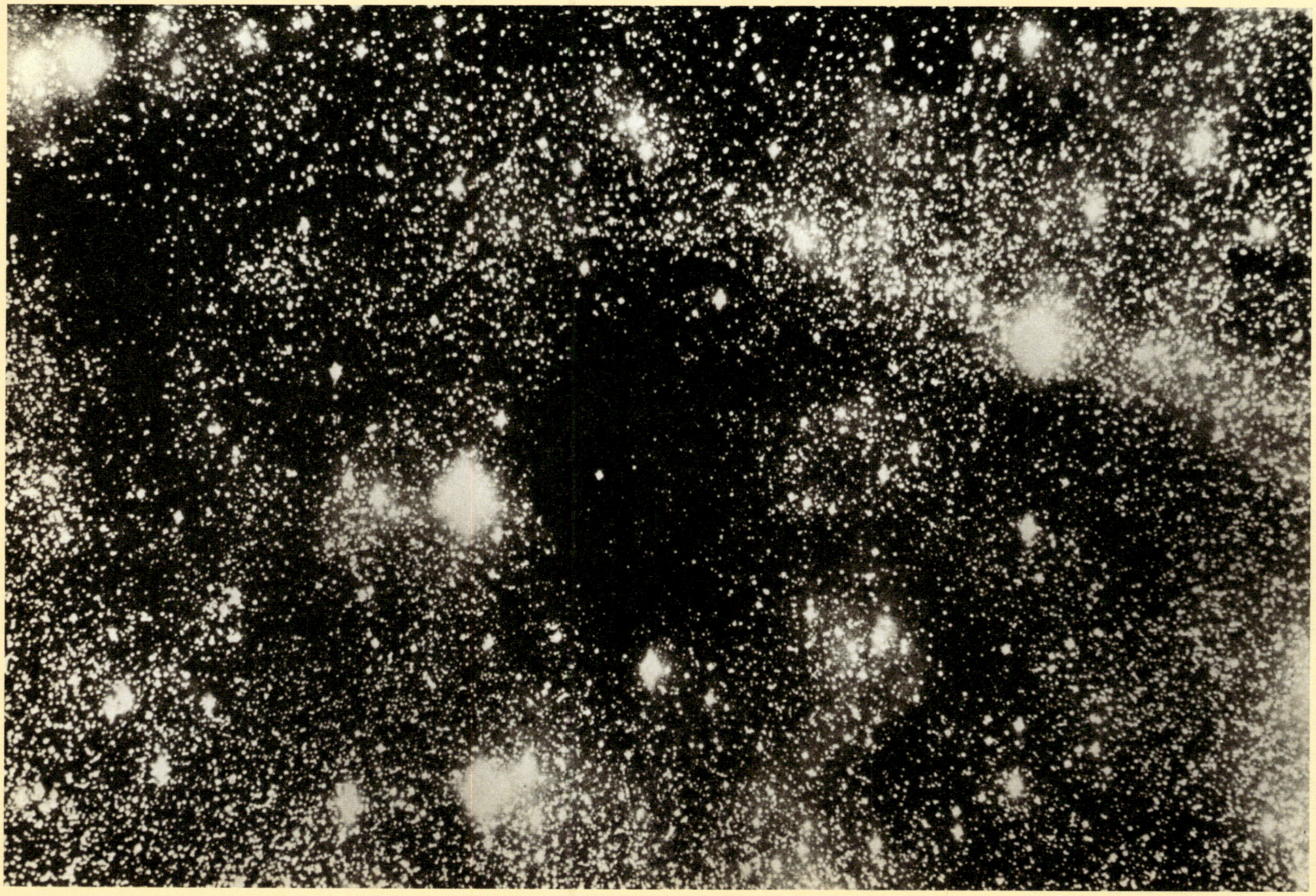

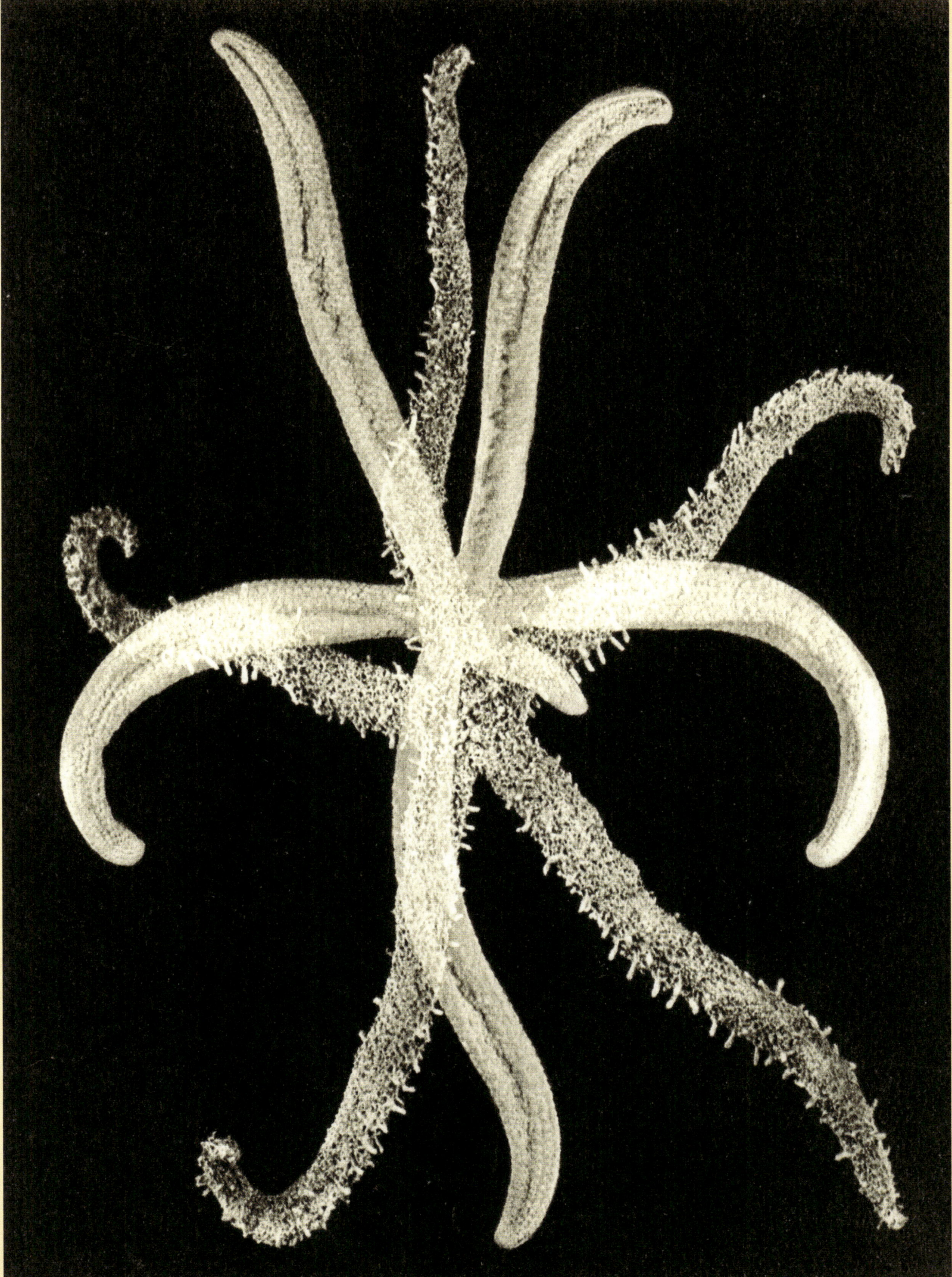

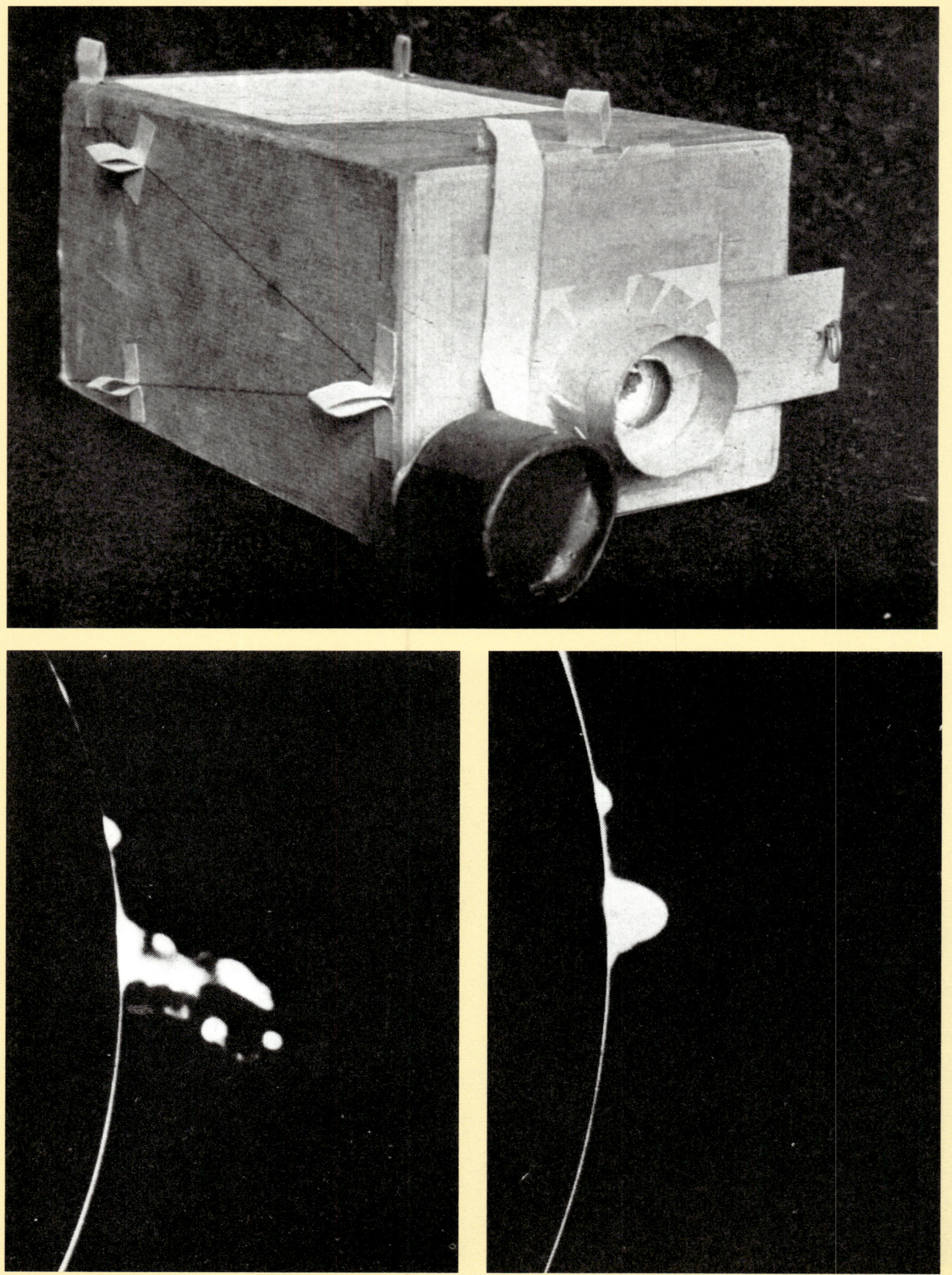

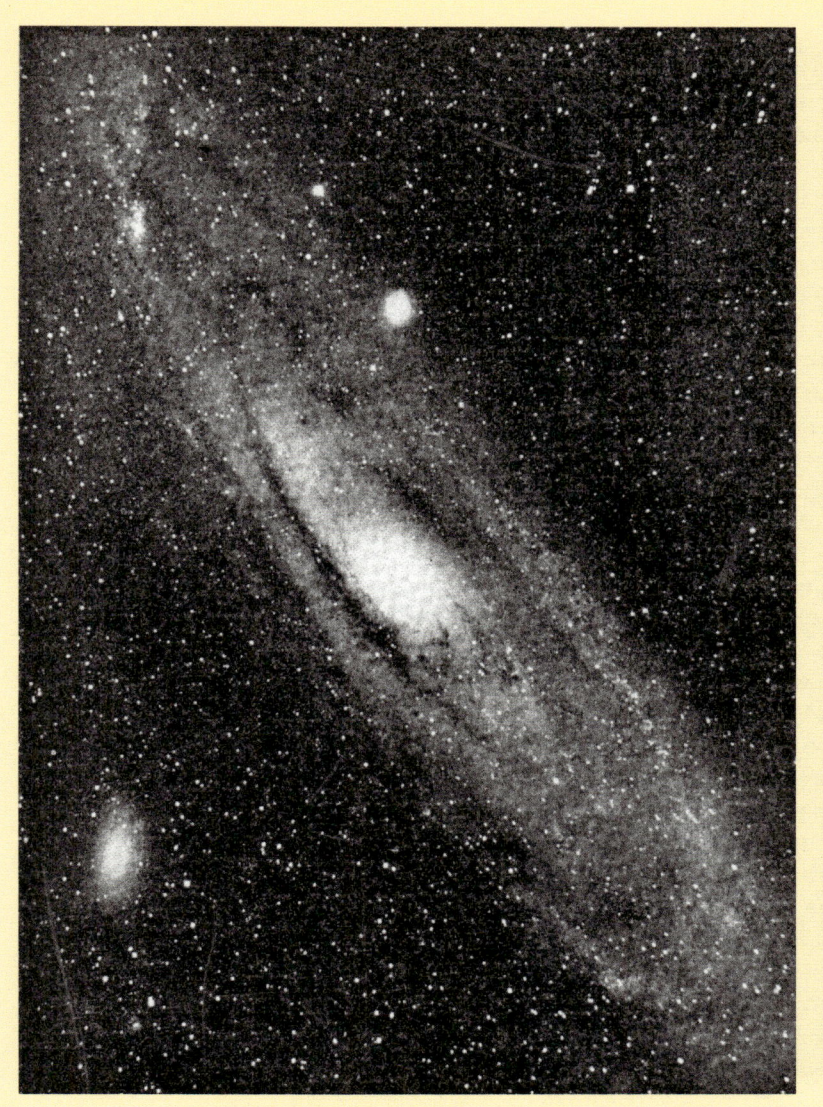
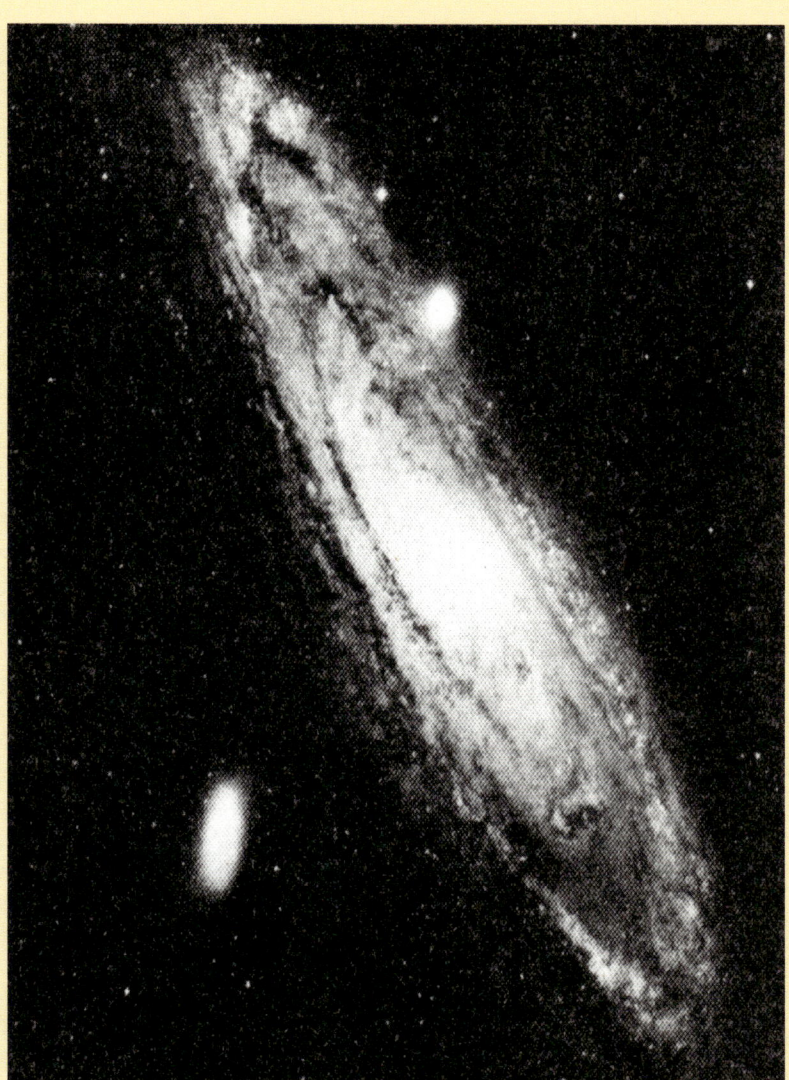

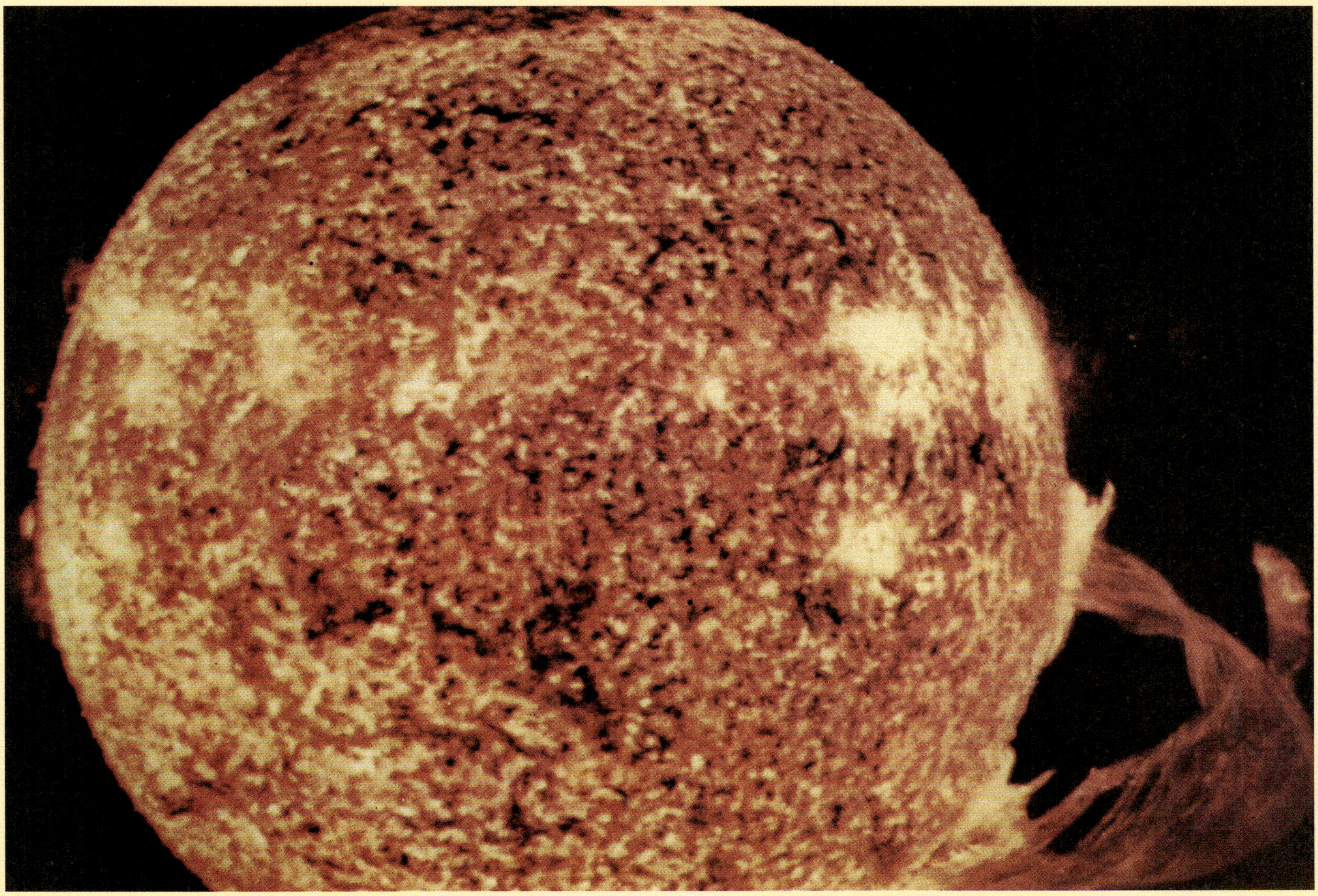

Awol Erizku
Mystic Parallax

Ashley James

In Awol Erizku's *Jaheem* (2020), an African mask is engulfed by fire, an orange-white burn so totalizing that the lapping flames light the steel-mesh fence against which the object is set. Energizing in every sense, *Jaheem* is a singular image, but the picture also coheres many of the aesthetics and subjects characteristic of Erizku's multivalent conceptual photographic practice: Africa and its diaspora; the mystical, the spiritual, and the surreal; creation both natural and cultural. High saturate color. Luminosity. Heat.

Fire is not seen but implied in *Quotidian Drip* (2018–20), the scene bathed in a warm orange, near-red, glow. A still life, the work demonstrates Erizku's open yet refined embrace of wide-ranging cultural reference points. Leather loafers—one shoe propped up on bricks—meet a Stanley-brand measuring tape, stacks of crisp Benjamins, a single rose stem in a clear vase, alongside a half dozen other dissimilar items. In one art-historical sense, this assemblage can be understood as purposefully nonsensical, engaging traditions of Dadaism and Surrealism. A photographic scrim that a C-clamp would conventionally clasp gets enigmatically replaced by an Ashanti "Akuaba" fertility doll. Behind it, a *maneki neko*, "lucky cat," peeks out from behind a jar. To stop at the absurd, however, would risk occluding the ways that Erizku's arrangements are constructed with intentions toward meaning-making of a kind. The unconventional construction visualizes the syncretism and multiplicity characteristic of contemporary global life, and, perhaps, especially Black creative life: leather, flowers, dollars, labor. At the same time, through selection, placement, and staging, these stable (and ofttimes staid) referents and symbols are cracked open and made anew both ontologically and aesthetically. There is no single reading of any object or juxtaposition, each unfurling along unending chains of signification. A bumblebee is a sartorial flourish . . . an ecological touchstone . . . a simple flash of gold.

This persistent signification is especially true in the case of Erizku's treatment of cultural objects from the continent. In *Quotidian Drip*, the faint profile of the Queen Nefertiti bust—ubiquitous within the Western imaging of African cultural import—is enclosed within a semitransparent jeweled cube. Barely visible but resolute, she is both familiar cultural referent and distanced glistening form. In *Love Is Bond (Young Queens)* (2018–20), Nefertiti is again present, with a quintet of young Black girls encircling a pedestaled bust of the royalty, while playing ring-around-the-rosy. In Erizku's imaginings, Africa is not only ancient but also mythical, technical, experimental, futurist, innovative, (e)strange(d).

It is also cosmic. In *Moon Voyage (Keep Me in Mind)* (2018–20), a picture that features two individuals in a ballroom-like embrace, a female figure wears what appears to be a stylized African mask pigmented in blue. Her silk dress and arm-length gloves bring tradition to the image, while the mask presents an electrifying portal to the mythological alien. The energy powering *Moon Voyage* is not solar but lunar, a green celestial light under which the two dance. But even without fire, the same sensibility that guides work such as *Jaheem* is present here, as it is in all of Erizku's still lifes, portraits, and tableaux. It is an approach marked by intuition, style, history, and opacity. A reverence and a confidence. Heat.

Opposite:
Love is Bond (Young Queens), 2018–20;
page 62: *Fit it, critic, get it, hit it, run it, drill it, wet it, I'm in it, really. Split it fifty-fifty. Ball, Reggie. Ready, set, go!*, 2021;
page 63: *Jaheem*, 2020

Ashley James is an associate curator of contemporary art at the Solomon R. Guggenheim Museum in New York.

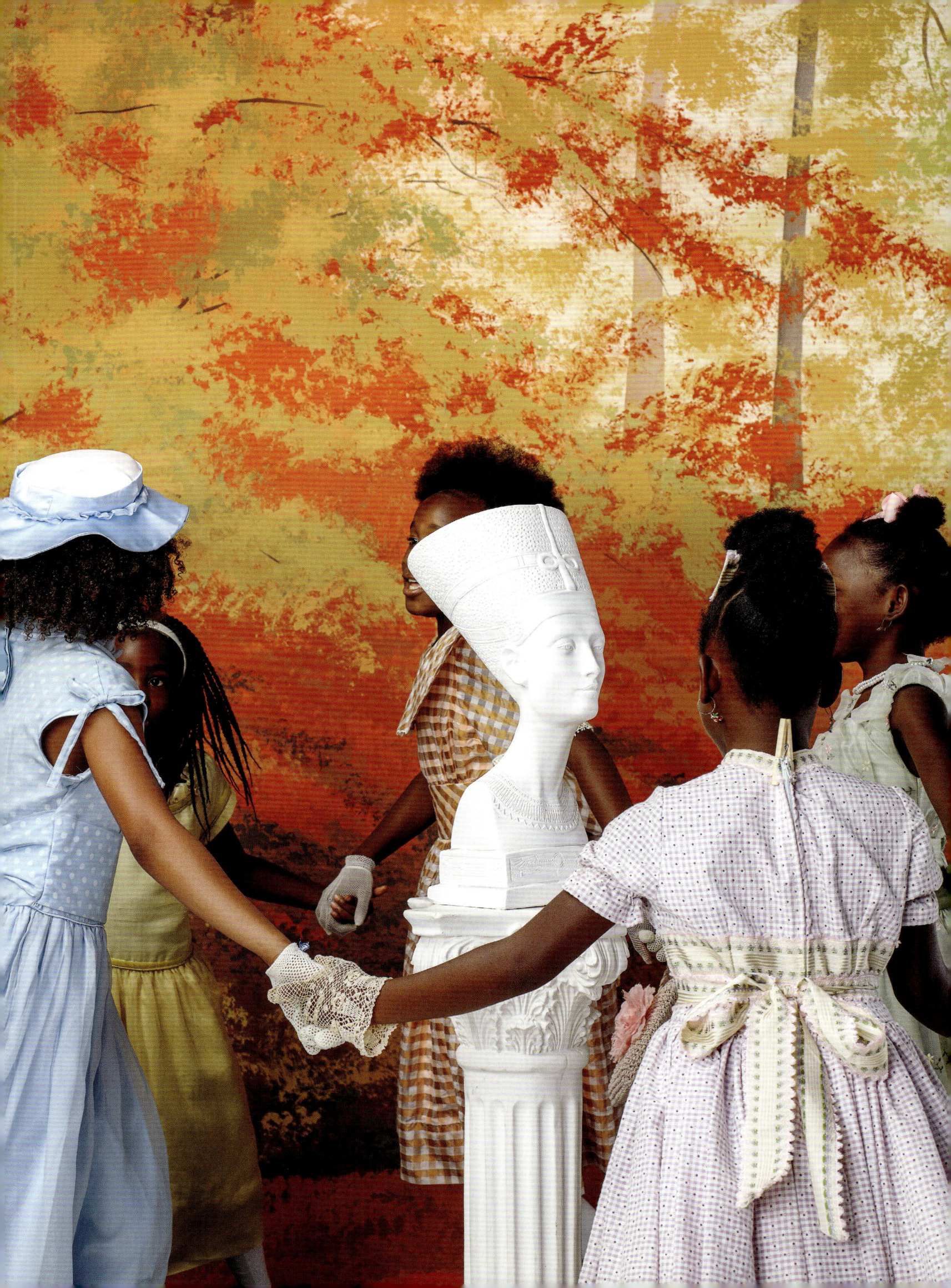

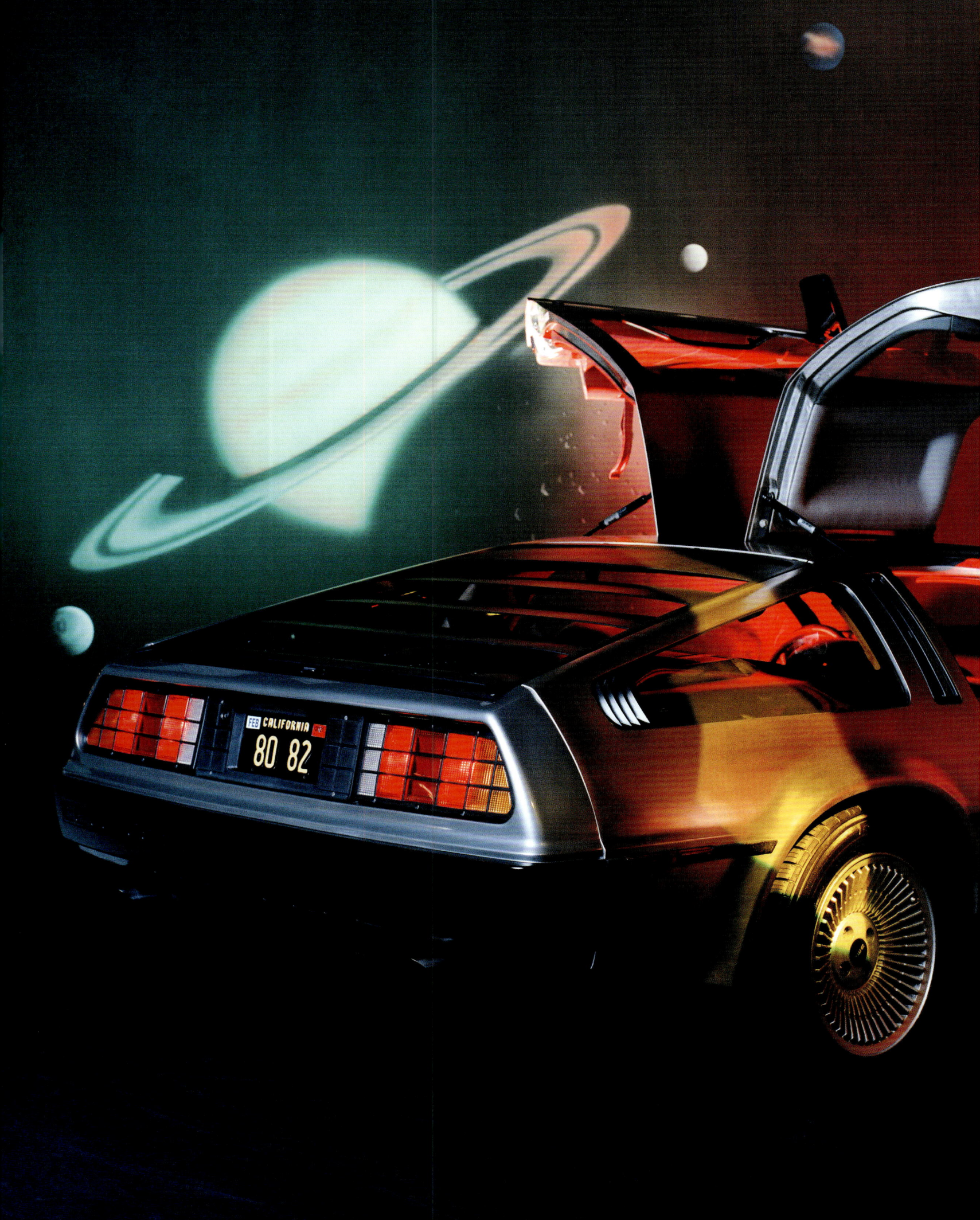

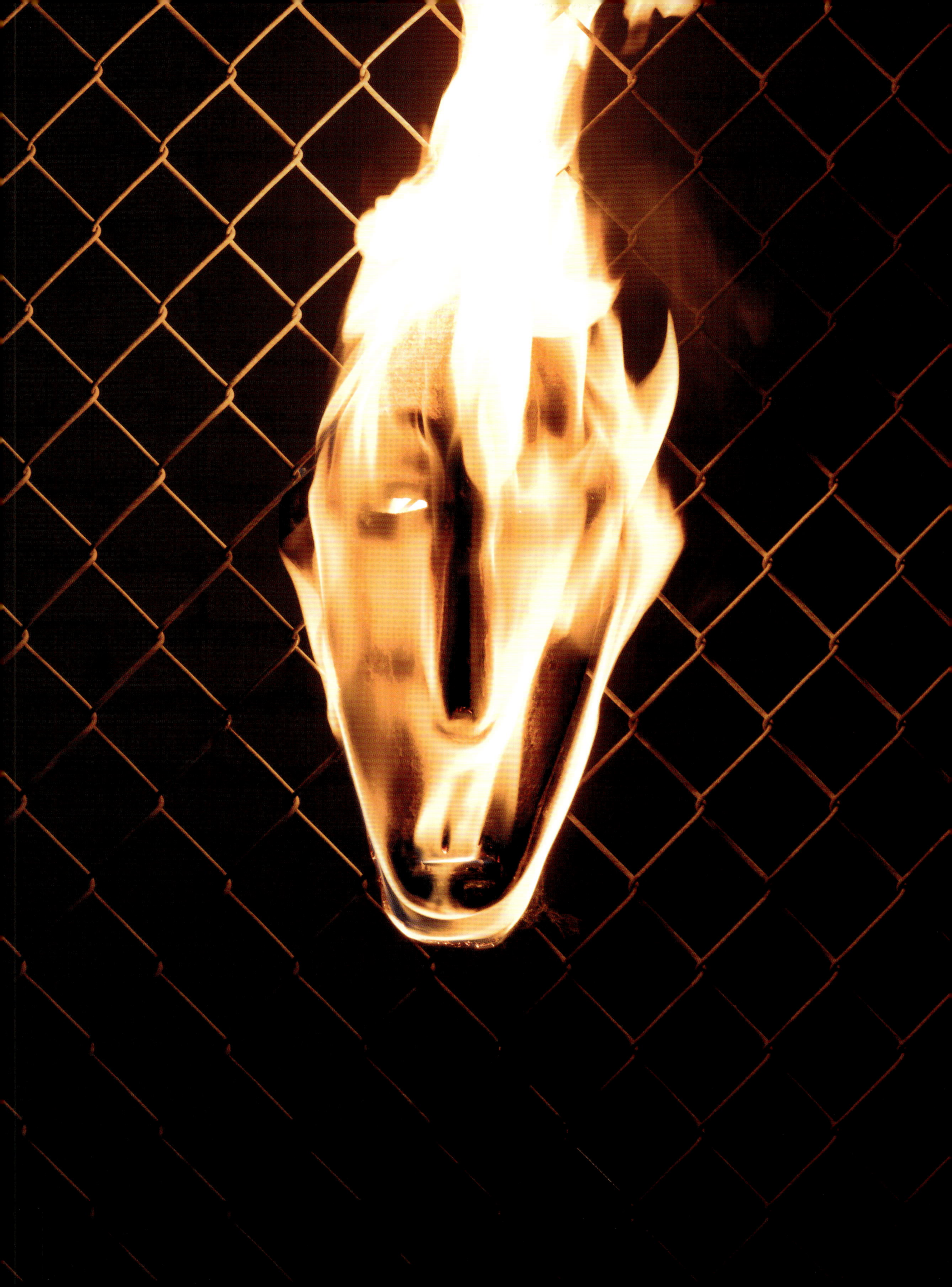

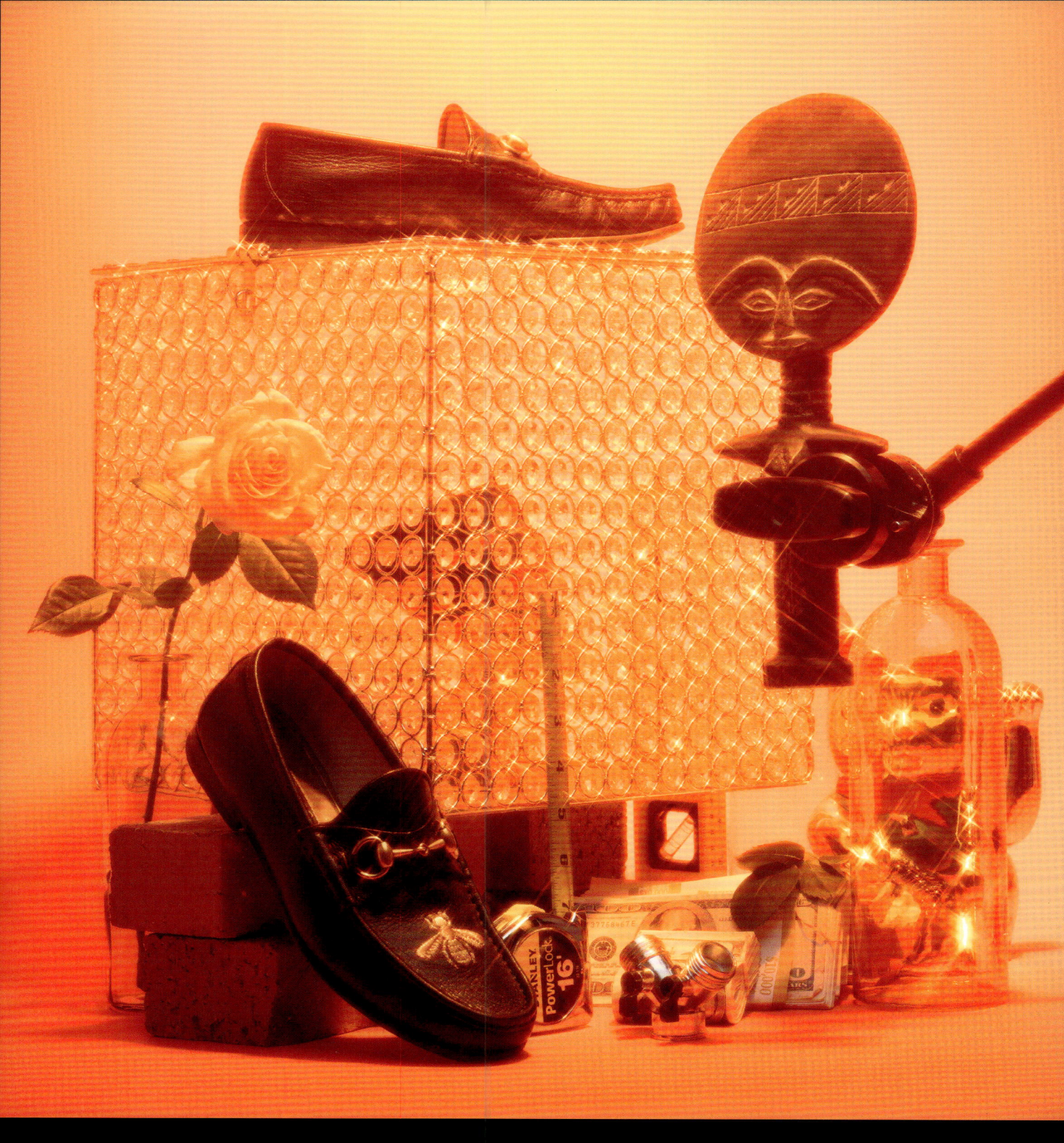

This page:
Quotidian Drip, 2018–20;
opposite: *Reverend Dr.*
Robert Turner kneeling in
front of a surviving wall
at the bombed basement
of The Historic Vernon
AME Church, 2020;

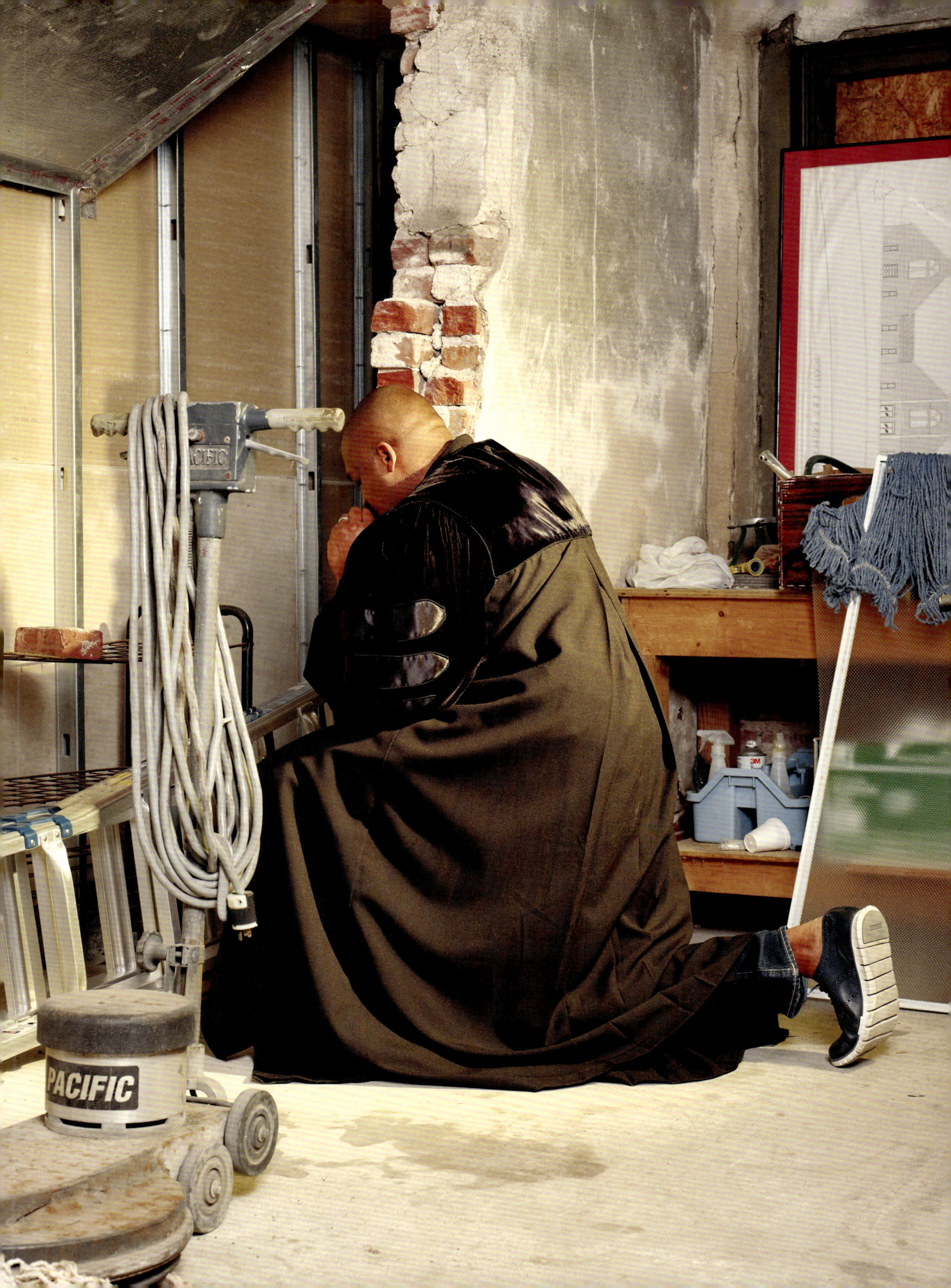

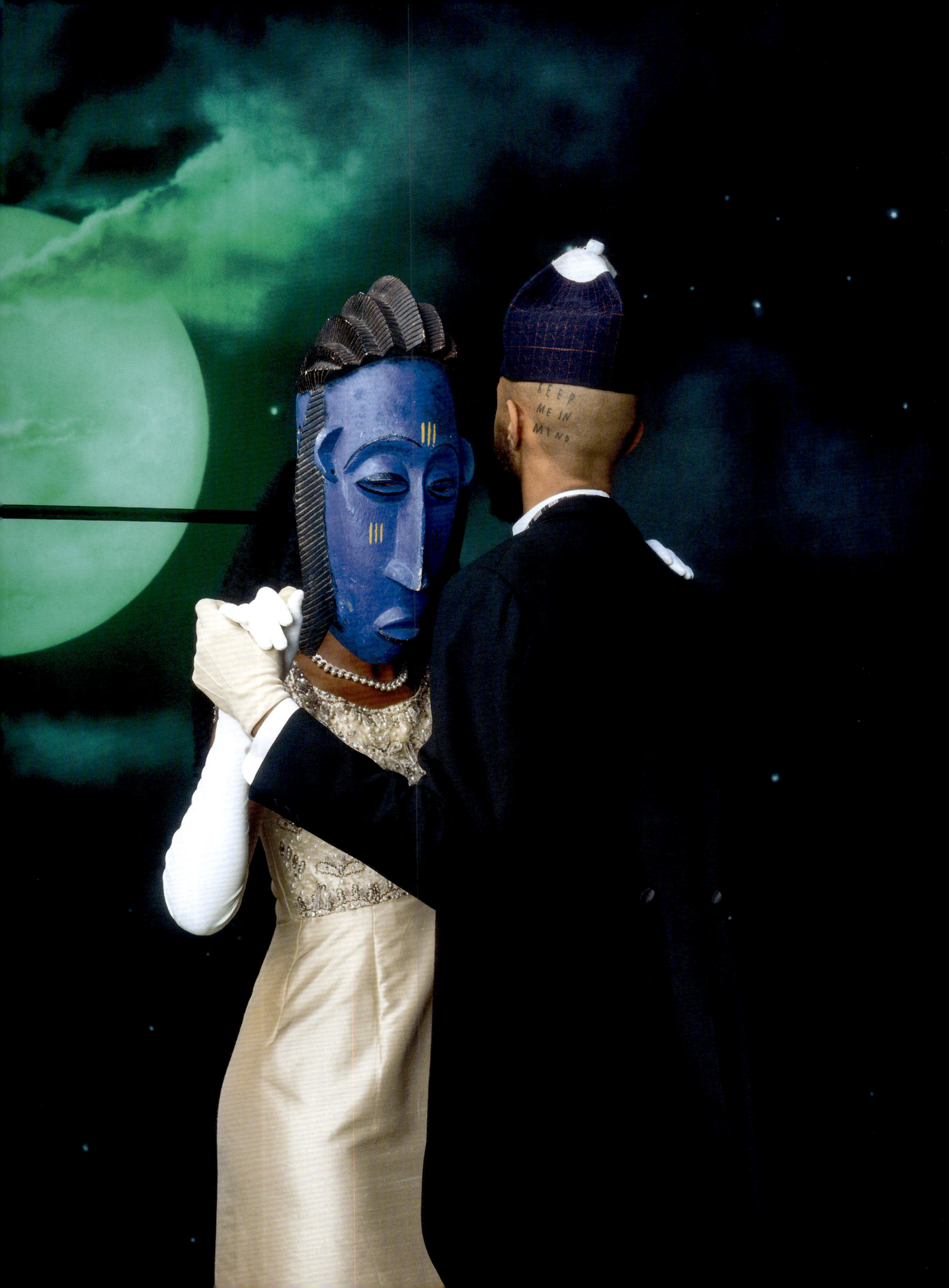

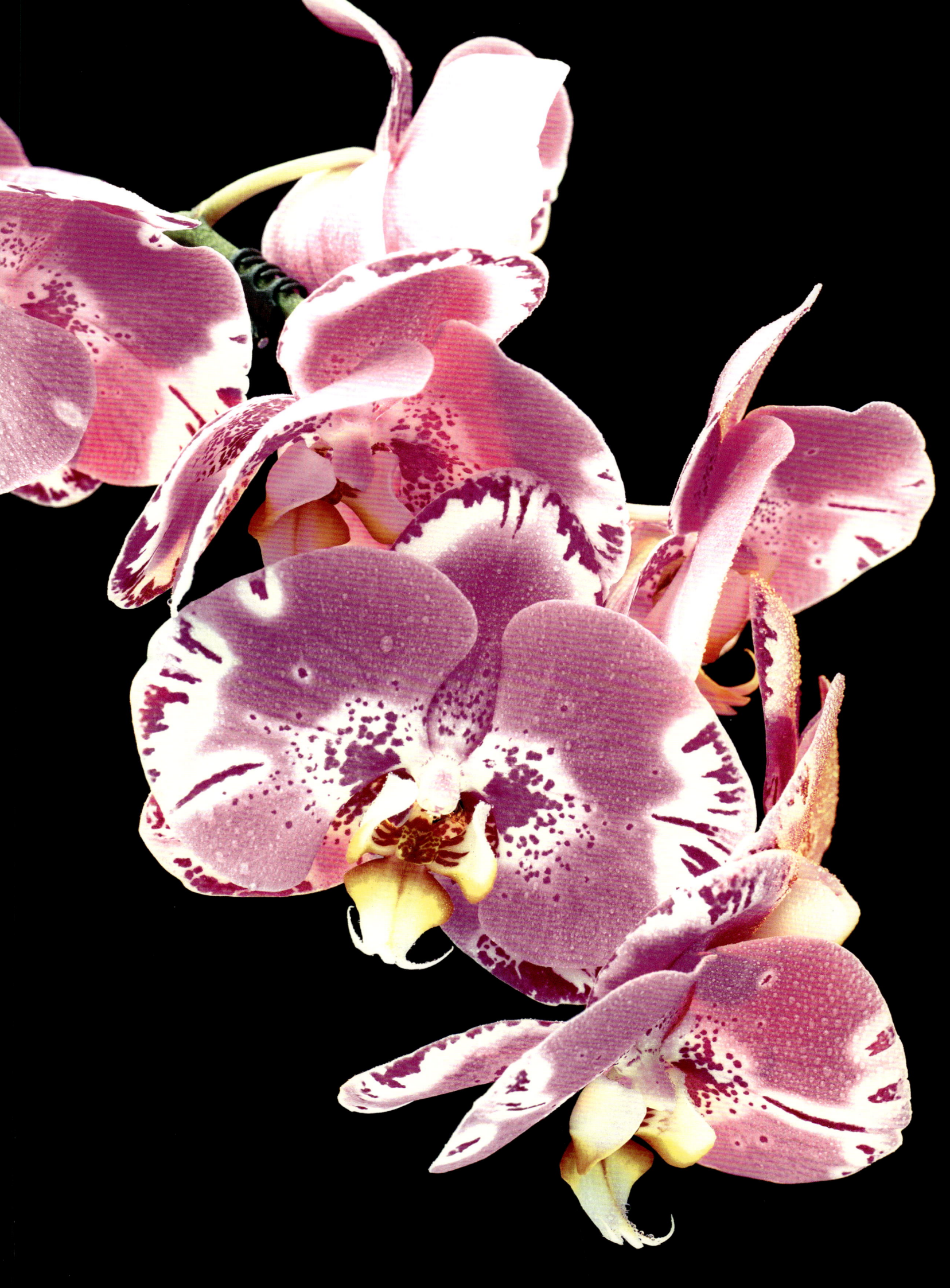

THE WORLD OF JUDITH JOY ROSS

Rebecca Bengal

Judith Joy Ross wants to show me her garden. As she throws open the back door to her home in Bethlehem, Pennsylvania, a large brown rabbit flashes across the yard, a comet trail vanishing into a maze of plants vivid and green against the gray sky. Ross turns to me, her face bright with excitement, "Did you see that?" I am reminded of a story I had heard, how once, while driving in rural Pennsylvania, Ross had seen something in a kid's face that caused her to pull the car over abruptly, drag her 8-by-10 camera out of the car, and call after two boys, aged twelve or so. Within moments, as Ross disappeared under the cloth and the boys began to arrange themselves before her lens, the alchemy of their connection became palpable.

Those particular photographs did not materialize—there was a problem with the film that day—but the Judith Joy Ross pictures

that do survive are the representation of thousands of such lightning encounters dating back to the late 1970s and first widely introduced at the 1985 *New Photography* exhibition at the Museum of Modern Art in New York. Ross is a master of the formal portrait, exquisitely executed with astonishing emotional clarity, as if she could see straight into the innermost lives of the earnest schoolchildren and tormented teenagers, the ennobled gas station attendants and car rental reps, along with veterans, senators, mourners, and protesters, most of them in the United States, most of them not far from Hazleton, Pennsylvania, the former coal-mining town where she was born and raised. These people form her photographic universe. "She has this extraordinary antenna," former MoMA curator Susan Kismaric, who has worked closely with Ross over the years, told me recently. Kismaric was along for the ride when Ross was

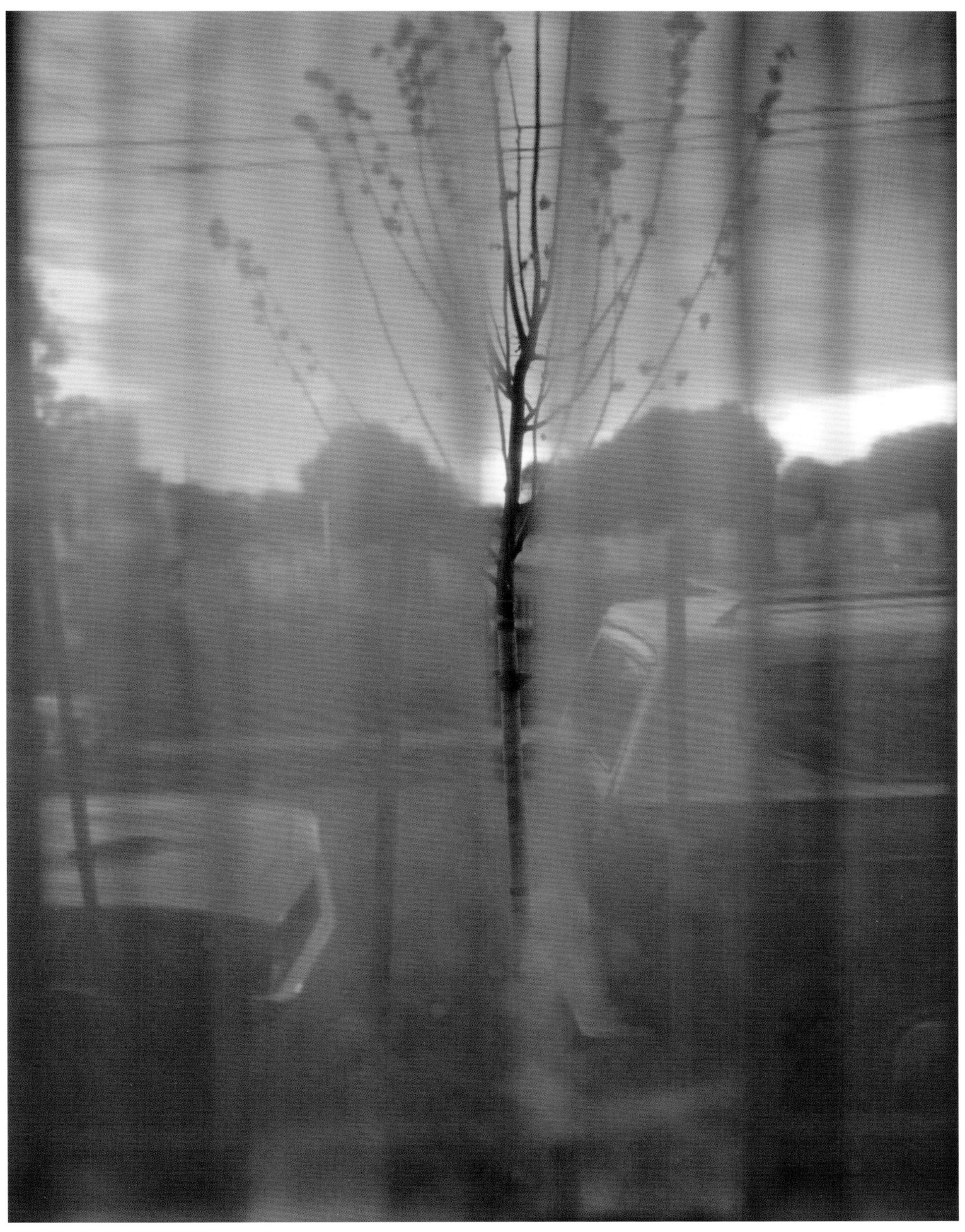

305 North Tenth Street,
Allentown, Pennsylvania,
1983

Ross's pictures are holy in their awkwardness—the teen with the dark gothic bangs wielding a rake, the way the girls clasp their hands over their bathing suits.

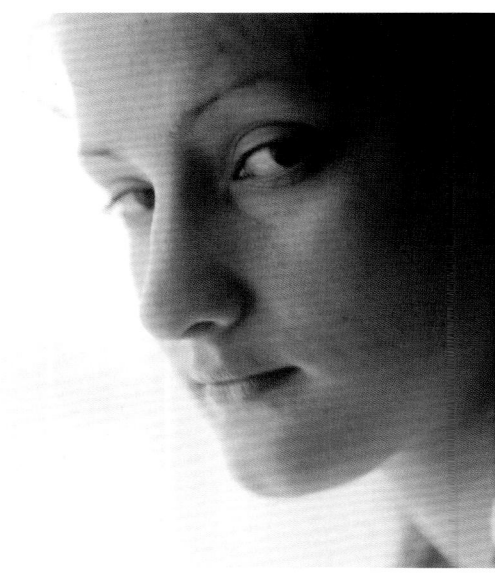

Celia, 1980

photographing in Minersville. "Judith never projects, she never condescends or judges, but she intuits."

In person, Ross is gentle, emphatically honest, devastatingly funny, frequently cursing—all at once. White blunt-cut bangs frame her face; she wears glasses in an outdated prescription. She rarely is idle for long, but when a thought overtakes her, she is apt to rest her entire head in her hands to fully consider it. She greets me on the porch of her yellow house, which, much to her dismay, overlooks construction that will soon obscure her view of Bethlehem, where she has lived for more than half her life. Inside is a home wholly devoted to photography, from the darkroom in the basement to the archives in the attic. "I long for two thousand square feet to store all this shit," she says. There is a large computer monitor in the dining room; its table holds recent contact prints. For her major retrospective, set to open in September at Fundación Mapfre, in Madrid, and travel through Europe, custom photographic paper was made to replace the now discontinued printing-out-paper Ross relied on for years.

In the early 1980s, when photographers could simply show up in person on an appointed day at MoMA and drop off their portfolios for review, Ross was called in to speak with John Szarkowski, the photography department's director, who, looking at her first major series, *Eurana Park* (1982), asked if she knew the pictures of the German photographer August Sander. Ross lied and said she didn't. "I was like Judas denying Christ," she says. "I didn't want him to think I was cheating." Szarkowski, who bought two of the pictures, offered reassurance: "It's okay, Judith. It's called tradition to be influenced by another's work." She had, in fact, studied Sander's pictures closely—how he photographed straightforwardly, centering the person in the frame. Sander's monumental series *Menschen des 20 Jahrhunderts* (People of the 20th Century), begun in the 1920s and proceeding for decades, identified and grouped subjects by occupation and social class. Ross isn't nearly as taxonomic; she is guided by a rapt, intense, wholehearted belief in the individual. (Ross disputes that Sander categorized people.) Her idiosyncratic printing practice—contact prints on printing-out-paper that are then toned with gold—enhances the fundamental uniqueness of the individuals she encounters. "No two prints by Judith are the same," says Joshua Chuang, who is curating Ross's retrospective and editing the accompanying catalogue. "Her way of experiencing humanity is through photography."

When she was coming up, Ross entered a world dominated by the iconographic portraits of Richard Avedon, Irving Penn, and Diane Arbus, pictures often first published in magazines, where they had to leap off the page. Ross's work, in a range of subtler tones, operates differently. Her contact prints are almost never bigger than the 8-by-10 dimensions of the negative. To enlarge them, she believes, could be "exploitive." Of the prints' scale and intimacy, Ross says, "They are asking you to come closer, and say hi."

"Like Diane Arbus and like Lisette Model, Arbus's teacher, she is working with the idea of the self, the tension between who one is and who one projects to the world," Kismaric explains. "With Arbus, one still sees something of that struggle; in Judith's pictures, outside the cosmopolitan world, it feels as though they're working against futures that were prescribed for them. The questions become more complicated."

Just as complicated is the question of why a photographer so revered by other photographers remains, to an extent, under the radar. The photographer An-My Lê once recalled how, when Ross visited her in New York, she'd play a game of guessing who on the subway Ross would choose to photograph; the fact that she was always wrong cemented Lê's awareness of Ross's empathic intuition. "Her work is beautiful in its transparency," Robert

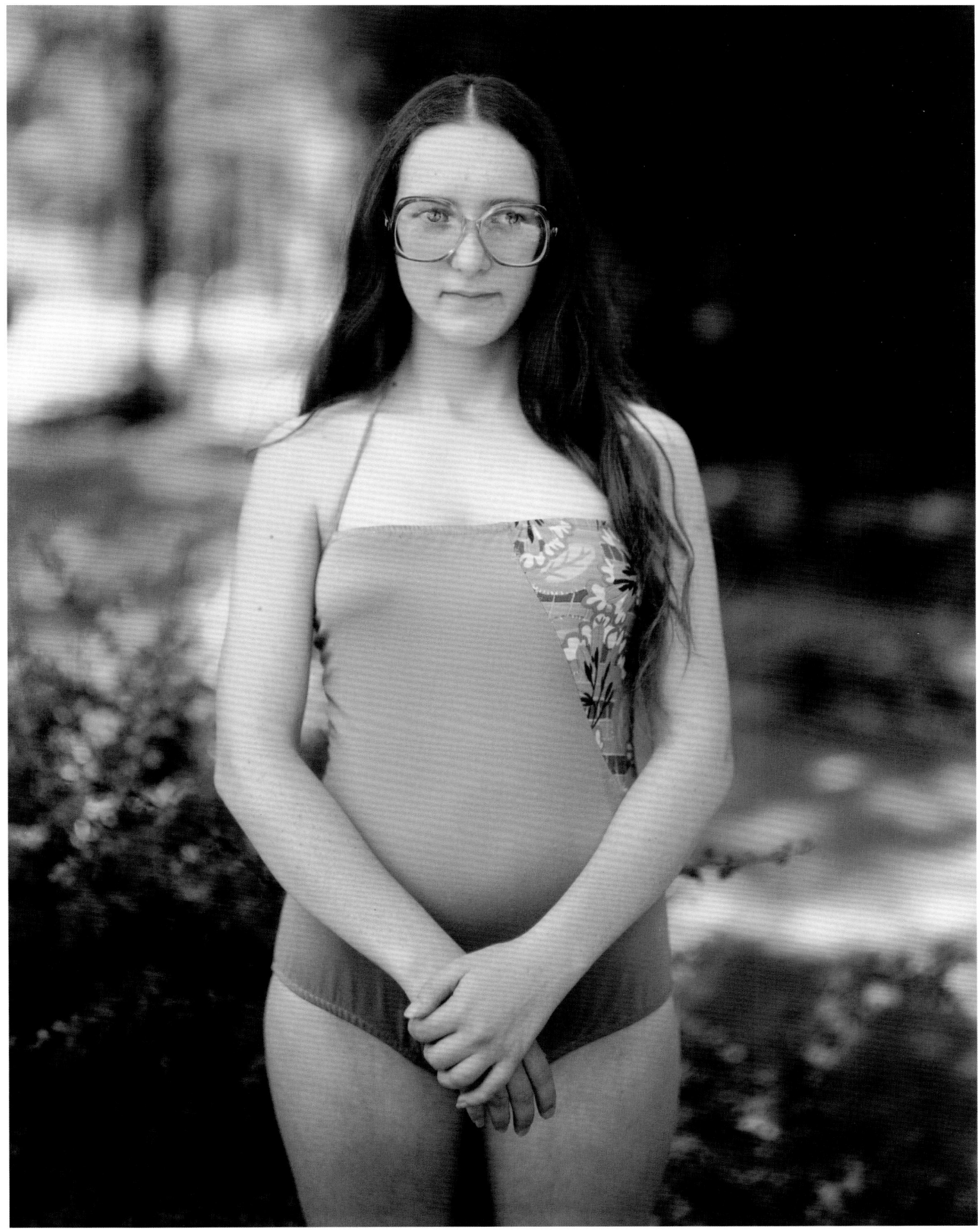

Untitled, Eurana Park,
Weatherly, Pennsylvania,
1982

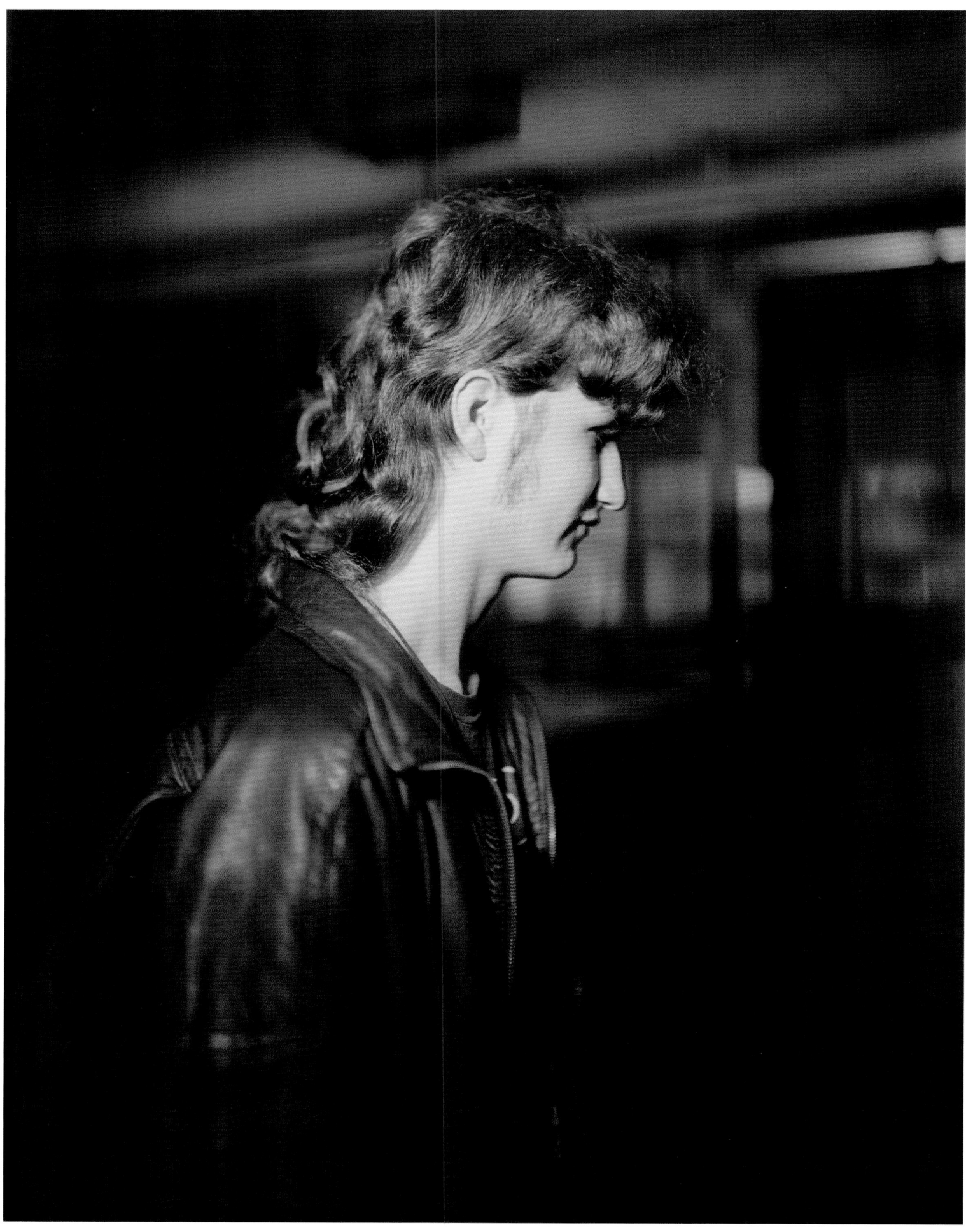

This page:
Timmy Wright, Shop Class,
Hazleton High School,
1992; opposite: Untitled,
Eurana Park, Weatherly,
Pennsylvania, 1982

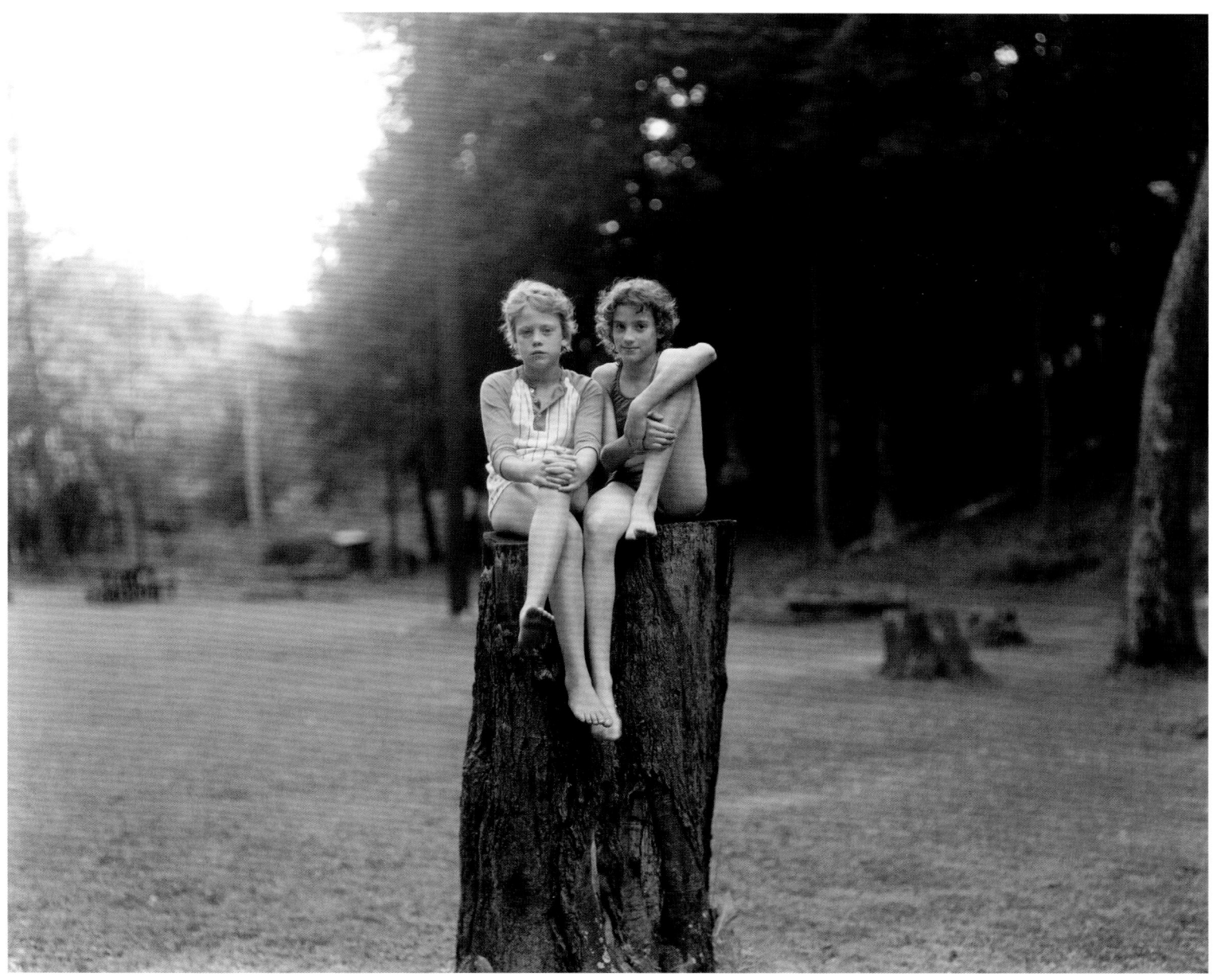

Adams writes in his book *Why People Photograph*—it's "a record of compassion." Gregory Halpern, a photographer who teaches at the Rochester Institute of Technology, has called her "the greatest portrait photographer to have ever worked in the medium." The photographer Paul Graham, who has taught with Ross at Yale, fell first for her Vietnam Veterans Memorial pictures. "It's one of the dirty little secrets of photography," he told me recently. "People act like they want to photograph rocks and houses and trees but what they really want is to have the gumption to photograph people the way Judith does."

Photobooks dominate Ross's shelves along with images by friends, such as Chris Killip, who died in October 2020. "I can't understand how his pictures can be so beautiful," she exclaims. "Tiny little people shown this big, yet every one of them is seen as an individual! Such humanity. Oh, my God. He is missed." Cabinets in nearly every room are filled with boxes of prints and negatives. To a visitor, the house can feel like the brain's memory chambers. Ross claims her own memory is foggy, but whenever a gap emerges, she herds me upstairs to look through the cabinets of boxes of prints to supply the story.

Above her dresser, framed works by her heroes mingle with family pictures. "That's our summer home, where my heart is," she says, pointing at a photograph of a cabin in the borough of Weatherly, Pennsylvania, where Ross grew up daydreaming and playing with her brothers among the creatures in the woods. "That's my mom, that's my dad, that's my Atget," she says, pointing out a

print of the Panthéon, a revered gift from her brother Edward. The influence of the French photographer is evident in a few of Ross's early personal pictures: One of her mother, a piano teacher, shown in profile, "looking with some sadness at jewelry at the Met," on a trip she and Ross had taken to New York. One of her father, reclining on a forest floor, dressed in a suit, appears romantic and elegiac. "Fucking suit and a tie in the woods!" Ross says, laughing. It could have been made after a day at the five-and-dime store he owned in Nanticoke, a former mining town where other relatives also had shops selling candy and secondhand books. "He used to let me help out, paint faces on the mannequins," she recalls. "I'd put eyeliner on them; I made them even worse. But he never minded. He just wanted us nearby."

Ross made her first photographs in the mid-1960s as a student at Moore College of Art and Design, in Philadelphia. At the IIT Institute of Design, in Chicago, where she earned an MA in photography in 1970, she felt disconnected from Aaron Siskind's experimental-minded program. "I was lost," she says. "Eventually, I didn't go to class. Including the Literature of Alienation. I should have gotten at least a C because I never went. I mean, what's wrong with these people!" The lost feeling lingered for a decade. Ross went to Bethlehem, where she taught at Moravian College, simultaneously giving herself the photography education she felt she never received in school, via Eastman Kodak materials and the exhibitions she'd see (Arbus and Bruce Davidson, among others) and books she'd buy (Sander, Atget,

Lewis Hine) in New York, two hours away. Eventually, she began photographing again.

In 1982, the devastation she felt over her father's death carried her back in time. The beloved summer cabin was lonesome in his absence. Ross took her recently purchased 8-by-10 view camera a few miles away, to a public swimming park in Weatherly. In her mind, the children and teenagers she met there at Eurana Park represented a time of innocence before the first experience of grief. The pictures are holy in their awkwardness—the teen with the dark gothic bangs wielding a rake, the way the girls clasp their hands over their bathing suits—barely visible surroundings briefly lifting them out of their lives. In some, droplets of water can still be seen on skin, evidence of how quickly Ross must have forged these connections.

"I photographed people from the get-go. Even though I didn't know how to have them in my life. That's probably why I'm good at it," Ross says. "Something happens, I see them intensely, and we never see each other again. I know it's just a photograph. I know I'm being delusional. But I like to think I'm capturing the real thing."

"But if you didn't think that it was the real thing in the moment, could you even make the picture?" I ask. Ross shakes her head emphatically, no.

Over the years, the arc of her work has expanded in scope to wider communities, public institutions, and national politics, projects for which Ross has sometimes earnestly sought the permission of mayors and civic organizations. But the true subject is both as simple and complicated as every human she meets. In 1983, thinking she would do a series about the United States and the Vietnam War, she traveled to Maya Lin's granite memorial in Washington, D.C., and found herself drawn to solitary expressions of grief.

The distinctions between her projects became apparent in her printing techniques. "In Eurana Park, certain browns were happy," Ross says. "When kids were pubescent they turned gray. For me, I didn't get puberty. I wasn't a happy camper with sexuality." Tones for Ross exist on a psychological register, darkening or morphing over time. "Certainly Vietnam was gray. And the gray got so extreme. Pictures from Nanticoke, they might be an exquisite gray with a dash of purple in it that was melancholy. Or a brown shadow on a gray print. A gray print means something."

In 1986, armed with a Guggenheim grant, one good suit, a makeshift shopping cart for her equipment, including a suspicious-looking box swathed in duct tape to hold her camera, and an inborn fear of authority figures, Ross set out for Capitol Hill—"gray with highlights and a hint of brown in the shadow." She photographed Strom Thurmond "with his five-foot-tall shoulders and shrunken apple head, surrounded by his French furniture. . . . This awful racist person but I was seduced by his presence." Her skill at creating instantaneous connections, and the magic ritual of bringing out the view camera, were crucial in these fifteen-minute appointments. In the faces of the members of Congress, humanized in Ross's frame, it is possible to glimpse, briefly, an aspect of their private selves, not far removed from her young swimmers and workers back in Pennsylvania.

In the early 1990s, when money was tight, Ross began cleaning houses. "Does it look like I'd be a good maid?" she joked, waving at her stacks of archival boxes. "I carried superglue with me on the job; I broke everything." It was in the midst of this time that the photographer John Gossage called to tell her she'd won a Charles Pratt Memorial Award of $25,000. First, she retorted, "How do I know you're John Gossage?" and then she called the owners of the house she was supposed to clean that day to say she wasn't coming. "I'm Cinderella! I just got a grant!"

From 1992 through 1994, she returned to the same public schools in Hazleton she'd daydreamed through while growing up. Again, the goal was idealistic. "I wanted people to pay their taxes. I wanted people to care about public education," Ross says. "I

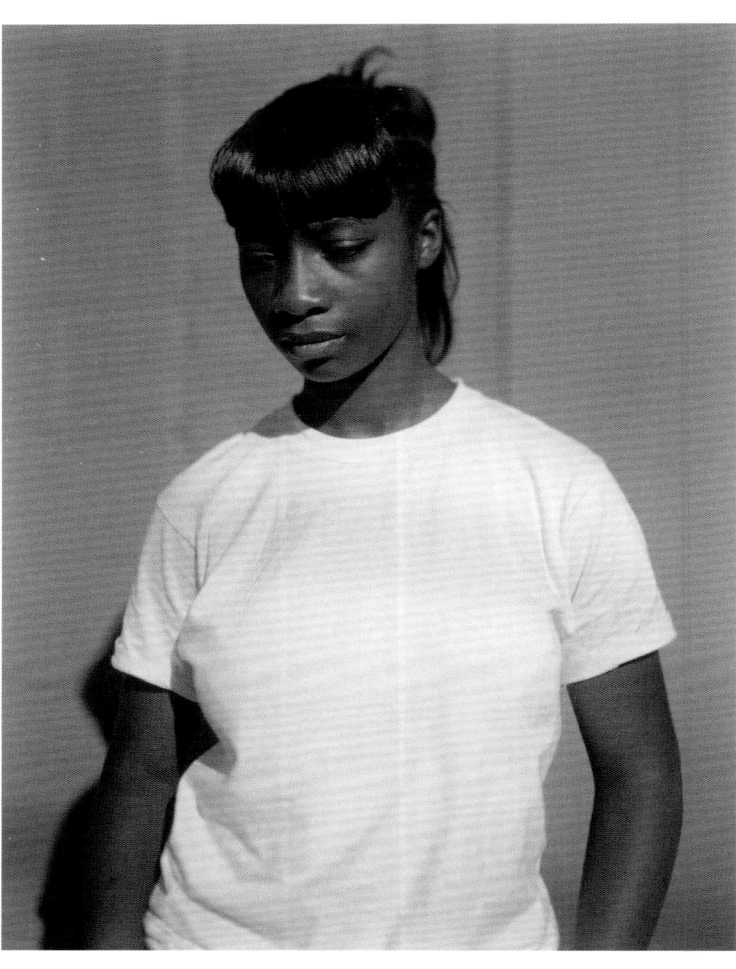

Philadelphia, Pennsylvania,
1998

certainly didn't care about mine. I thought school sucked." Ross's Hazleton pictures are singular in their acknowledgment that school can indeed suck, and in their eerily personal portrayal of the vastness and discomfort and yearning and angst of adolescence— the pride of a perfectly brushed mullet or a cascade of sprayed hair. "These are *their own selves*," she says. In a print displayed in her front room, a boy stares at the camera through glasses so thick you long to tell him they'll be considered cool in twenty years. But here, he simply is a high schooler briefly showing his vulnerable self. Ross's framing preserves this, acting as a protective shell.

Protest the War (2007), an unassuming little book published by Steidl and Pace/MacGill, her gallery at the time, is about the size of a trucker's logbook or a horse-racing pamphlet. Ross, hoping the pictures could change people's minds about who a nonviolent protester is, had wished it would be distributed at gas stations, "right next to the chewing tobacco and the beef jerky and the breath mints." The fervent, believing expressions of her protesters never made it into this montage, but Ross herself again went to Capitol Hill, hand delivering copies at congressional offices. At the heart of her work is a profound identification with the singular person and a belief in what society can and should be, the rift that exists between the two, and the person confronting the specter of change. "I see you, and, please God, I want to get what I see before it's gone," Ross says. "Once you get out the camera, you get discombobulated and you have to find it again. You may not be finding the same thing."

Ross says she is not interested in photographing people anymore. Or, that she does have a new idea about photographing people that she is intent on pursuing, but she doesn't want to talk about it yet in a public way. She is recovering from eye surgery that she claims made her vision worse. The world has been so uncertain.

Last year, in the days before the U.S. presidential election was called, Ross began to photograph trees. "Maybe it's sacrilegious to talk about them this way, but I do see them not as people but as individuals," she says. We get in Ross's car, stickered Make America Green Again, and she points out favorite elms as we drive to a cemetery in Bethlehem, from which you can glimpse, through a veil of ropy vines, the cemetery that Walker Evans famously depicted in *A Graveyard and Steel Mill in Bethlehem, Pennsylvania* (1935). "He couldn't have photographed from here, because everything's the same tone," she notes. Ross comes here for walks, not pictures. "The subject of death is so enormous, who can photograph it?"

She is pleased when I notice that, instead of camera equipment packed in her car, an animal cage rests on the backseat. Later, I will think how *cage* or *trap* feels like the wrong word, especially for someone who lights up when she describes seeing a muskrat in the wild and tells me she cannot bear to have dogs anymore ("because you love them more than your family, of course"), especially when I learn that it is for the groundhog that lives under her porch and sometimes ventures to the back steps, standing on its hind legs. She speaks of it in a way, I think, that might apply to some of the people in her pictures: "Sometimes, I think I should try to catch it," Ross says, "and take it to a happier place."

In September 2001, Ross began to make portraits at another site of mourning—an overlook on the Eagle Rock Reservation in New Jersey where people come to stare toward New York at the spot where the Twin Towers once stood. Silently, Ross would slip a handwritten request to anyone she wished to photograph. A day after our visit, I drive to Eagle Rock. I try to pick out the people whom Ross might approach, and I am sure I am wrong. On my way out, I notice a young couple walking rapidly away from a marshy thicket, carrying a long trap seemingly identical to the one I'd seen in Ross's car. The cage is empty; whatever they have brought with them, they have now released.

Rebecca Bengal is a writer based in New York.

Ross is guided by a rapt, intense, wholehearted belief in the individual.

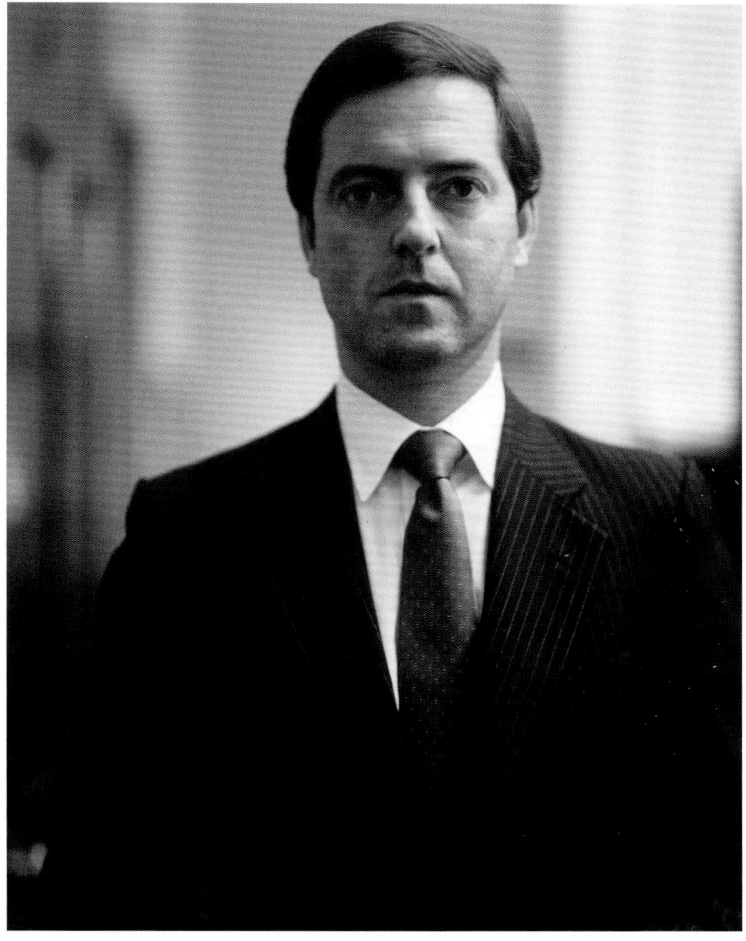

Congressman John P. Hiler, Republican, Indiana, 1987

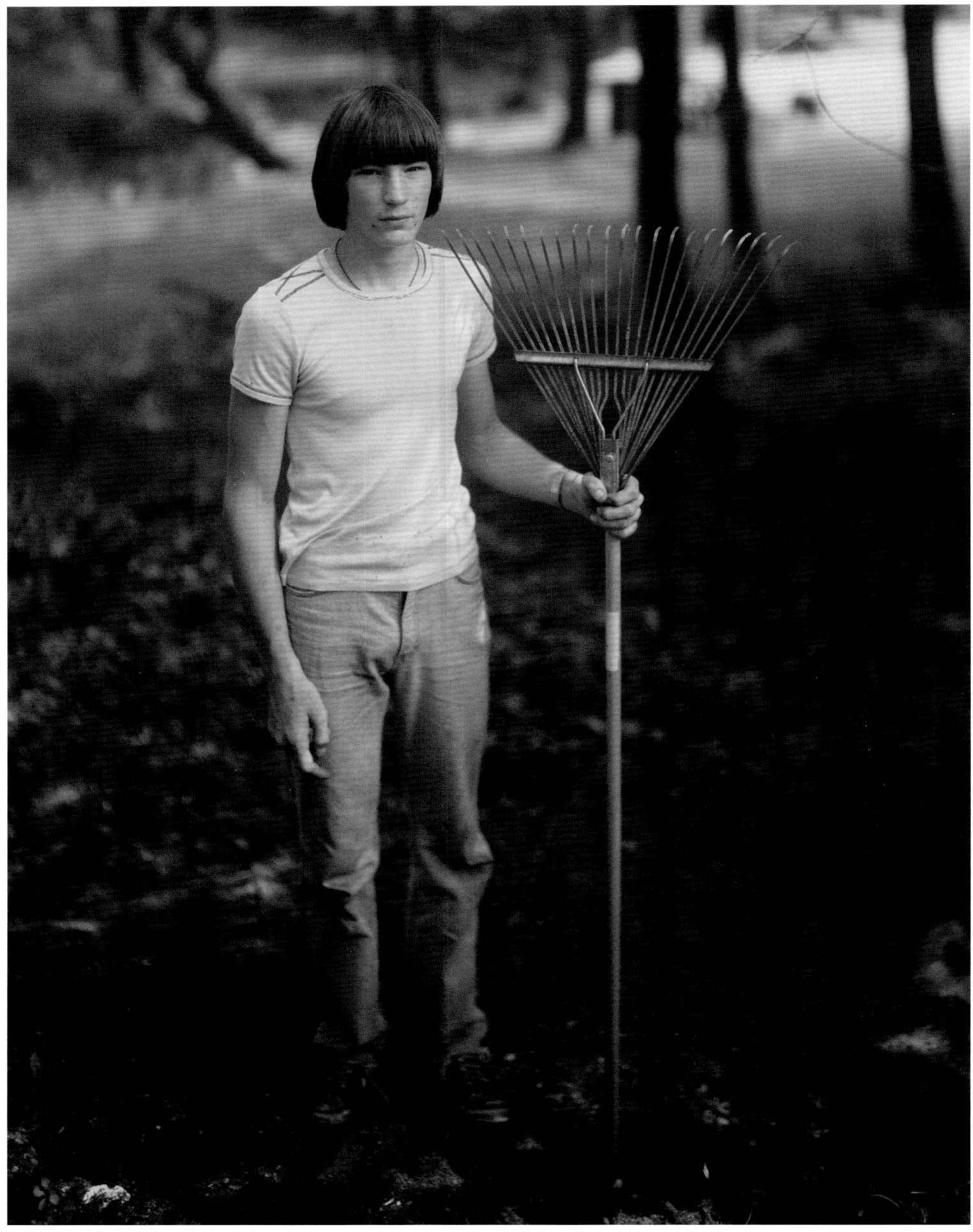

Untitled, Eurana Park,
Weatherly, Pennsylvania,
1982

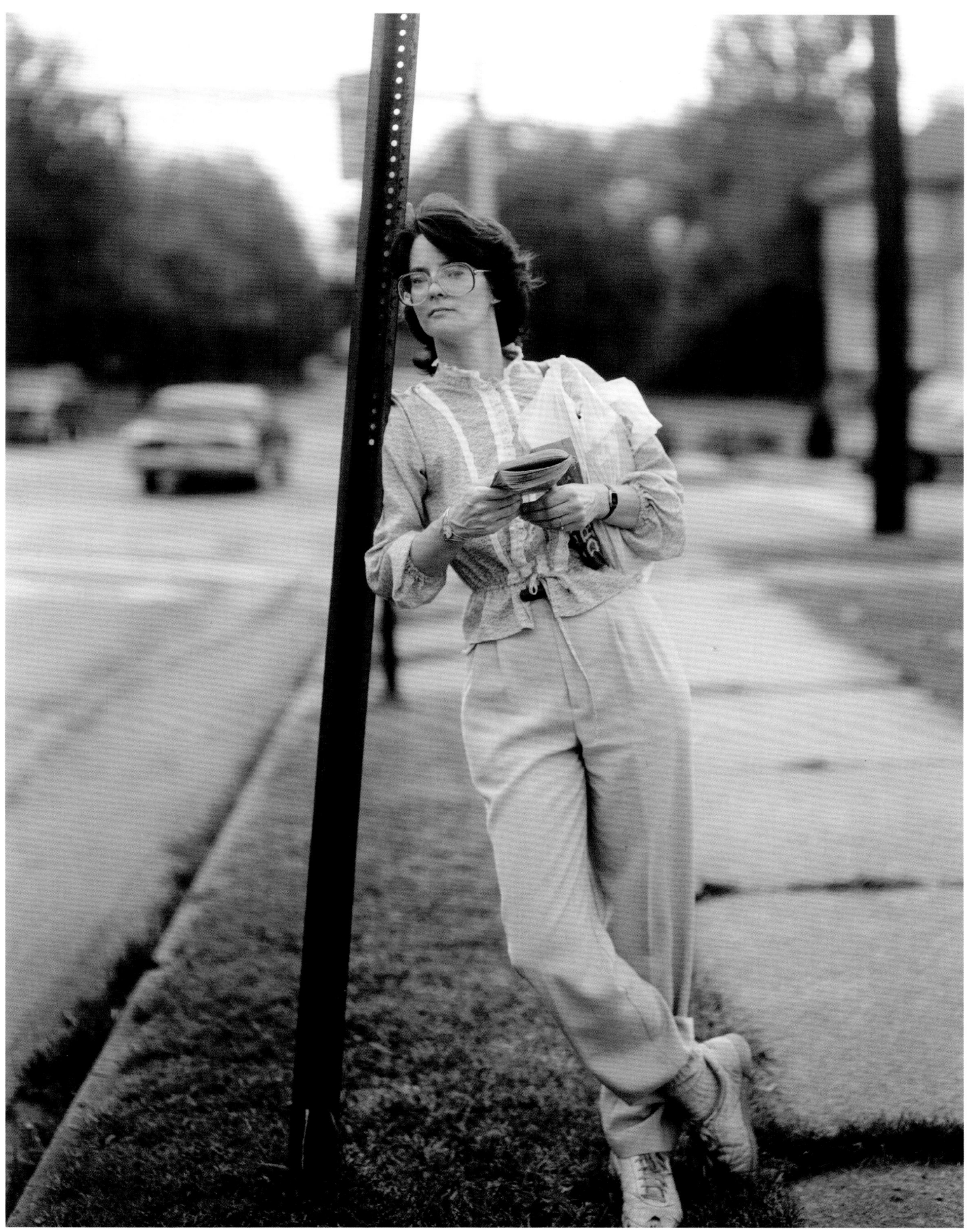

Bus stop, Bethlehem,
Pennsylvania, 1989

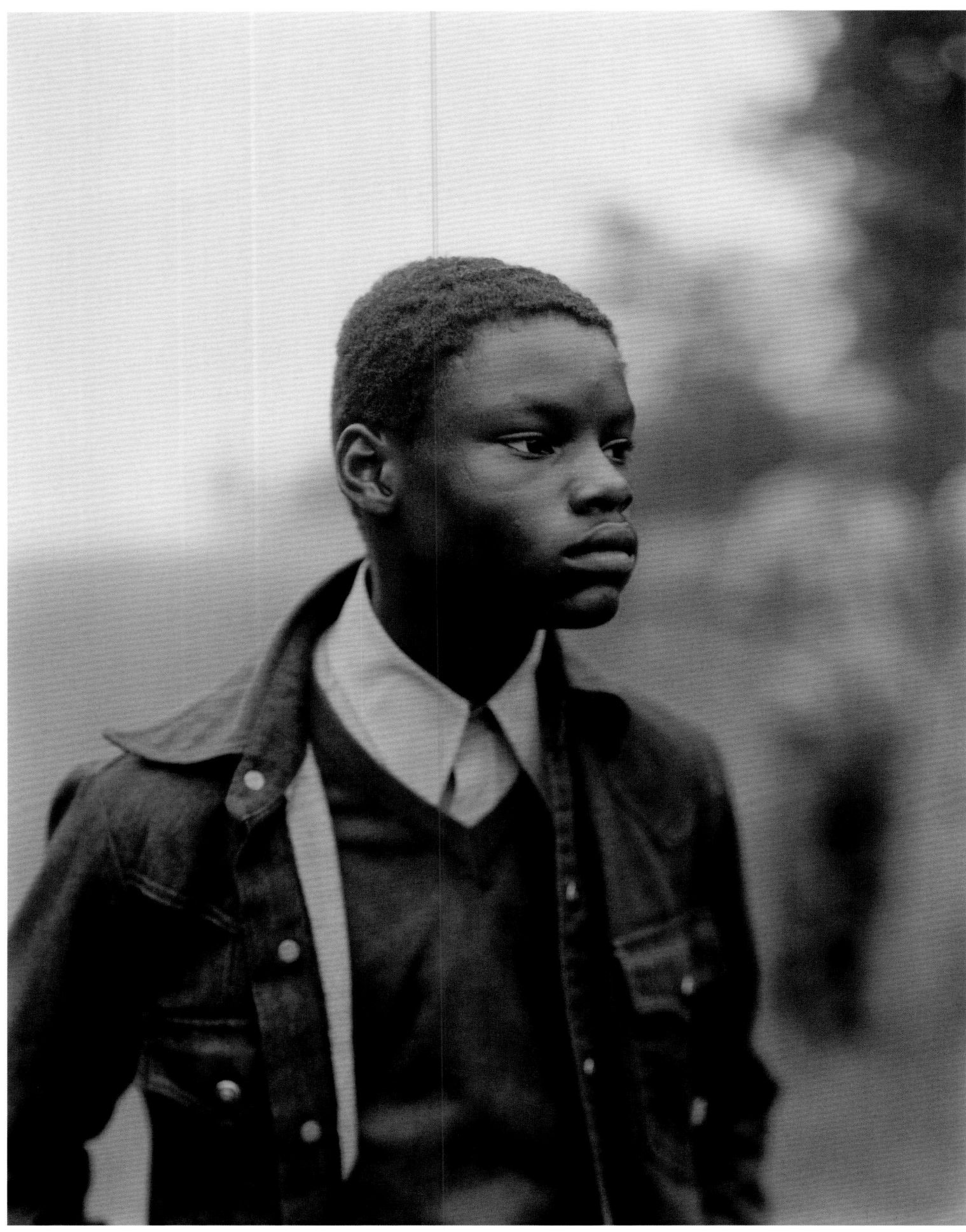

**Untitled, Vietnam Veterans
Memorial, Washington,
D.C., 1984**

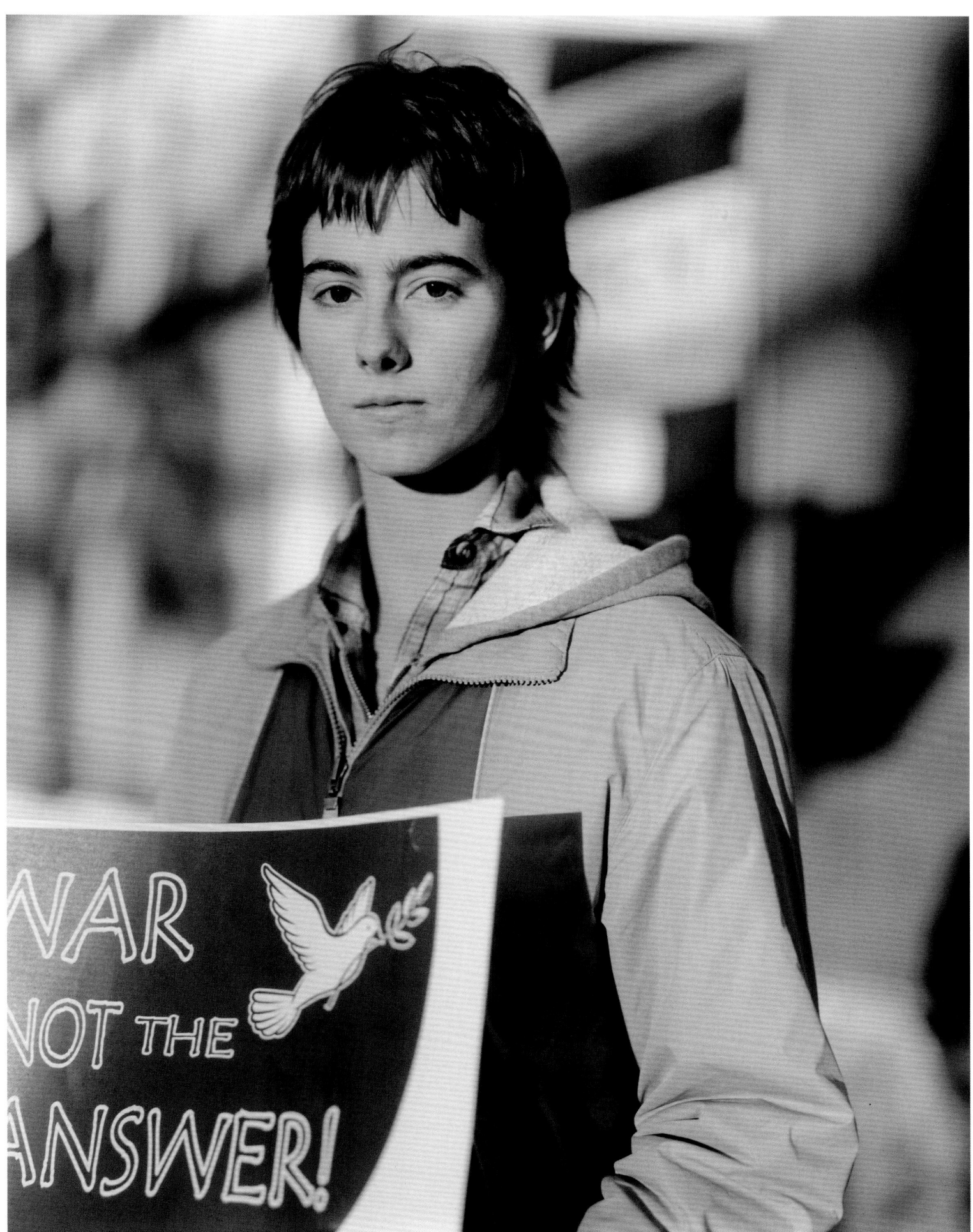

Annie Hasz, Easton Circle, Easton, Pennsylvania, 2007
All photographs courtesy the artist and Galerie Thomas Zander, Cologne

Jim C. Nedd
Carnival

Daniel Berndt

Reflecting on the relationship between oral tradition, history, and power, Jim C. Nedd's work asks how cultural and visual codes, along with mythology and customs, serve as forms of both resistance and belonging. Born in Italy and now residing in Milan, Nedd spent most of his childhood in Colombia. While his mother remained in Europe to support her family back home, Nedd was raised by his relatives in the town of Valledupar. "Even though I had a very strong feeling of being Colombian," he told me recently, "I knew that there was a place on the other side of the ocean where I somehow belonged as well." This sense of in-betweenness, from his experience of migration and exposure to different cultures, has defined Nedd's artistic practice.

Nedd combines a documentary approach with staged and stylized elements to create a distinct hybrid aesthetic. Playing with the glamorous and psychological aspects of fashion photography that aim to trigger and resonate desire, he puts a visual language dominated by intense contrasts, artificial light, and an almost haptic quality in dialogue with scenes captured spontaneously in natural settings.

Colombia's carnival culture and the popular street parties called *verbenas* are recurring themes. *Guacherna* (2018), for example, showing the backside of a woman covered with a white substance, refers to the nocturnal parade ahead of the carnival in Barranquilla and the custom of throwing cornstarch at people during the festivities. This tradition originated on the Canary Islands in the seventeenth century as a carnivalesque imitation of the aristocratic families that ruled the island from the motherland. Across the ocean, the tradition became an expression of race relations, especially on occasion of the Carnival of Barranquilla.

Water is another prominent motif in Nedd's photography. *Loango* (2020) specifically refers to the tale of Catalina Loango—a woman from San Basilio de Palenque who was abducted by a Mohan, a supernatural being sometimes described as a white man with long hair and backward-pointing feet. Disguised as a fish, he dragged Catalina Loango down to the bottom of a river and kept her captive as his mistress. When her mother died, she reemerged from the water, ghostlike and singing, to take part in the mourning ceremonies.

San Basilio de Palenque is said to be the first freed-slave town in the Americas. The myth of Catalina Loango is "related to the fear of the waters, and the idea of water as a portal rooted in the experience of the Middle Passage," Nedd explains. "Many enslaved people believed that if they jumped overboard, they would be returned to their family and friends in their village or to their ancestors in the afterlife. But the tale, for me, is about a form of mutation as well, about how certain beliefs or customs transform into something else, gain different meanings in different places."

In addressing these mutations, Nedd inevitably reveals the undercurrent of politics in his work. "Every Colombian is marked by memories of violence, and since the 1960s, the political situation hasn't really changed. On top of this, Black bodies have always been extremely politicized," he says. Yet Nedd's photography also tells a deeply personal story. For him, Colombia "is still a place where intensely beautiful things happen." He embraces this beauty as well as the ghosts of the past, creating work that lingers in the in-between.

Opposite:
Parque de la Leyenda,
2020; page 82:
Alsadir, 2018; page 83:
Guacherna, 2018;
page 84: *El Rey*, 2020;
page 85: *Loango*, 2020
All photographs courtesy
the artist and Sandy Brown,
Berlin

Daniel Berndt is an art historian based
in Zurich and Berlin.

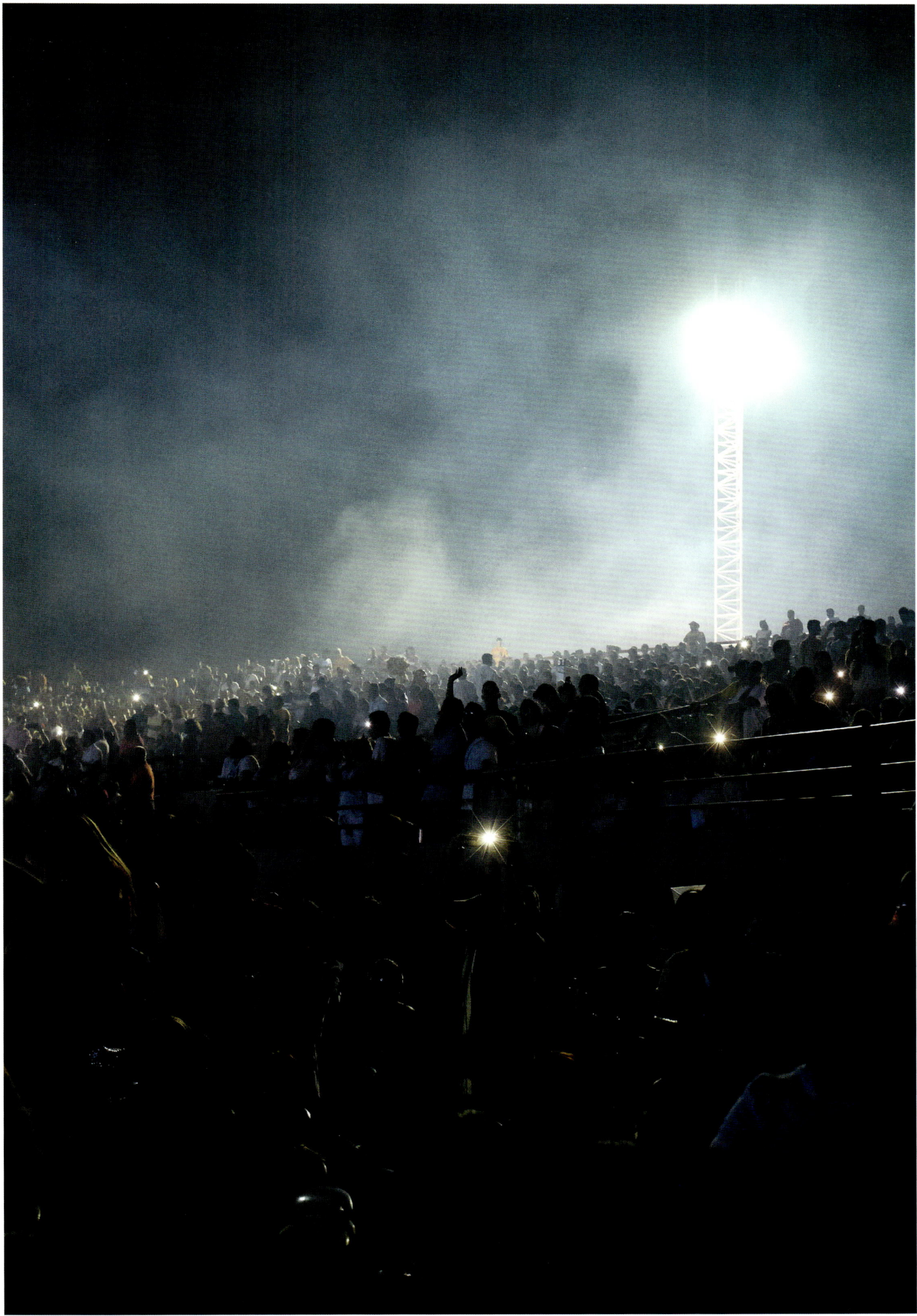

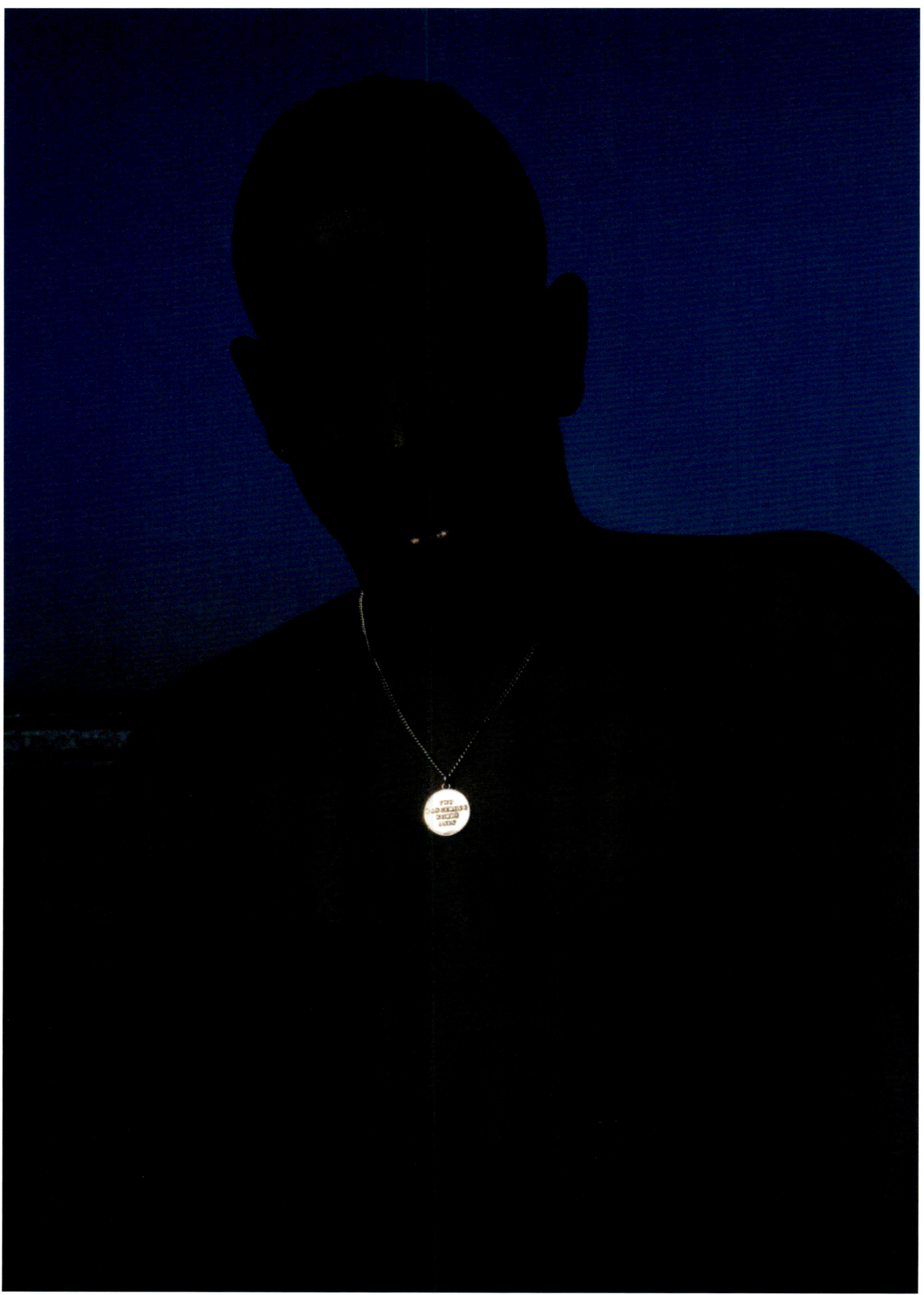

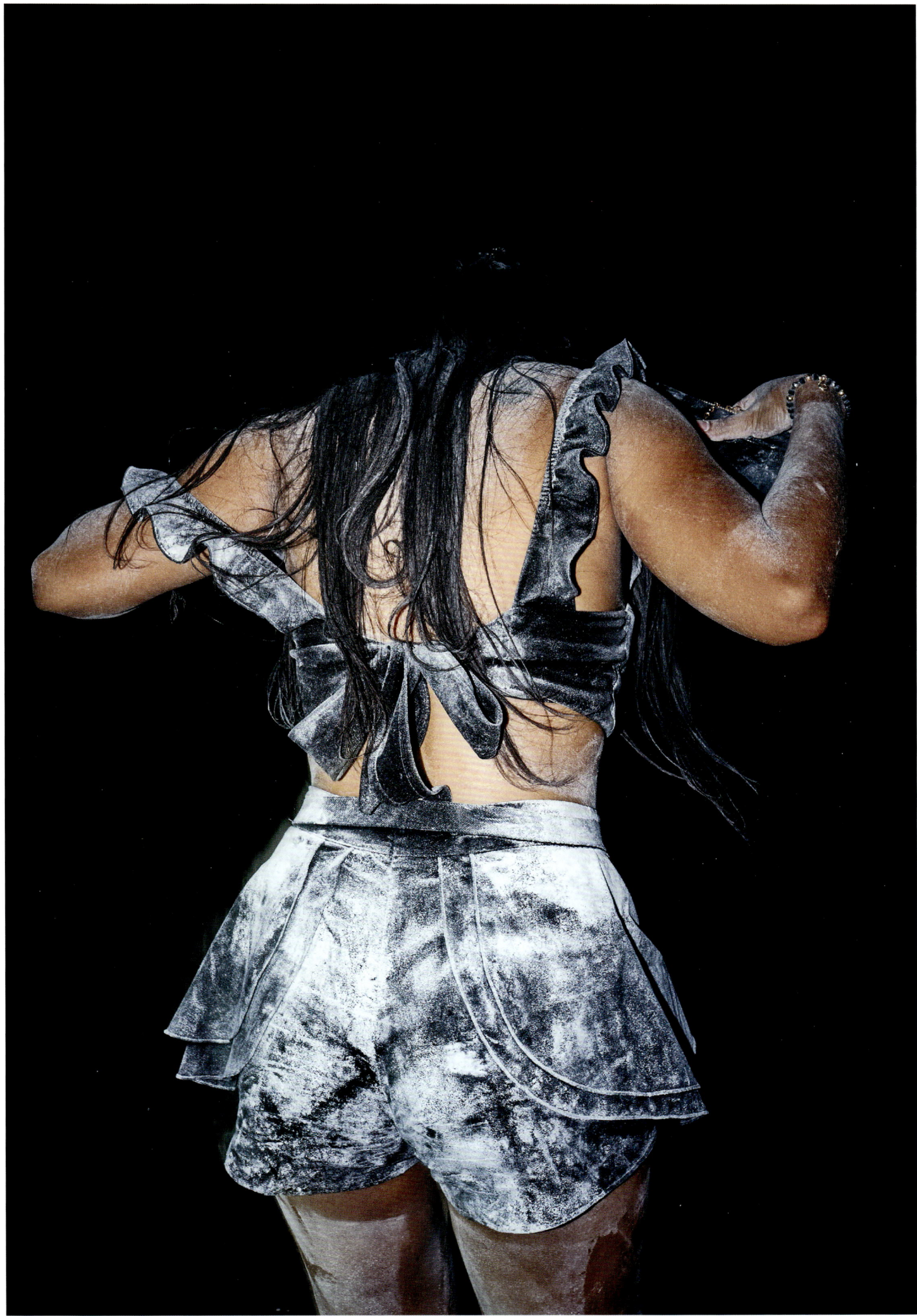

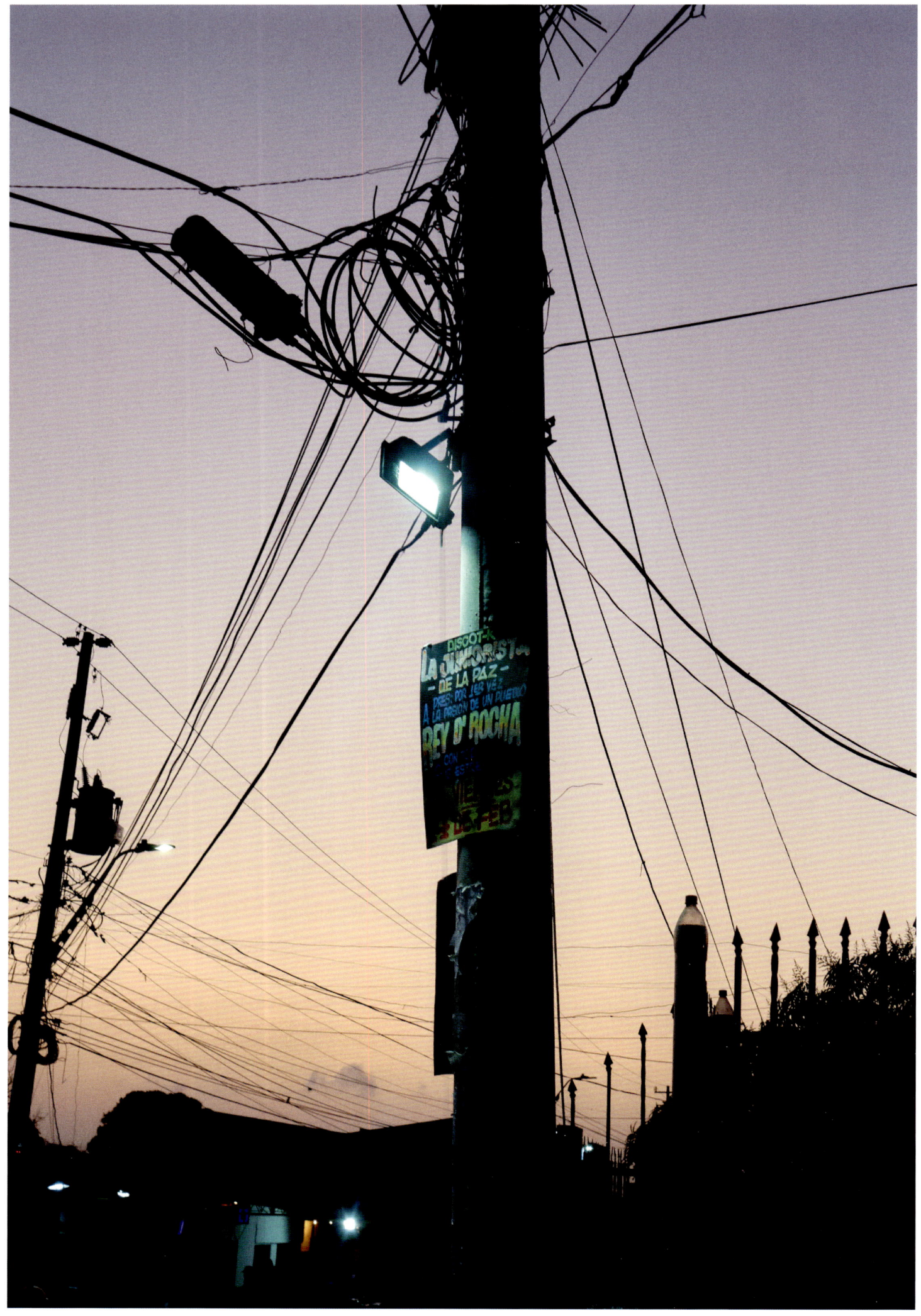

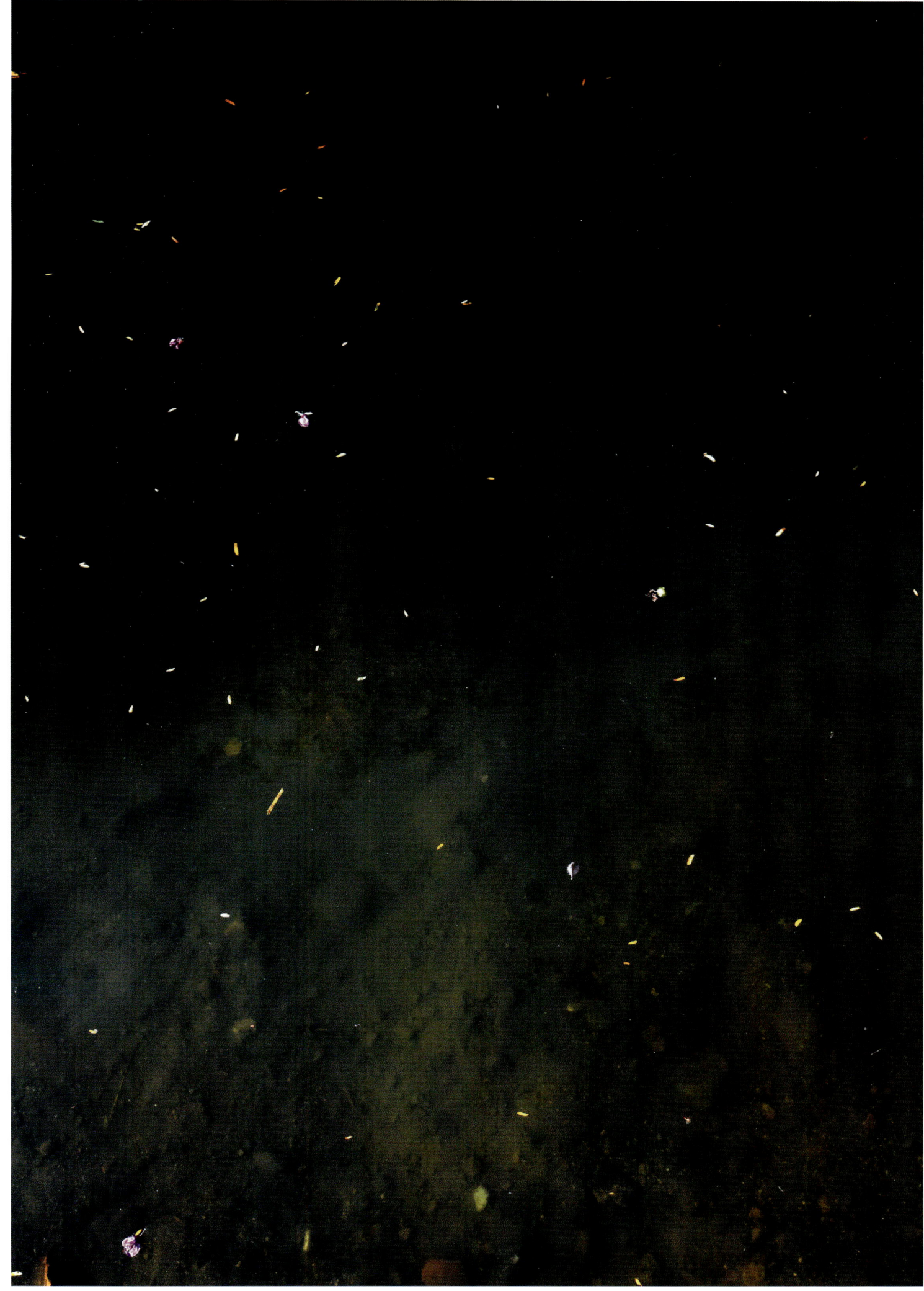

In Japan, where I've made my home for thirty-three years, it's not uncommon to see people bowing to a telephone as they speak into a receiver. Ceremonies are held in temples every year for sewing needles that have given themselves up to make a kimono. My Kyoto-born wife was taught to apologize to a table if she kicked it in a fit of six-year-old pique. We can bring the same care to objects, my neighbors teach me, as we do to one another; that might be the heart of reverence, of humility—and of the mystery known as clear attention.

I think of all this when I survey the art of Tom Sandberg. Always, it seems, the late Norwegian artist was training his lens on the objects that we overlook: Not the people enjoying lunch, but the paper bag beside them, so vivid we can almost hear it crinkle. Not a jet cutting through the heavens, but the emptiness that surrounds it. There are vehicles—cars, planes, and buses—in much of his work, and yet the images are about movement of a subtler kind, maybe emotional: misty and precise as smoke rising from a stick of incense (or a cigarette?), they focus not on the cars outside but on the way a wind stirs a filmy curtain.

This mix of specificity and absence is deepened by the fact that Sandberg, though he did have a solo exhibition at MoMA PS1 in New York, in 2007, chose to live along what most might consider the margins. Throughout his career, he was partly sustained by donations of food from friends who worked in restaurants. In the early 1970s, he worked as an assistant dogcatcher in England, where, while studying photography, he encountered another old master who produced black-and-white analog evocations of light, Minor White.

Much like White, Sandberg was fluent in the art of suggestion. His pieces are all untitled. They sit calmly in the midst of all that they do not disclose, and so, very often, take us far beyond all we can see. I don't know what to make of the reflections of all those faces in a bus; when I look at the clouds swirling against a blackness, smoke gets in my eyes. As with classic pen-and-ink drawings, these images invite us to complete the picture ourselves. Everywhere, in the world we take for granted, Sandberg may be pointing out, are enigmas as open as that paper bag; much can be shared even when no words are exchanged.

Photography, Sandberg once said, is "a difficult dialogue between shades of grey." He worked long and hard, for more than thirty years, to find a thousand shades of "grey and mattness," barely deviating from his handmade aesthetic. Perhaps it's no surprise that he made a large portrait of John Cage, the man who not only wrote the book on silence but also showed us, in works such as *4'33"*, that what the artist offers us is not the whole picture; his collaborator is circumstance.

Cage was a great believer in randomness and the way everything around us can, if seen or heard in the right way, be taken as a work of art. We don't need to rely on man-made distinctions between what is interesting or beautiful or important and what is not. It is the eye—of the audience as much as the artist—that makes a picture and, in so doing, makes the world.

As I live with Sandberg's work, I keep coming back to some of Cage's haunting koans. "I have nothing to say and I am saying it." And, "we are involved in a life that passes understanding and our highest business is our daily life." Sandberg himself once remembered Robert Rauschenberg saying, "I don't know where I'm going, but I know I'll get there on time." Sometimes, the images here are so distinct, we can't look away from them; sometimes, so elusive, we look and look and still don't know what we're seeing. In all of his work, Sandberg—born in 1953 and leaving the world in 2014—is offering us attention so clear it feels like a secular prayer.

Tom Sandberg
Grayscales

Pico Iyer

Pico Iyer is the author, most recently, of *Autumn Light* (2020) and *A Beginner's Guide to Japan* (2020).

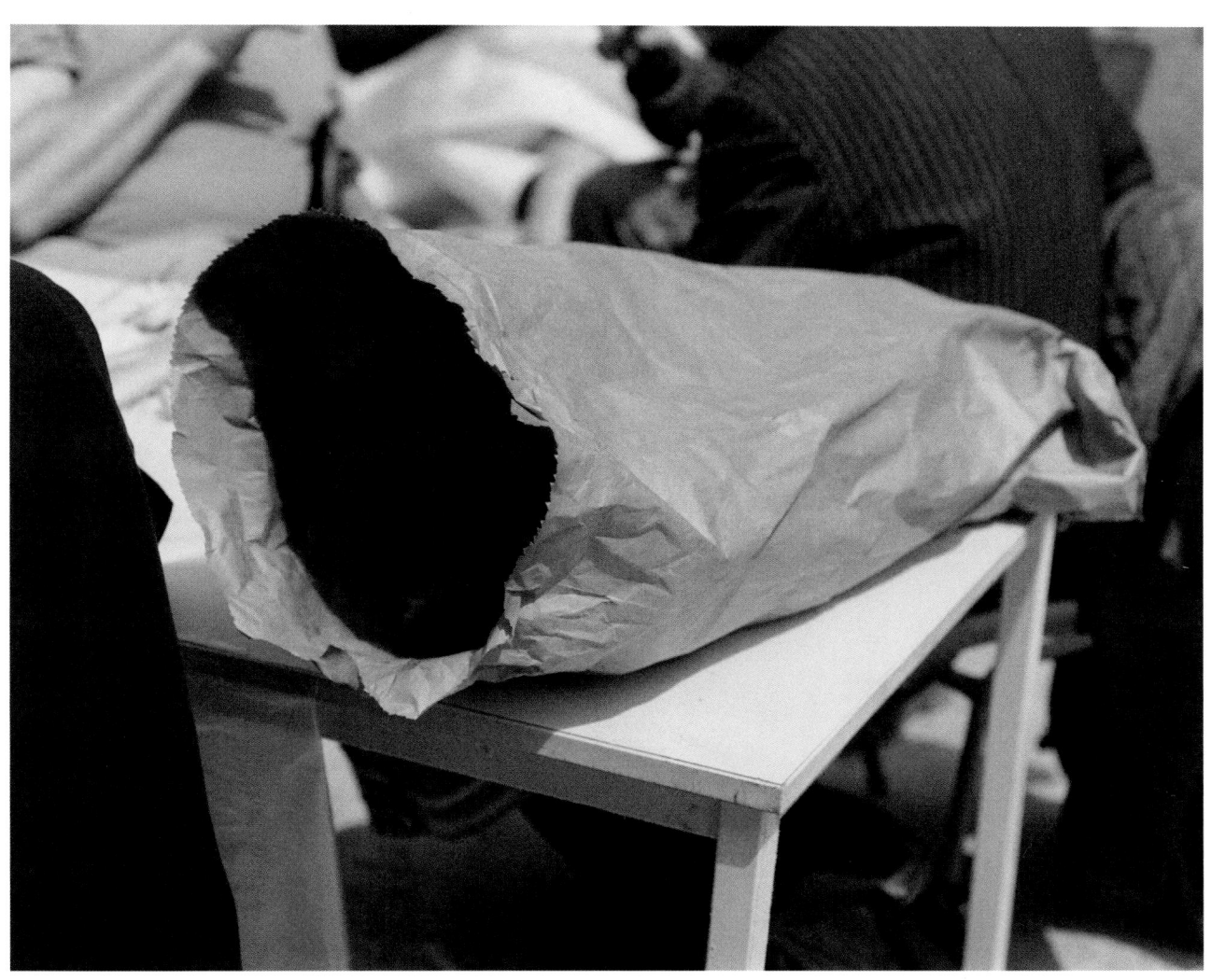

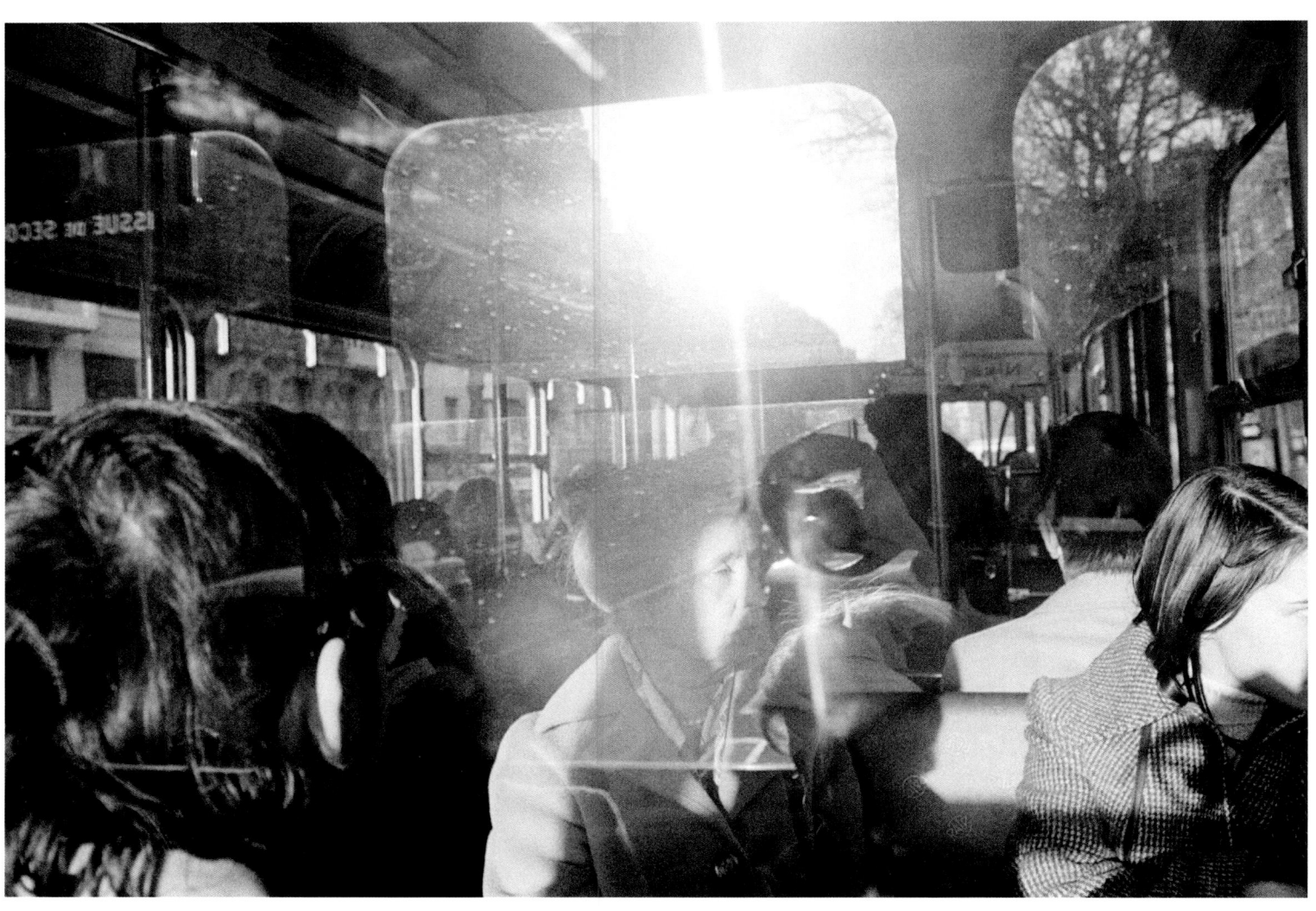

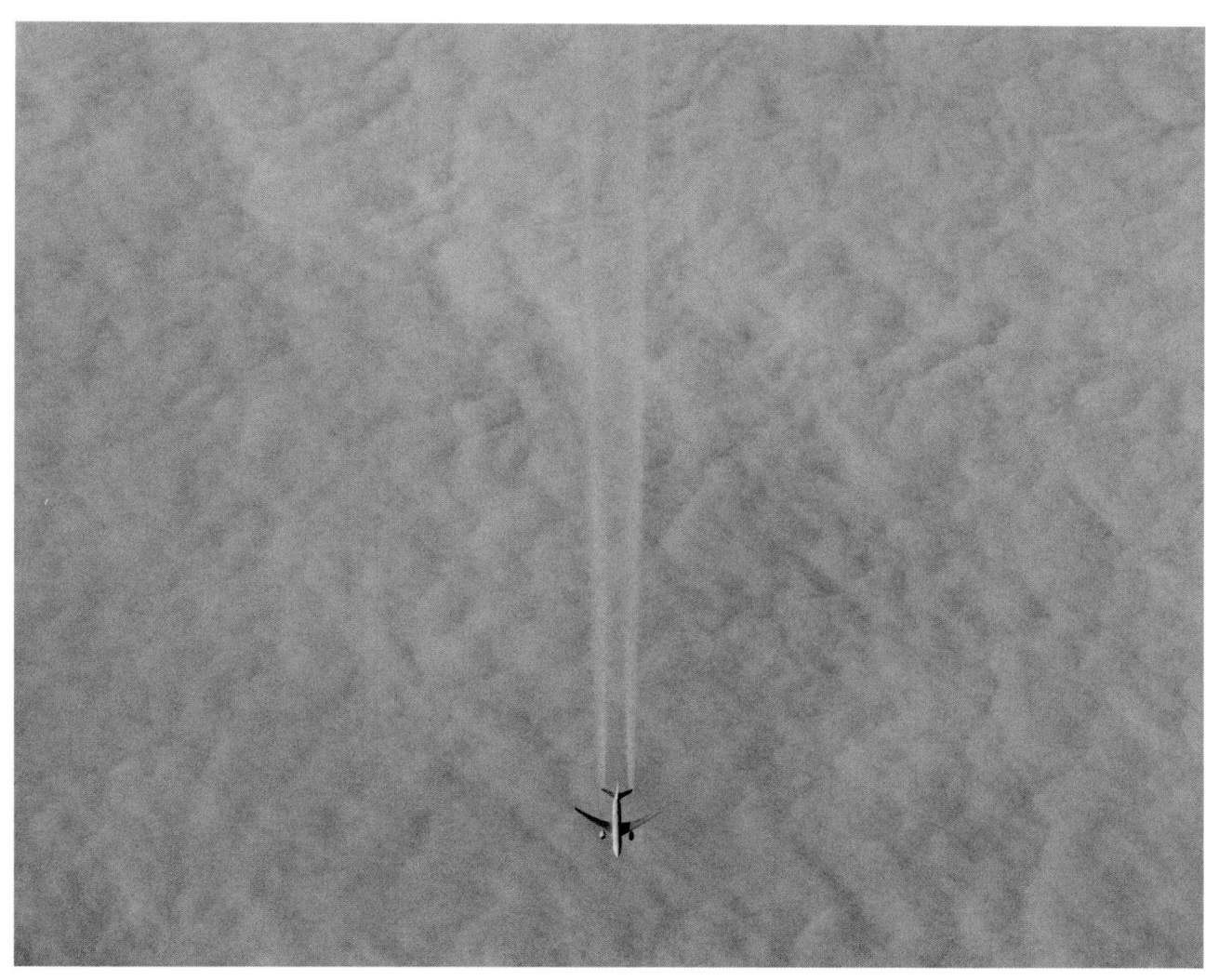

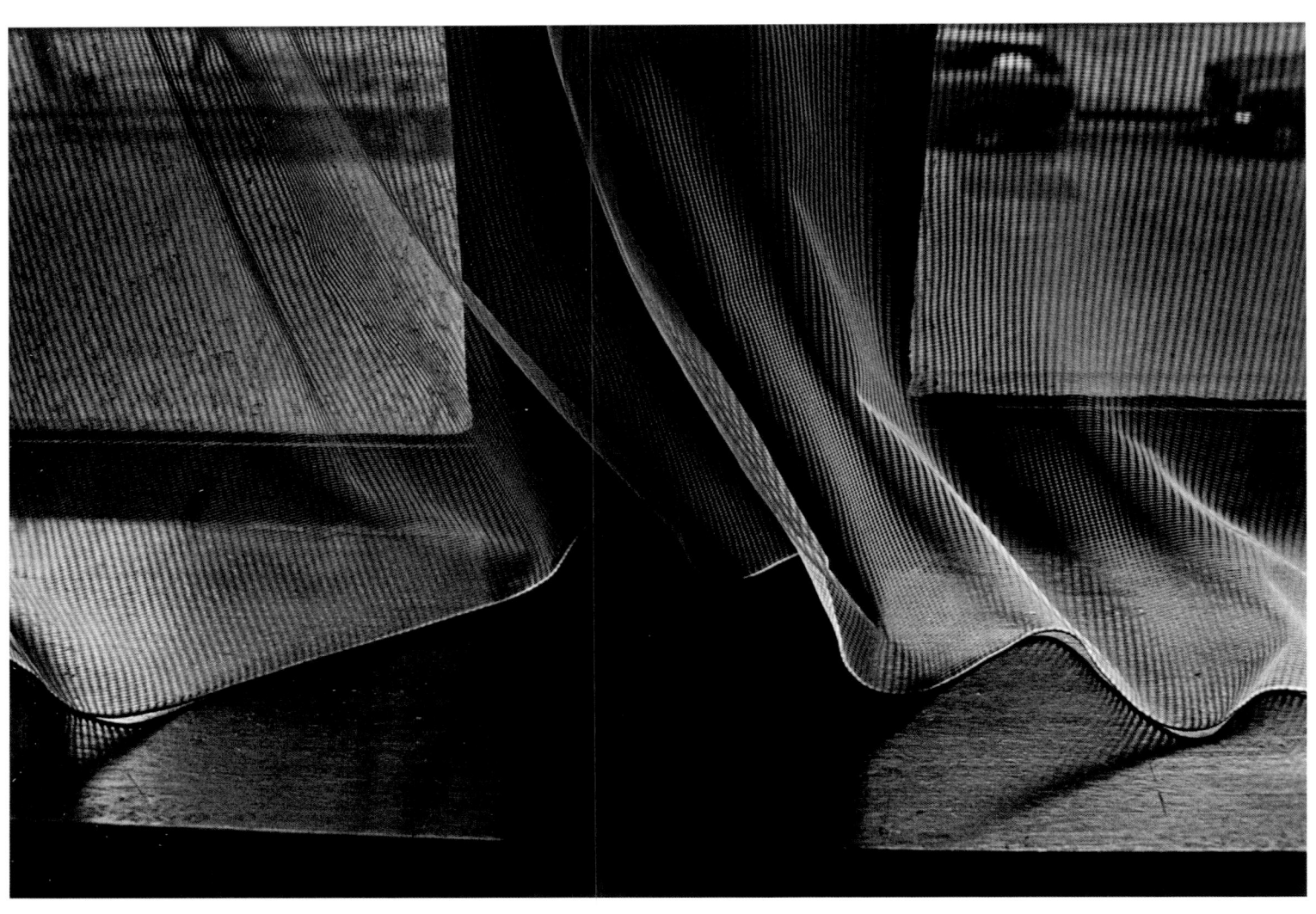

**All photographs *Untitled*,
1995–2008**
Courtesy the Tom Sandberg
Foundation

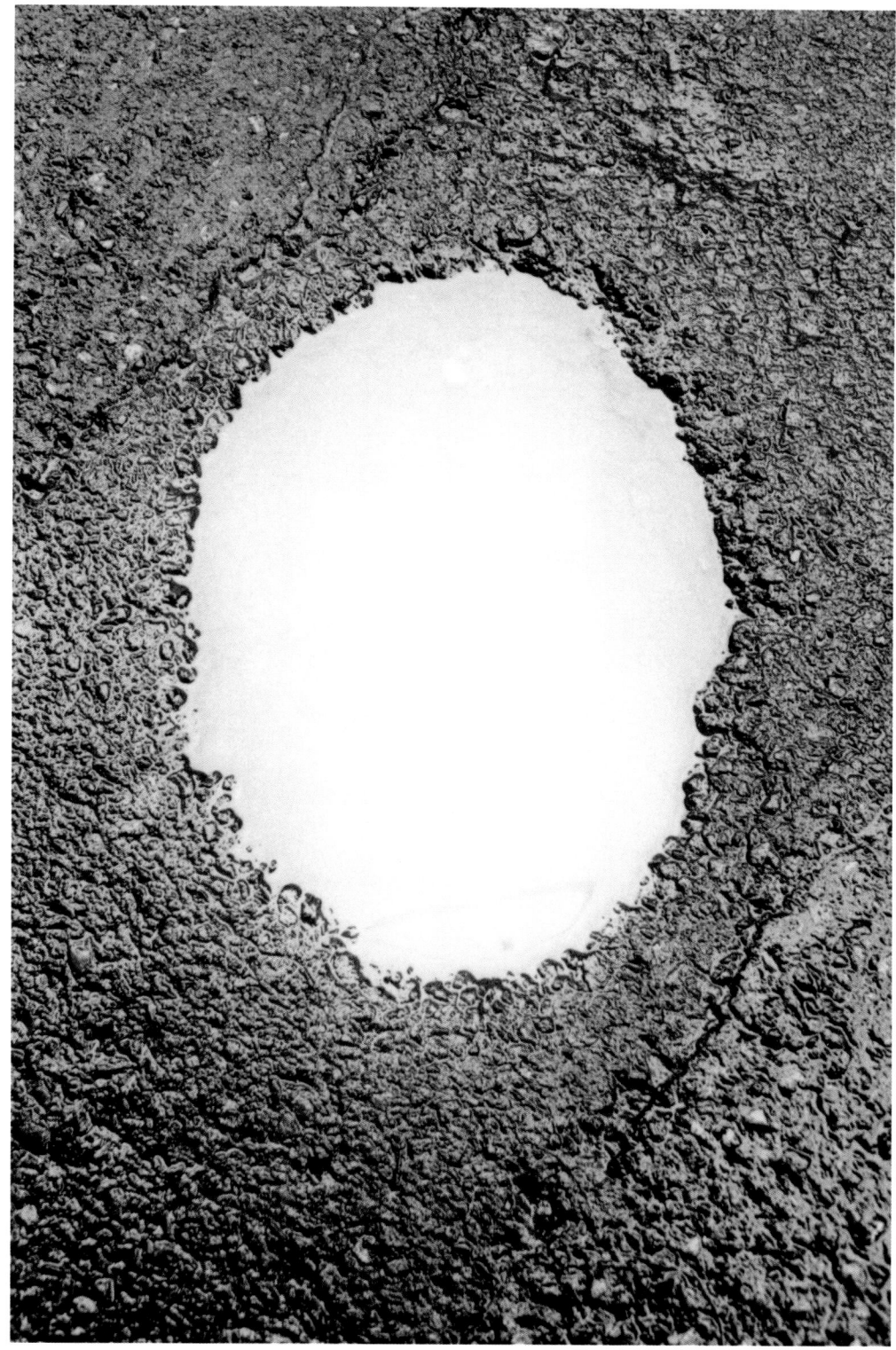

Tavares Strachan
Cosmic Atlas

Kaelen Wilson-Goldie

The artist Tavares Strachan makes enormous neon sculptures, immersive installations, and accumulative two-dimensional series that layer historical photographs of monarchs, explorers, and musicians over and under drawings, advertising images, traditional geometric patterns, and technological glitches such as the smudges from a printing error or the wavy lines and test patterns of television broadcast interruptions. His best-known projects take performance to an outrageously global, even cosmic scale—moving a four-and-a-half-ton block of ice from the Alaskan Arctic to a freezer in the courtyard of his Bahamian elementary school, in 2006, or placing a 24-karat gold canopic jar bearing the bust of Robert Henry Lawrence Jr., the first African American astronaut chosen for a national space program, into a SpaceX rocket that has been orbiting Earth since 2018.

Strachan speaks of his work in terms of a West African street festival where dance, poetry, music, and the performing arts are jumbled together in an exuberant whole. It's hard for him to separate out any one medium, to speak of photography, say, or sculpture, in isolation from his other modes of making. As he explained to me one day in early June, speaking from his studio in New York, so much of what he is trying to do, as someone who was raised in an Afro-Caribbean home (he grew up in the Bahamian capital of Nassau) but graduated from high-powered Western institutions (RISD, Yale), is about reconnecting the experiential elements of the former that were pulled apart by the organizational systems (and colonial undertones) of the latter.

Strachan compares the process of making the pieces in series such as *Notes on Exploration* and *The Children's History of Invisibility* (both 2018) to the loose structures of 1960s jazz, "with a little bit of dub and a little bit of hip-hop," he says, adding that "those genres speak to each other." They respond to a rift or a clue. "I think, visually, I'm doing something similar with images, textures, the pieces of a story." These works have the appearance of large-scale collage, but more often than not, they are made from images printed on layers of Mylar and vinyl mounted on acrylic or museum board. Strachan also calls them poems, assembled from a language that is never innocent or transparent but can be wrestled into a form that speaks to (and about) systems of power.

A work such as *The Stranger* (2018), for example, might begin with an image of Haile Selassie, the emperor of Ethiopia who galvanized public opinion, inspired the Rastafarian movement, and, incidentally but tellingly, kept massive pet cheetahs as his preferred symbols of power. From there, Strachan builds the surface sonically, adding a delicate line drawing of a maze; a Lion of Judah flag, which he used to see everywhere in his neighborhood as a kid growing up; a *Life* magazine cover featuring the astronaut John Glenn alongside a headline about women's intimate apparel; and a photograph of himself in a cosmonaut suit, his head obscured by an oversized, performative mask. He's particularly drawn to materials with double meanings, such as Native American textile patterns that not only are decorative but also serve as maps or other such communication channels.

"Duality allows for a certain level of elasticity in how we think about the world," Strachan says. "Instead of spending all this time thinking about how we are different, it allows for thinking about sameness, about overlapping and intersecting, about all kinds of complexity. My own history, my erased history through colonialism, my new history as someone who's been living in the United States for some time in a society that wants you to decide you are one thing or another—all of that goes into the work."

Kaelen Wilson-Goldie is a writer and critic who lives between Beirut and New York.

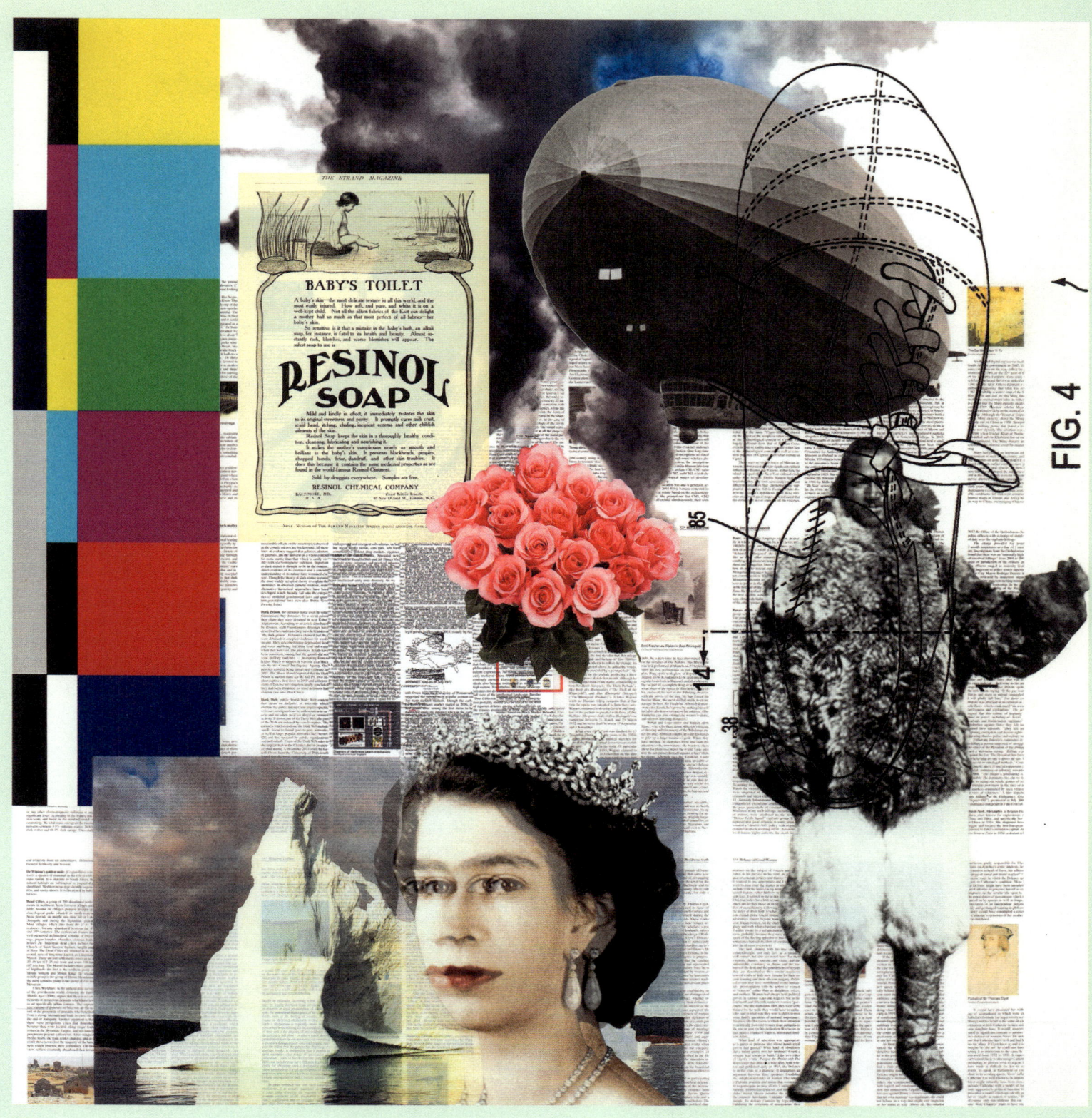

Resinol Soap, 2018,
from the series *Notes
on Exploration*

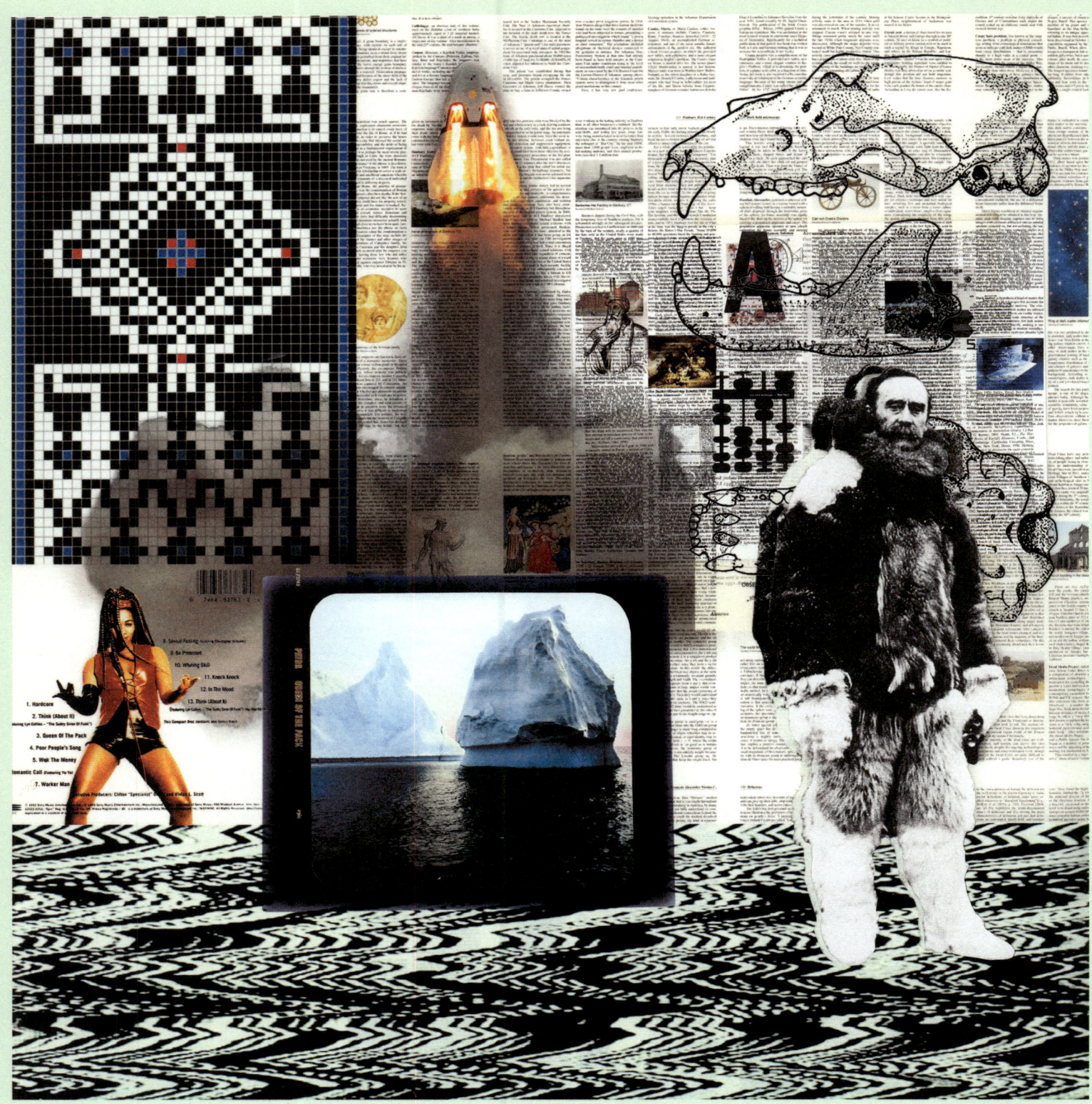

Rocket, 2018, from the
series *Notes on Exploration*

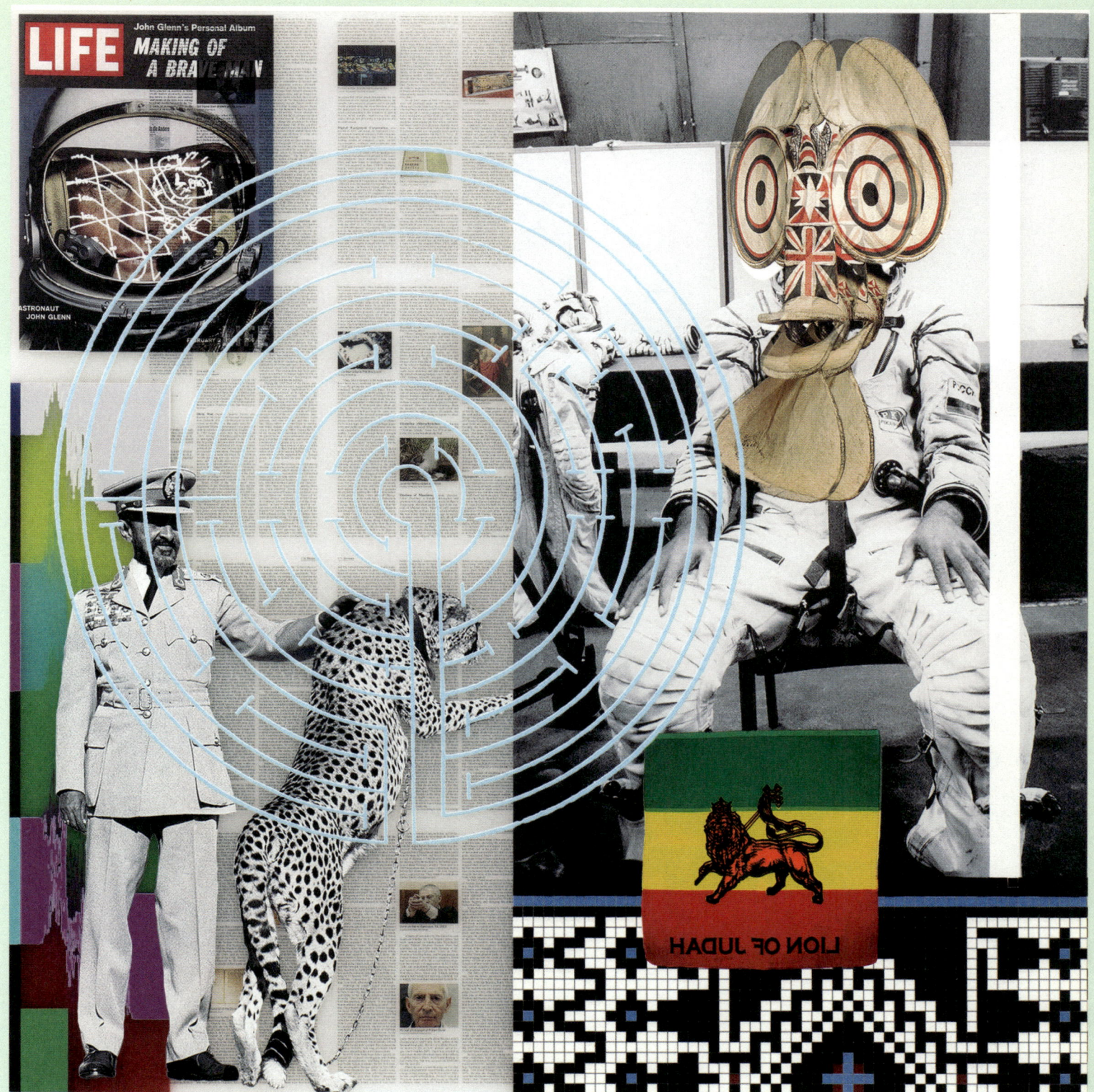

The Stranger, 2018
Courtesy Regen Projects,
Los Angeles

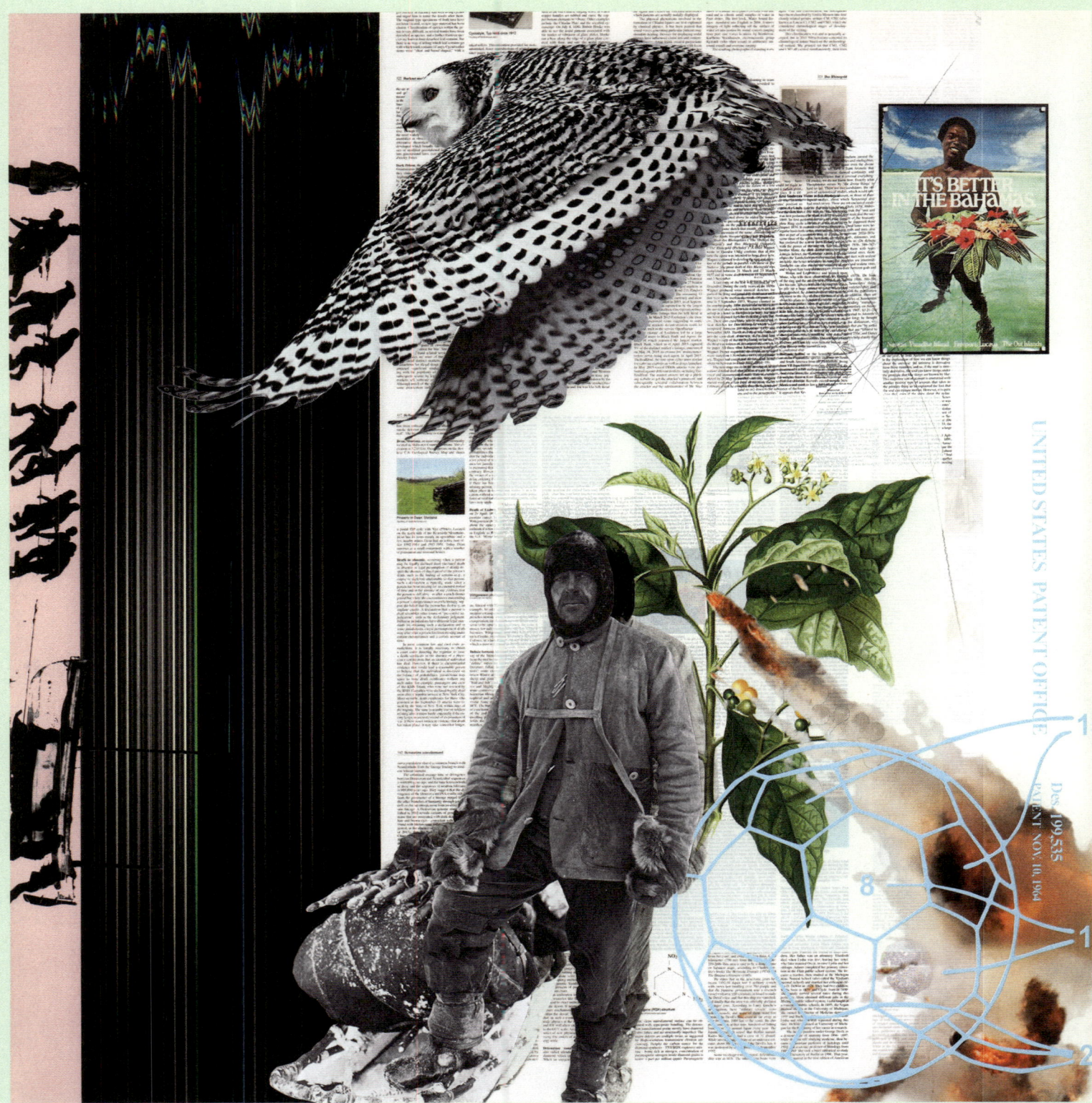

It is Better in the Bahamas,
2018, from the series *Notes on Exploration*

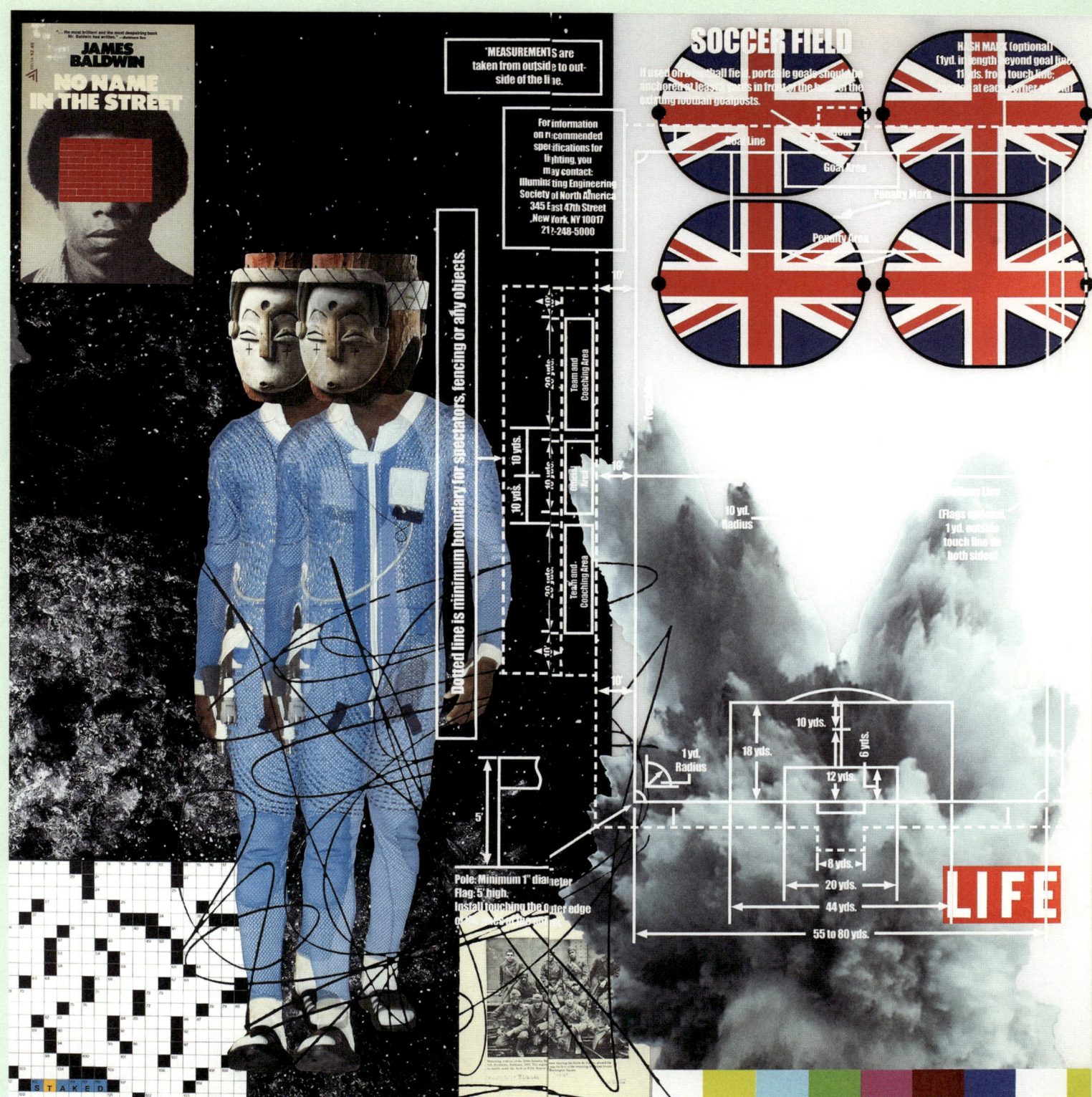

No Name in the Street,
2020
Unless otherwise noted, all
works courtesy the artist and
Marian Goodman Gallery,
London

Feng Li
Good Night

Xuan Juliana Wang

Thirteen years ago, while touring Buckingham Palace in London, Feng Li became enchanted by a colorful African parrot in one of the drawing rooms. A rush of awe and serenity overtook him—if only he, too, could have such a beautiful bird as a companion. The following year, an identical parrot landed on Li's balcony in Chengdu, the capital of China's Sichuan Province, and made his home there.

Events such as this led Li, a trained doctor of Chinese medicine who took up photography as a hobby in his twenties, to believe that there is some higher order in the universe. After quitting medicine, Li got a job as a civil servant in local government. Soon, he was taking photographs for the city's publicity department, recording community events and urban development, always with the aim of making things look beautiful and perfect. This day job allowed him to transition to becoming a professional photographer, as if by accident. Yet, even in his placid, promotional imagery, he could often detect an otherness, like the flip side of a coin, a kind of unspoken performance, a complication, a sinister character lurking beneath the surface.

In recent years, Li has lived in and photographed Paris and Berlin. The change in settings didn't prevent him from being able to find the subject of his fascination—people and how they reveal their true nature to his camera at unexpected moments. His photographs often unveil a scene in an absurd drama, and, in those buoyant flashes, there is just a whiff of tragedy. In each man-made comedy of errors, something is not quite right, but you can't bring yourself to look away. "You are born into a world before you can enter it," he says, "before you can even begin to grasp its power and complexity."

Recently, his parrot passed away, and after he departed, it was as if Li stopped seeing the vibrant colors that have characterized much of his imagery, which has earned him an international reputation. The series *Good Night*, taken from 2007 to 2021, is, by contrast, dominated by the color black. Viewing these images, you must accept that these incredible events pictured by Li in simple, alluring, and humorous compositions actually happened.

In one instance, Li told me, a car ran a red light as he was walking down the street. It crashed into a road sign, and white rabbits came flying out. Hearing the loud bang, Li walked up expecting to see a tragedy, but the driver had merely fainted. The rabbits, though, were theatrically spilling out of the car. In another, one afternoon, looking up from his desk at home, he witnessed a darkly dressed man, directly across from him, scaling the neighboring office building like a ghost. We also see a wild-haired little girl—the artist's niece—with her hand extended, playing with his pet bird, but in that instant she becomes a legend of dark authority. In still another, a woman encounters a dinosaur sculpture in a park.

Li delivers you to the front steps of this surreal world, where joy and grief, cruelty and fragility are distributed among kindred spirits. Each day, Li looks at his life completely anew, ready to accept the sublime. Something is profoundly amiss with the people in these photographs, and yet, we want to move even closer to them. "I like to believe these people were coming to look for me that day," he says of his subjects. "As long as I have my camera, I will be ready. I don't want to let them down."

All photographs from
the series *Good Night*,
2007–21
Courtesy the artist and
Concrete Rep. Ltd

Xuan Juliana Wang is the author of *Home Remedies: Stories* (2019).

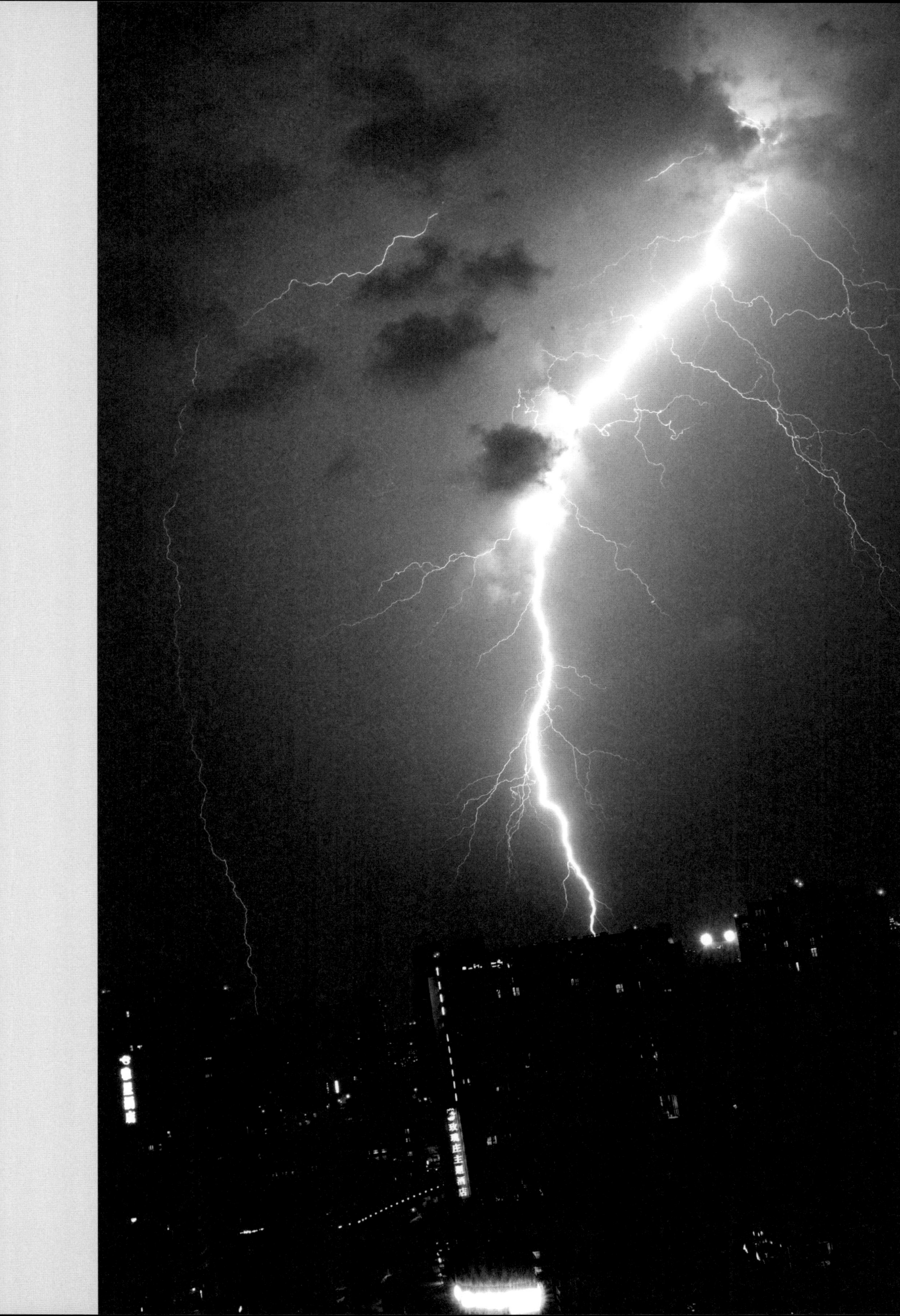

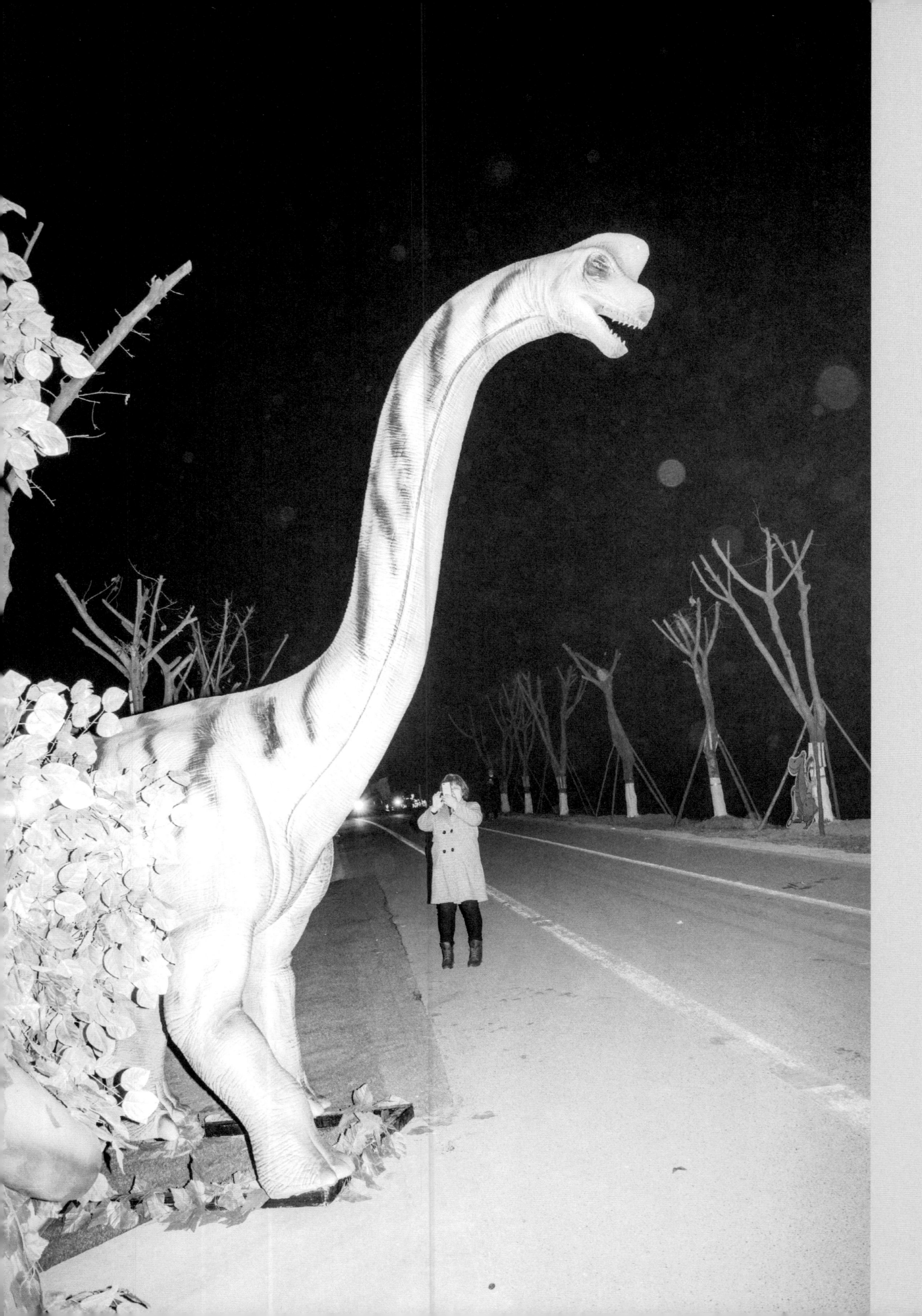

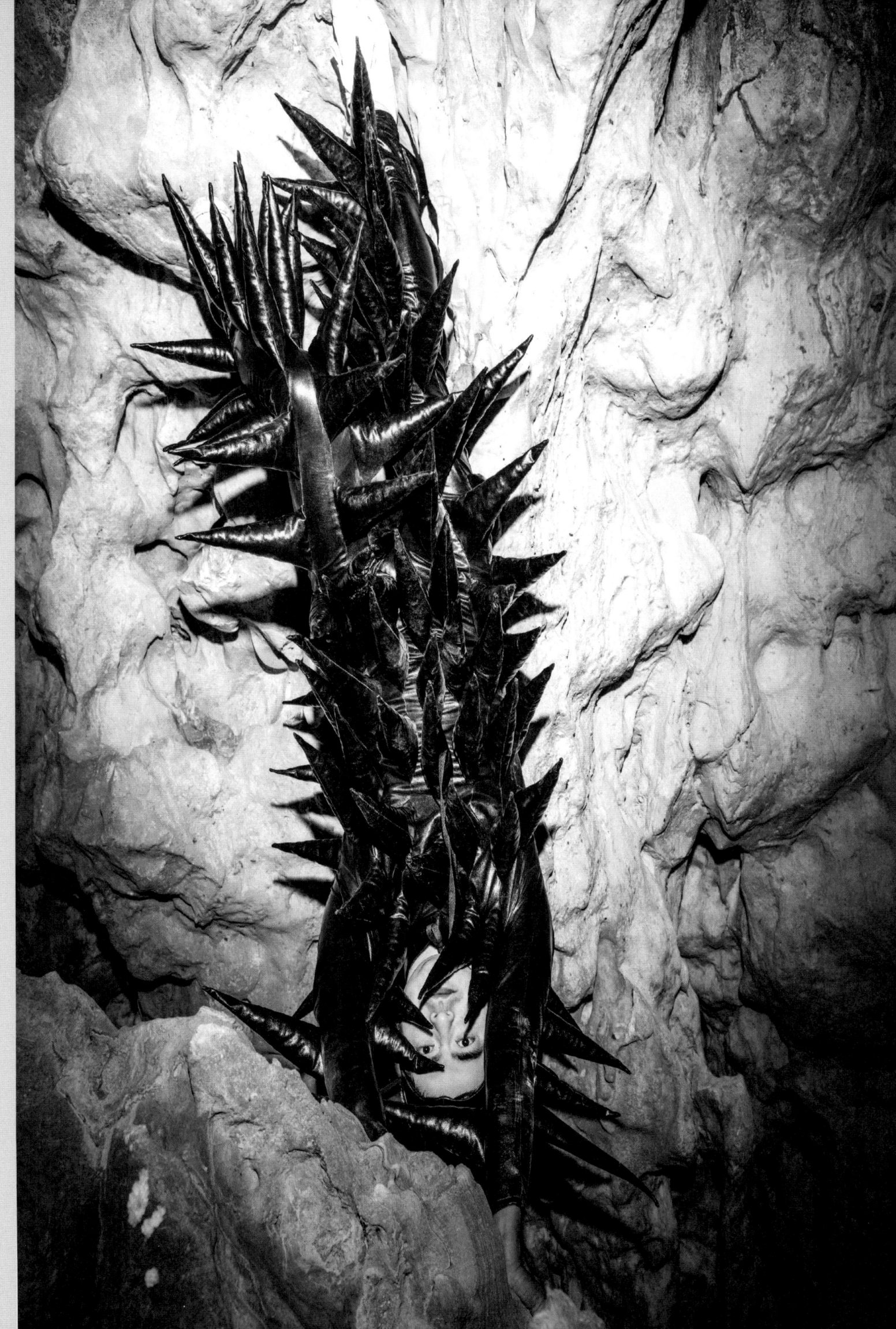

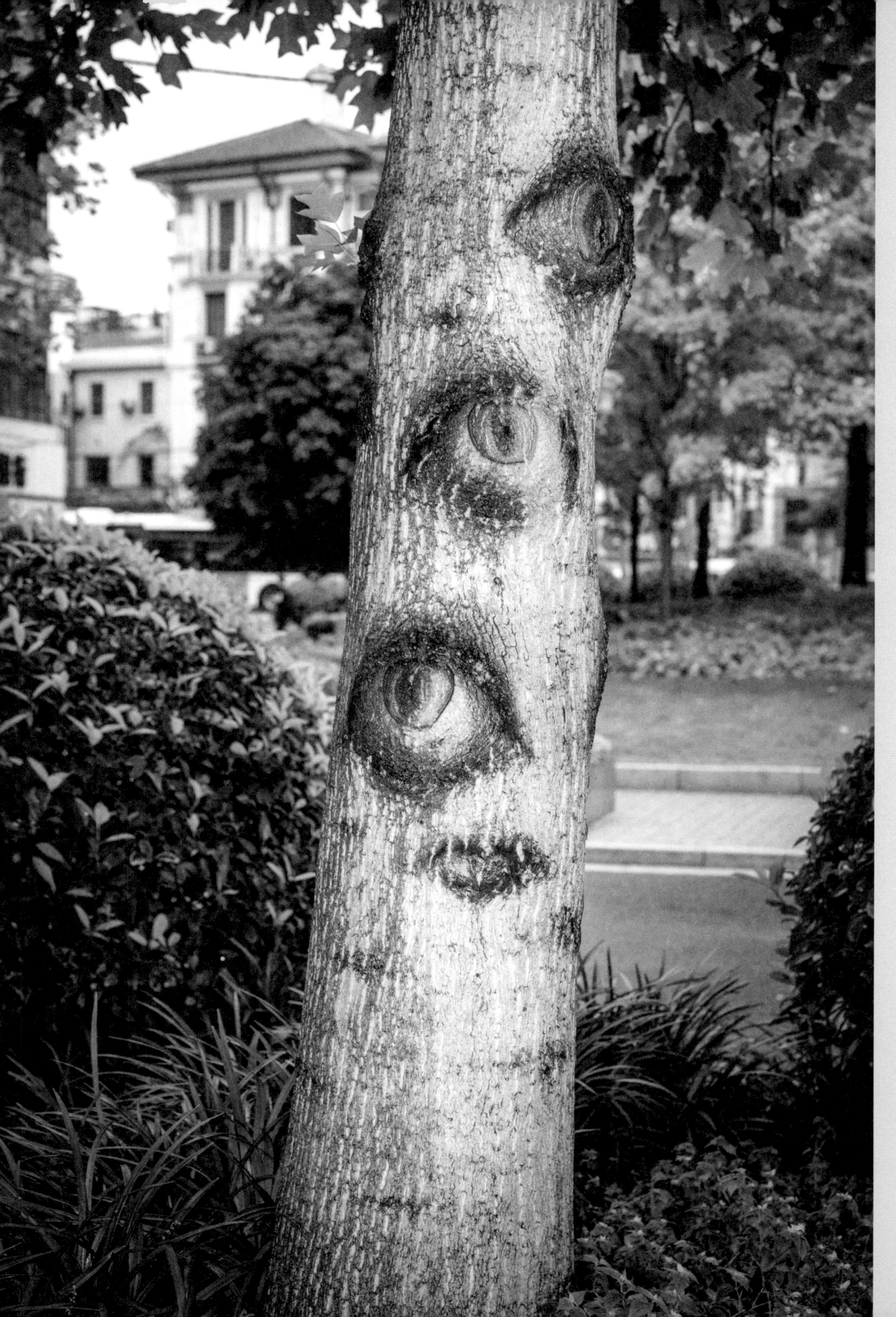

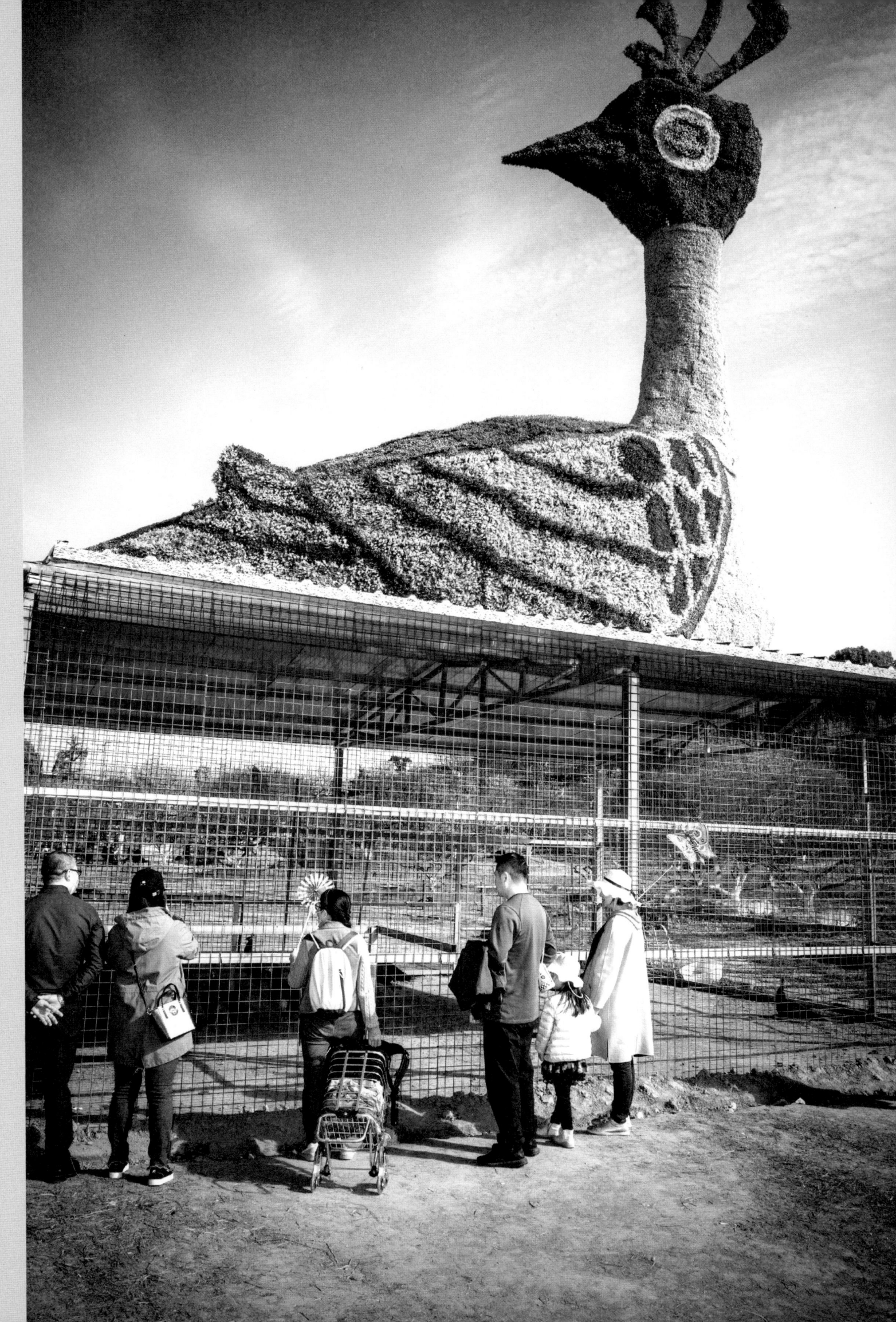

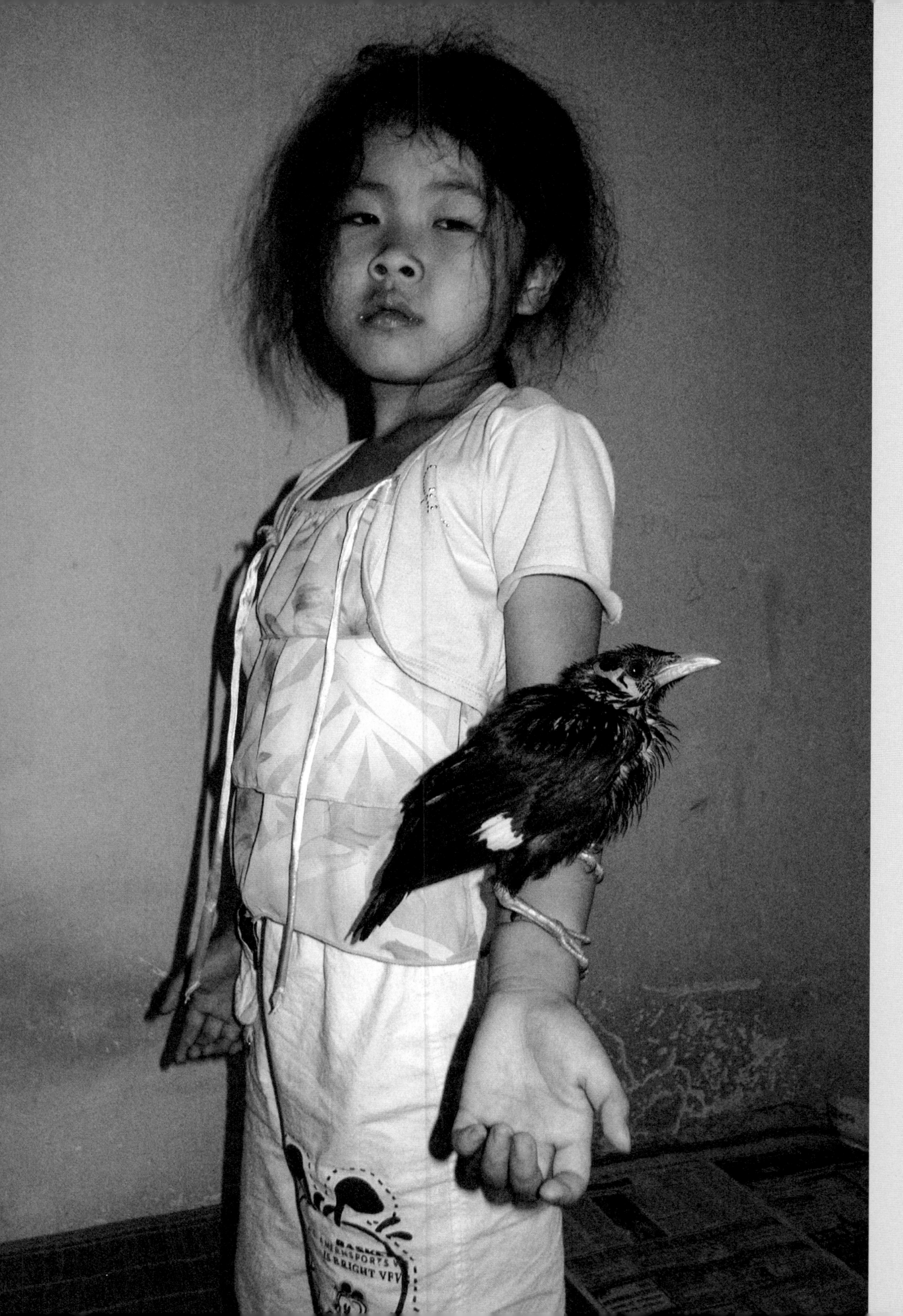

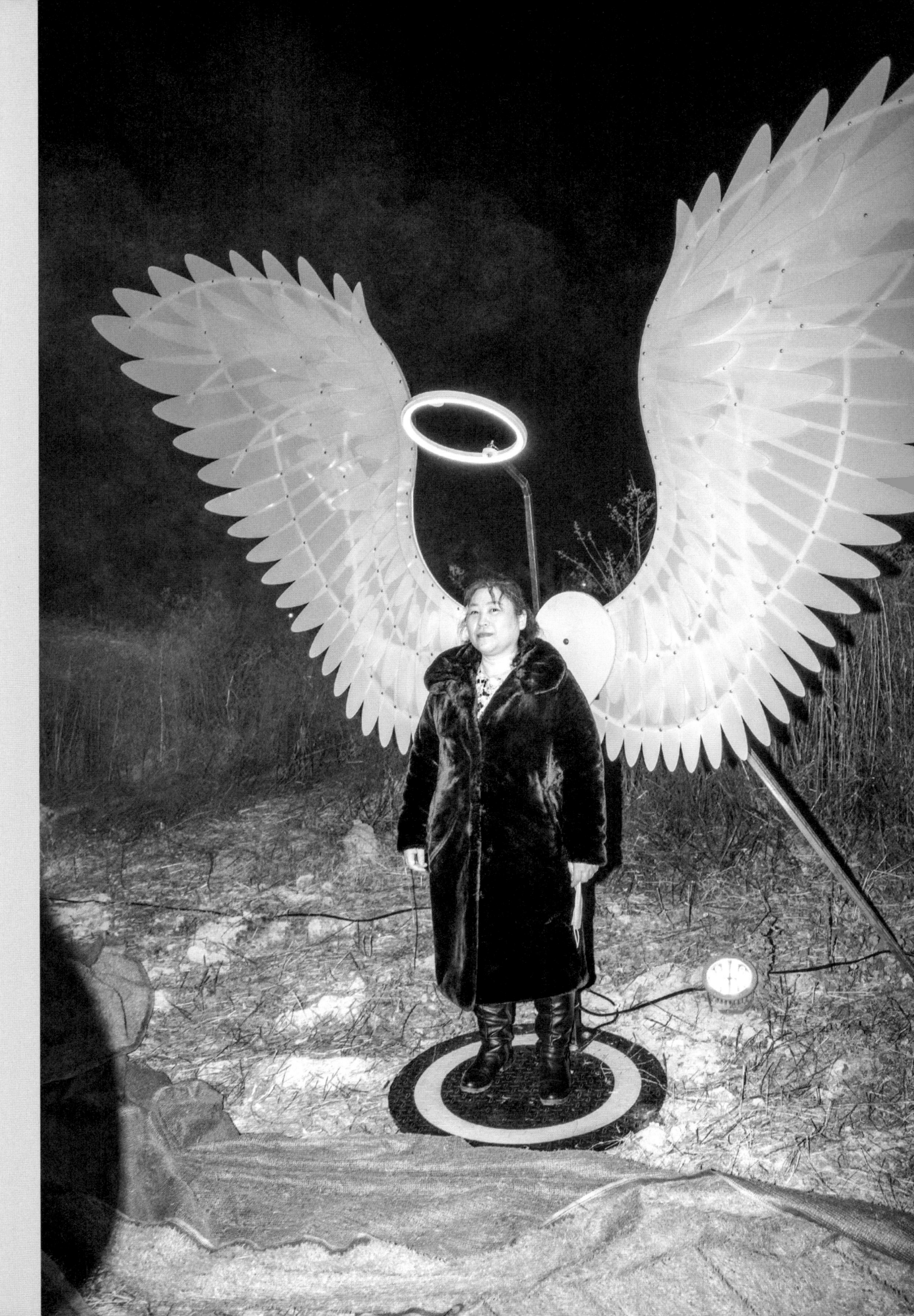

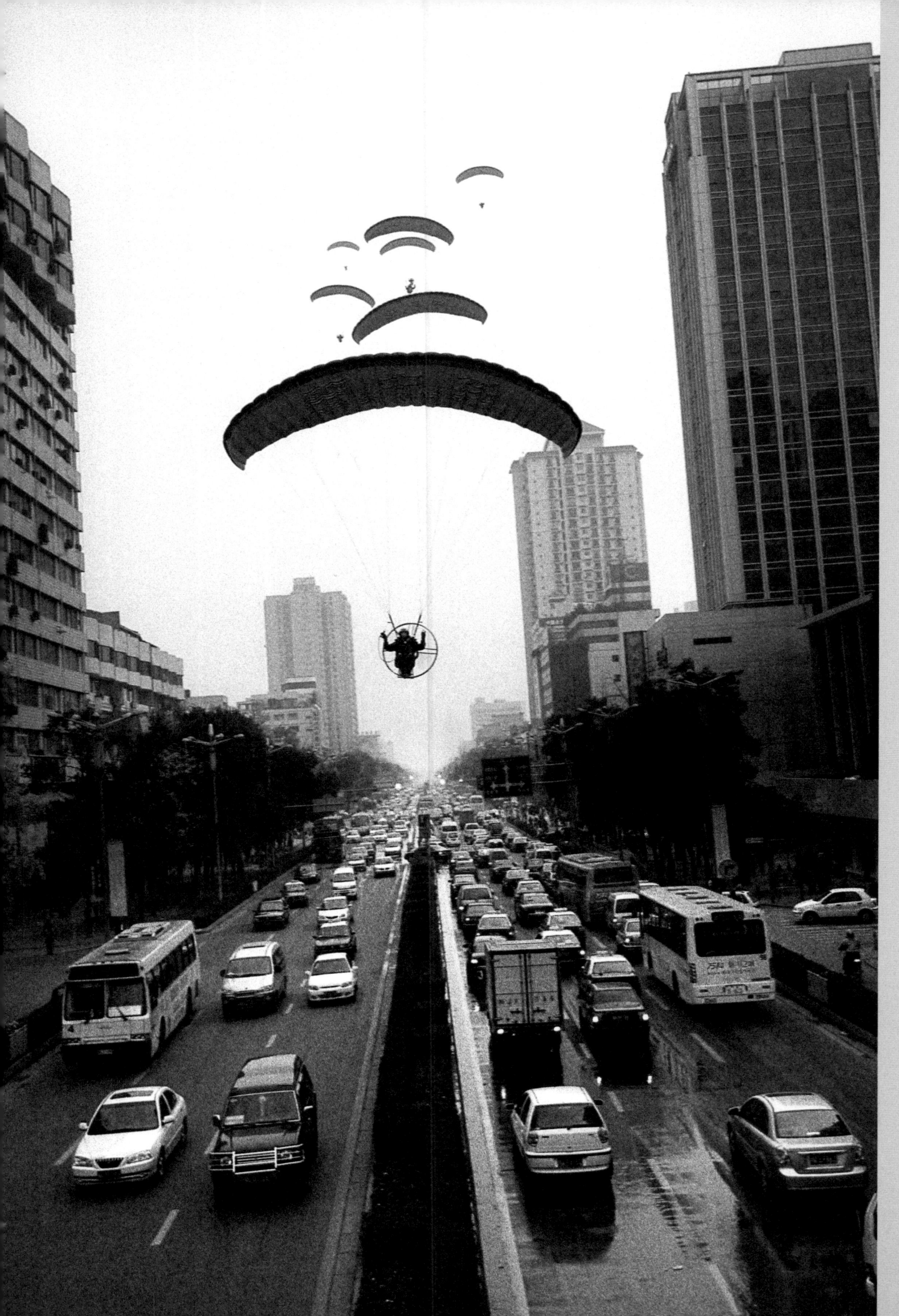

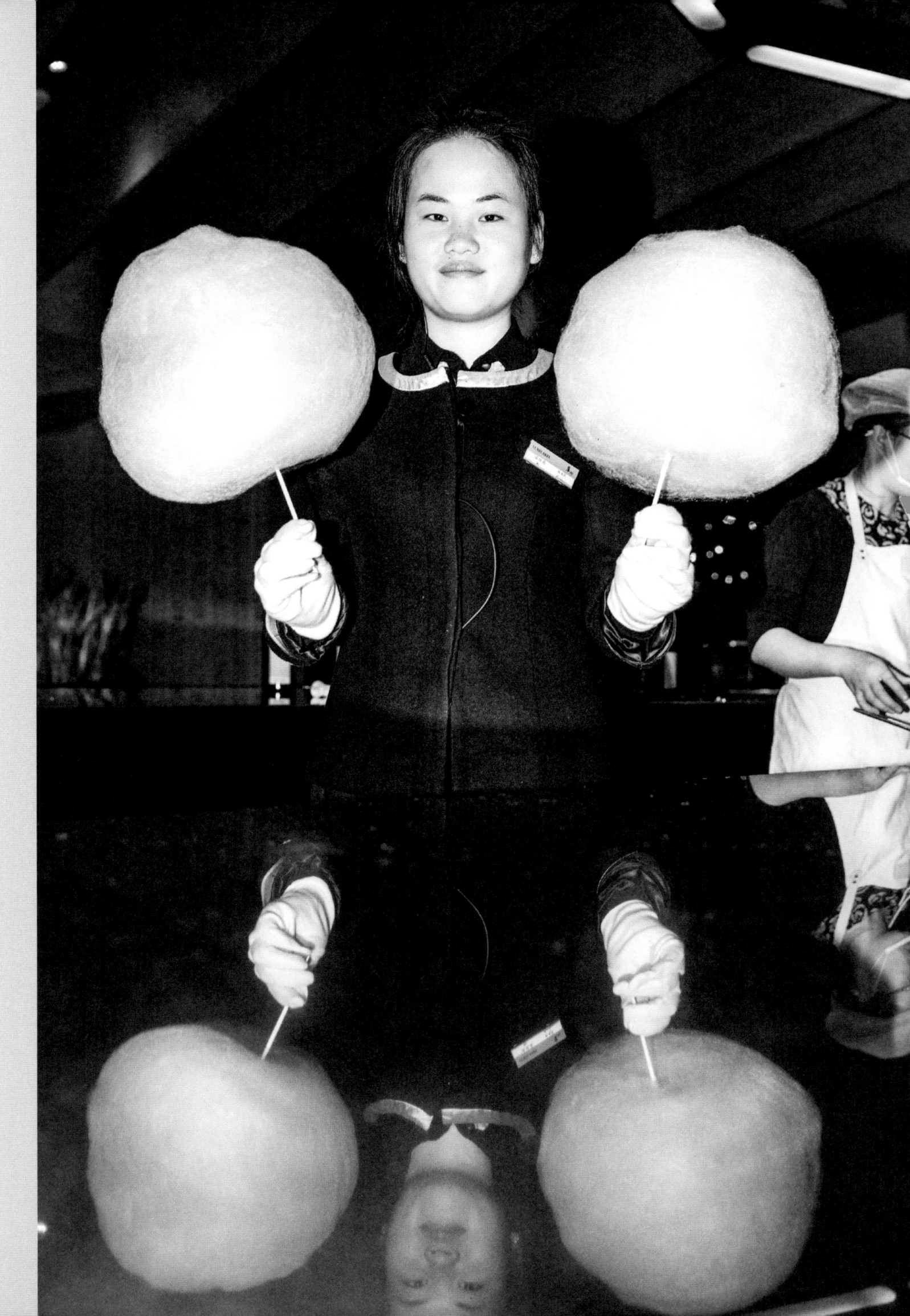

Pao Houa Her
My Grandfather Turned into a Tiger

Kong Pheng Pha

Our Hmong elders often narrate stories about Laos. In one, they carry bamboo baskets on their backs as they leisurely walk barefoot along the rugged mountainsides toward the rice paddy fields. Idiosyncratically shaped hills embellish the landscape, providing a panoramic view of steep valleys as green as dragon skin. Gibbons frolicking atop banana trees serenade passersby with their melodies, while Asian unicorns prance behind the emerald timbers. In another story, the elders transport us to wartime Laos, where mountains are set ablaze by cluster bombs. Rotting carcasses of water buffalos litter the bomb-stricken landscape. Bloodstained trails zigzag through the compressed jungles as the eyes of trees surveil lost wanderers. In this account, dead men become tigers, the most malevolent of all creatures. The tigers lurk behind bamboo huts, roaring through crevices exposed in the dead of night.

Pao Houa Her, a Hmong photographer born in Laos and raised in the United States, takes these conflicting geographies of Laos as frameworks for the series *My Grandfather Turned into a Tiger* (2017) to ask: How do Hmong in the United States imagine Laos when they do not have a direct connection to it? Which of these scenes—literal or allegorical—resonates with Hmong? After the end of the Vietnam War in 1975, Indigenous Hmong who served as American proxy soldiers in Laos were displaced into the West as political refugees. Many Hmong refugees resettled in Minneapolis–Saint Paul, Minnesota, where Her's family has lived since the mid-1980s.

Her's photographic repertoire draws on the fragmented temporalities and uneven geographies of worlds past to perform a visual narrative of how these disconnected histories unfold in the present. She always carries a camera with her in order to stage a photograph or capture an accidental moment with family and community members, both in Laos and Minnesota. Her imbues her photographs with lust and desire—for her subjects and for the homeland—with the need to grieve for the dead, now specters in our splintered memories.

"One challenge of my photography is to create a narrative that does not require a beginning or an end," Her told me recently. A circuitous trajectory of Her's work formulates a complex metaphorical dialectic: the blurriness of both prewar and war-torn Laos narrated by her elders. The country's distance—both geographically and metaphorically—seems closer than it appears. This circular vision materializes through a sequence of illusions that are simultaneously mundane, absurd, and chaotic.

Faux flora epitomizes a major hallucinogen in Her's work. "The floral makes something hard to look at beautiful to look at," Her says. The paradoxical pain and pleasure in looking requires a psychic reconciliation to disentangle the various oppositional elements within Her's photographs. How do we resolve the antagonistic impressions of Laos? Her does not claim to fulfill the expectations of our imagined geographies, but rather to draw from our contradictory archives of knowledge to adjust our gaze—and mind—beyond the visual medium.

Kong Pheng Pha is an assistant professor of critical Hmong studies and women's, gender, and sexuality studies at the University of Wisconsin, Eau Claire.

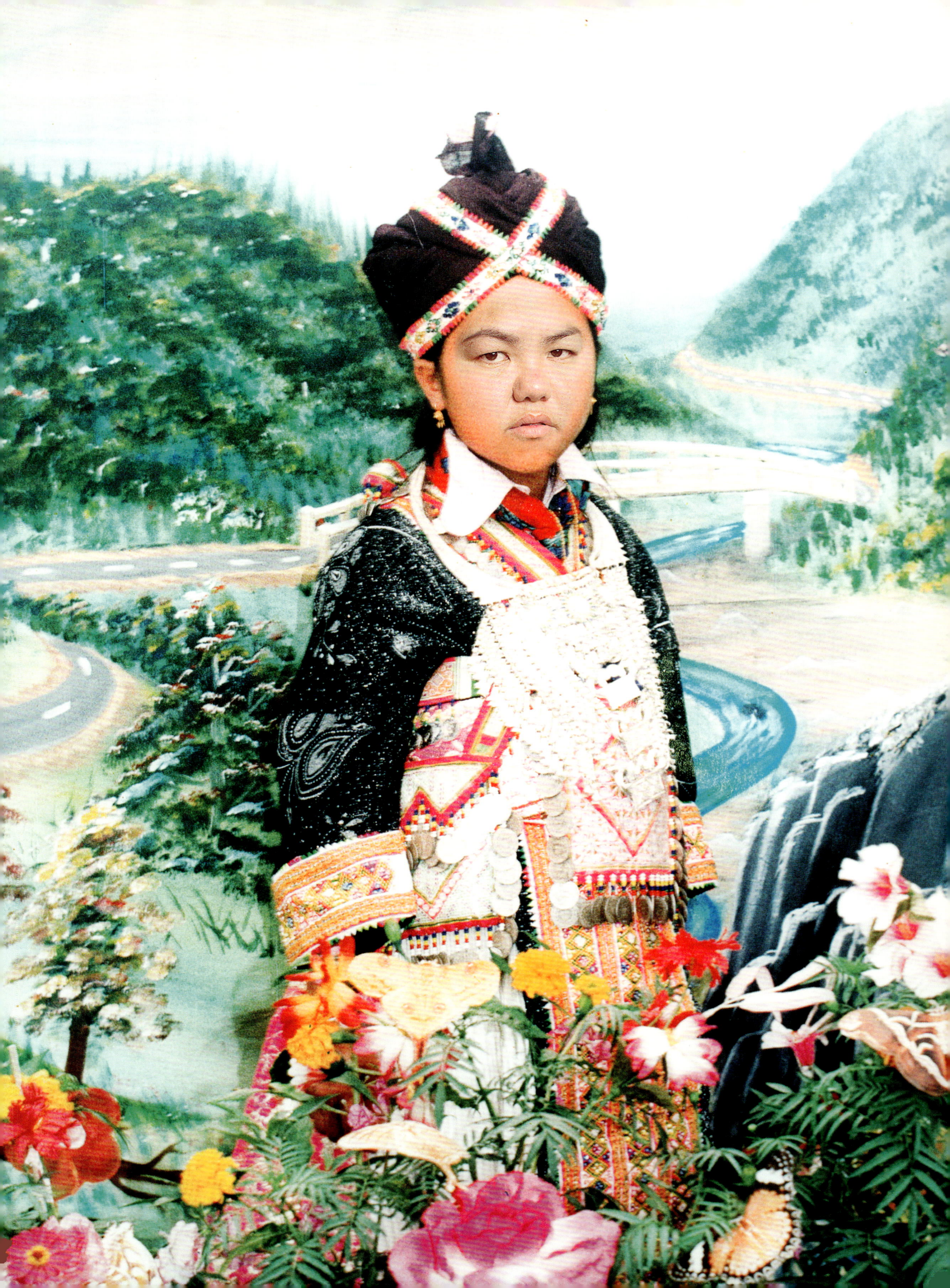

Previous page:
*My Grandmother's
Favorite Grandchild—
Pao Houa*, 2017; this
page: *Three Bachelors
at the Elder Center*,
2017; opposite: *Maroon
Backdrop*, 2017

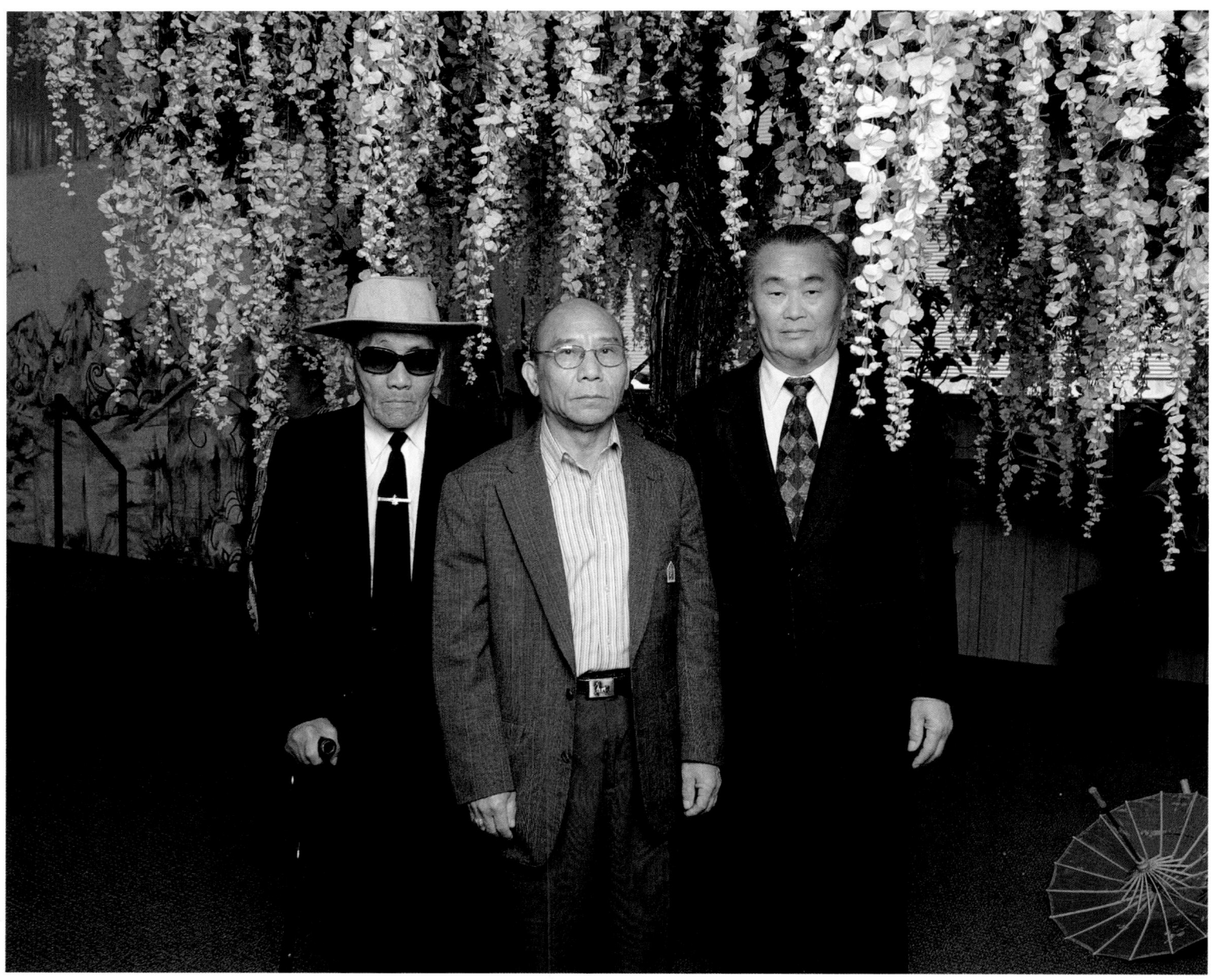

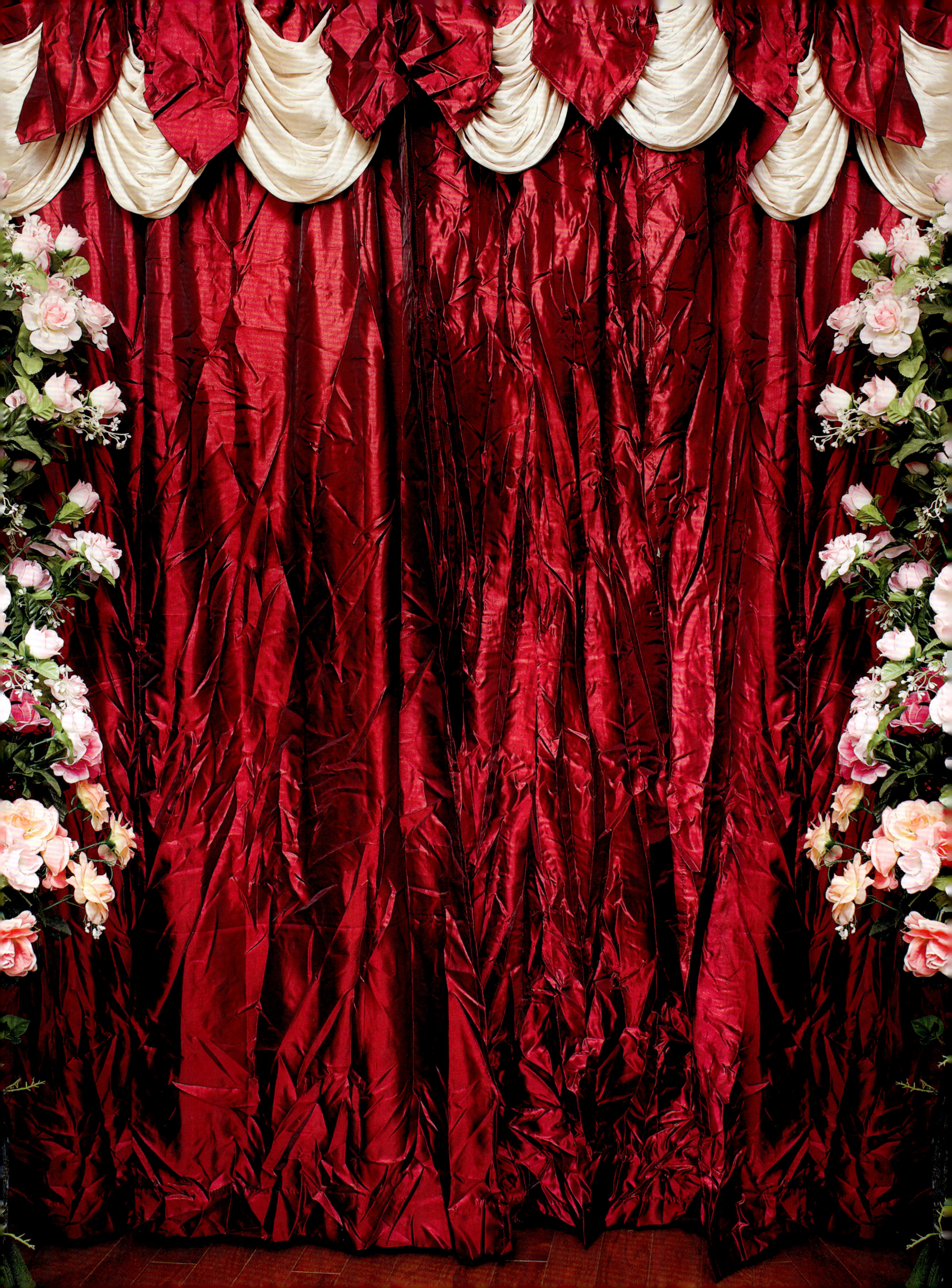

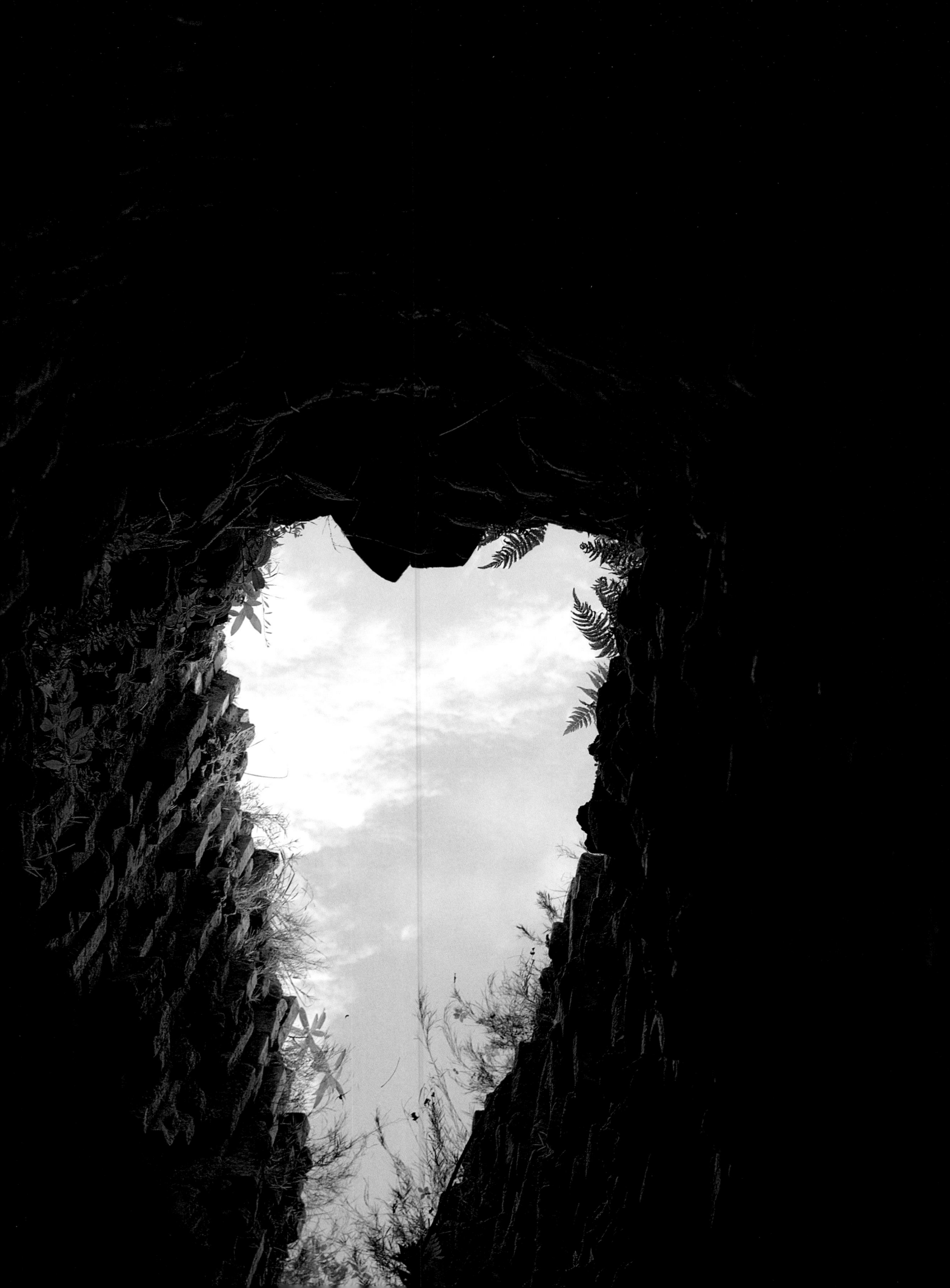

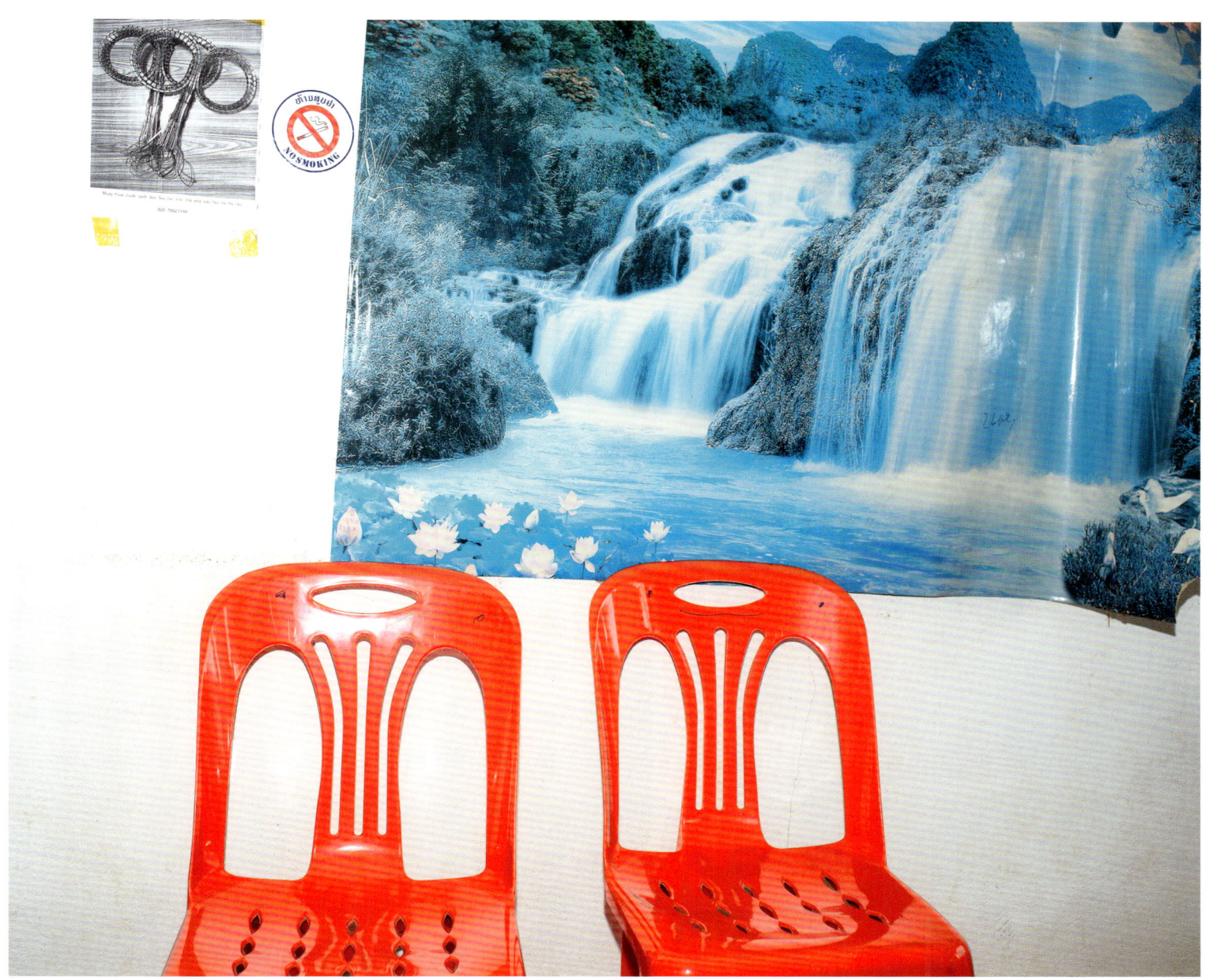

This page:
Prince Charming, 2016;
opposite: *Vince Crying*,
2017

All photographs from
the series *My Grandfather
Turned into a Tiger*
Courtesy the artist and
Bockley Gallery, Minneapolis

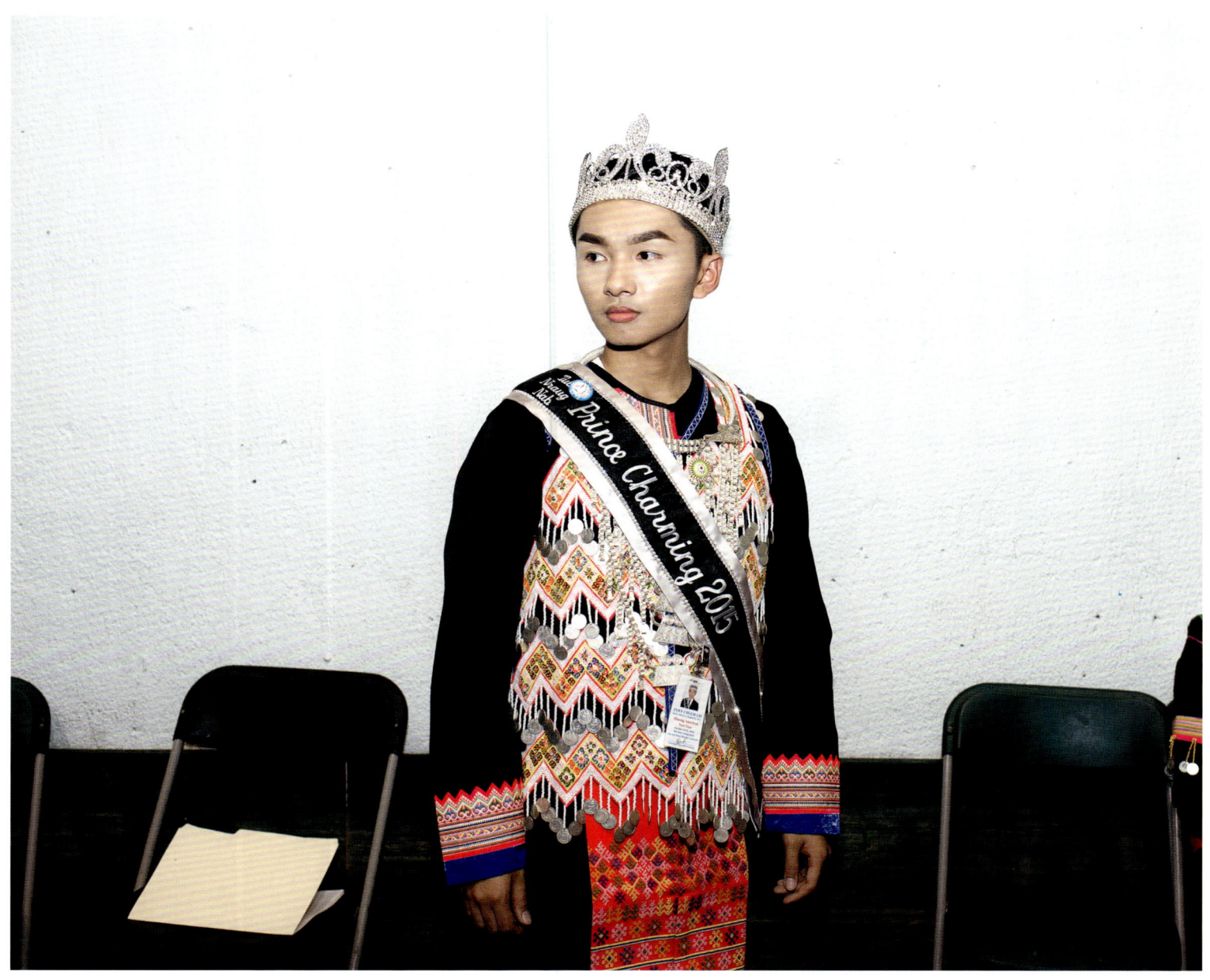

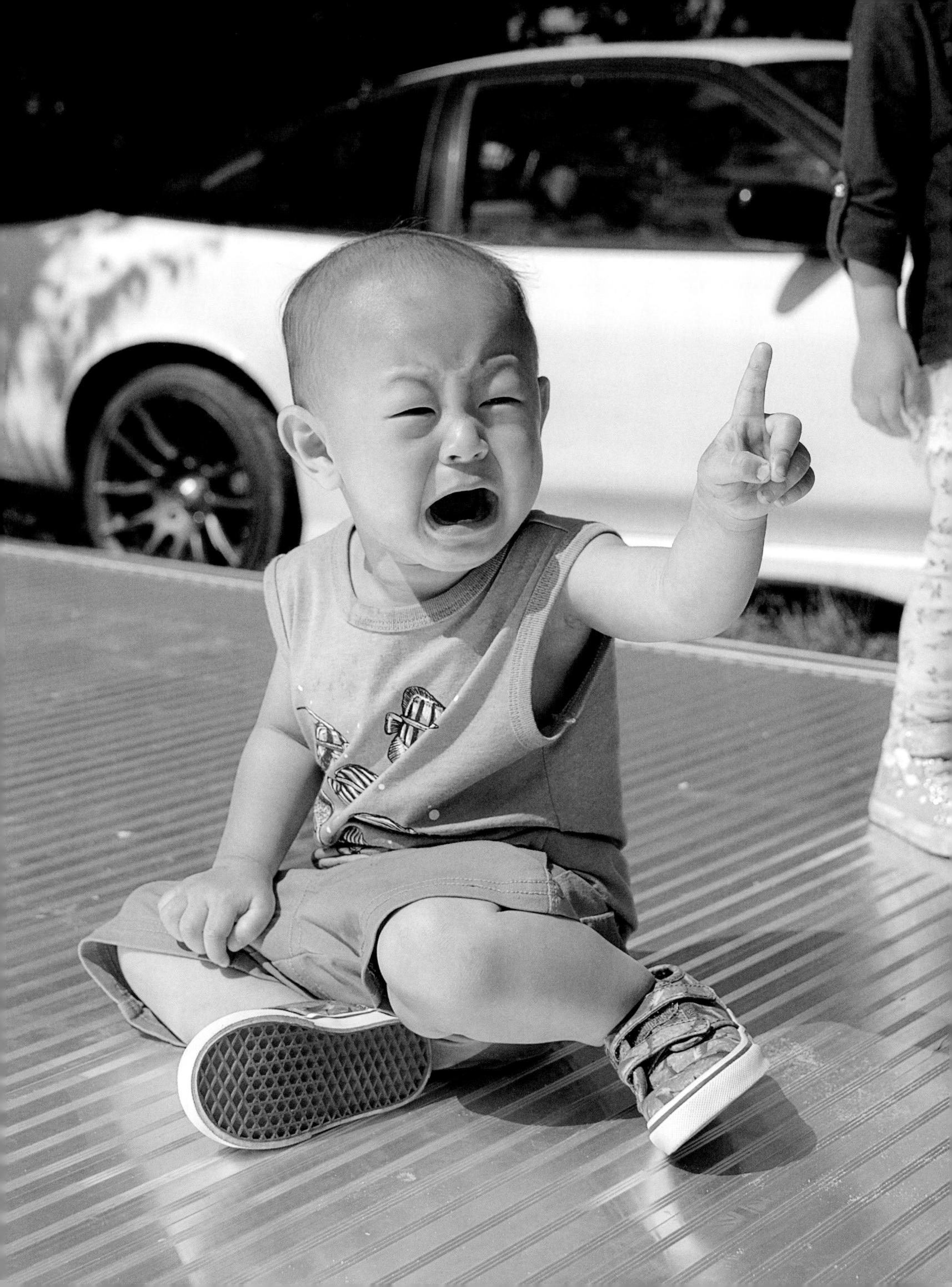

Dionne Lee
True North

Shiv Kotecha

The objects and ideas that appear in Dionne Lee's photographs, videos, and collages seem again and again to be involved with the problem of survival and with resistance against the systems of power that order the American landscape. Merging snippets from nineteenth- and twentieth-century nature photographs, Lee is motivated, she says, by the "difficulties of how to survey what is lost, what is stolen, or what was never even allowed to be." Her collages, often made with gelatin-silver prints and graphite, question how the natural world is wielded in America's colonial and photographic histories, and how that same history can be reworked to help repair our sense of the present. Soliciting our attention to what is elemental to building a world, the artist's layerings—of words, hands, twine—suggest how to survive within it.

I recently spoke to Lee, a New York–born, Oakland-based artist, about her evolving practice, which included having her bathroom rejigged as a darkroom, a COVID-19 lockdown necessity; about the many windows she's "always inside of" teaching photography online; and about her research as both a space of learning and a space of living. In *Between your hands into a hearth* (2019), Lee culls the active verbs from a guide on how to build a fire and projects them against a massive plume. The translucence of the print medium fills out the gas's illuminating shape. Thrown like a poem across the surface, Lee's handwritten words capture the tensile relations between the history of the land and the impending climate disaster: "eventually burn / against each other choose / and construct in keeping / (see opposite) / feeding cut strong / drill center / between your hands / into a hearth."

Drawing from examples of Black, brown, and Indigenous collectivity in the Northern Hemisphere—peoples marked by their eviction from the bounteous lands white Americans love to picture themselves in front of—Lee's frictional surfaces unmoor viewers from the trappings of colonial propriety, by interrupting the scenes with gestures of embodied interaction. In her 2019 collage *North*, Lee's own hands are held in the air to form the winglike gesture recalling the North Star that fugitive slaves used as a compass to flee the South.

Lee produced the 2020 collage *Wounds* beneath the loud helicopters surveilling the protests in Oakland after the deaths of George Floyd and Breonna Taylor, and the raging fire season that has eclipsed what Californians once called summer. Lee layers spirals drawn in thick graphite onto arboreal, monochromatic columns torn from print. Four poppies— California's state flower—appear doused in crimson red like cauterized lesions as well as symbols of remembrance. Lee's photographs imagine possible worlds without being baffled by time and memory. She speaks with her hands, and with them she articulates a future.

Shiv Kotecha is the author of *The Switch* (2018) and *Extrigue* (2015) and is a contributing editor at *Frieze*.

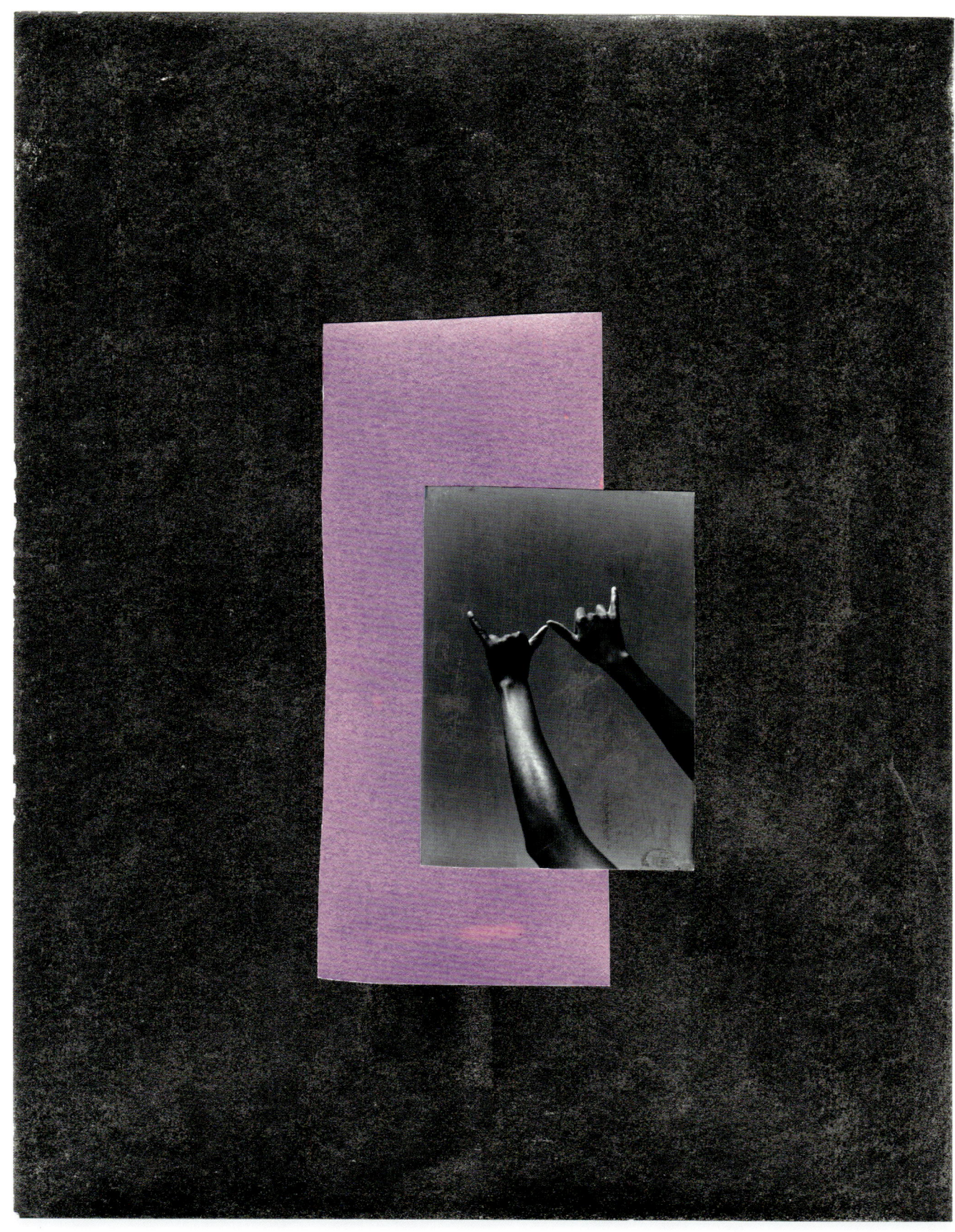

North, 2019

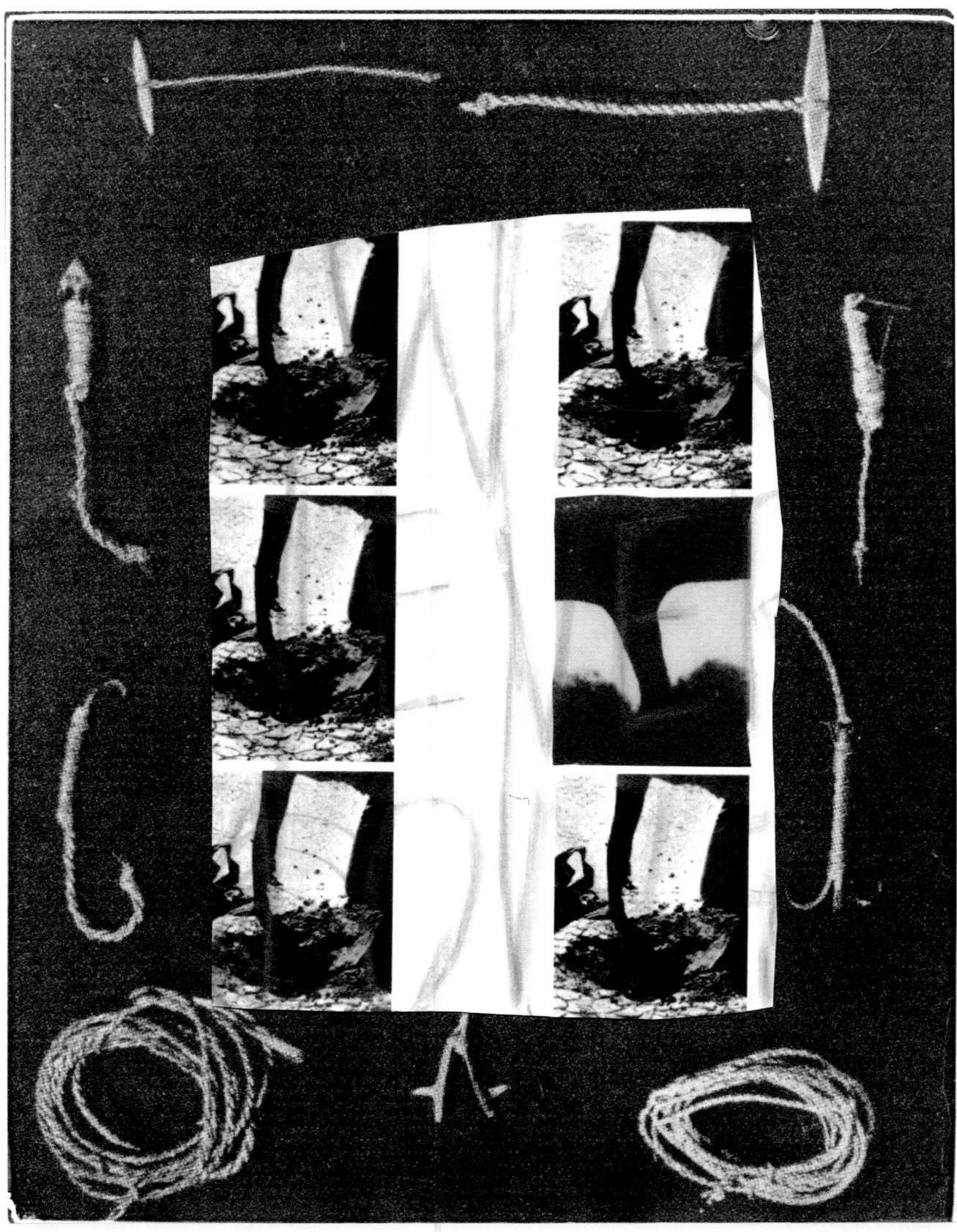

Warnings (1), 2019

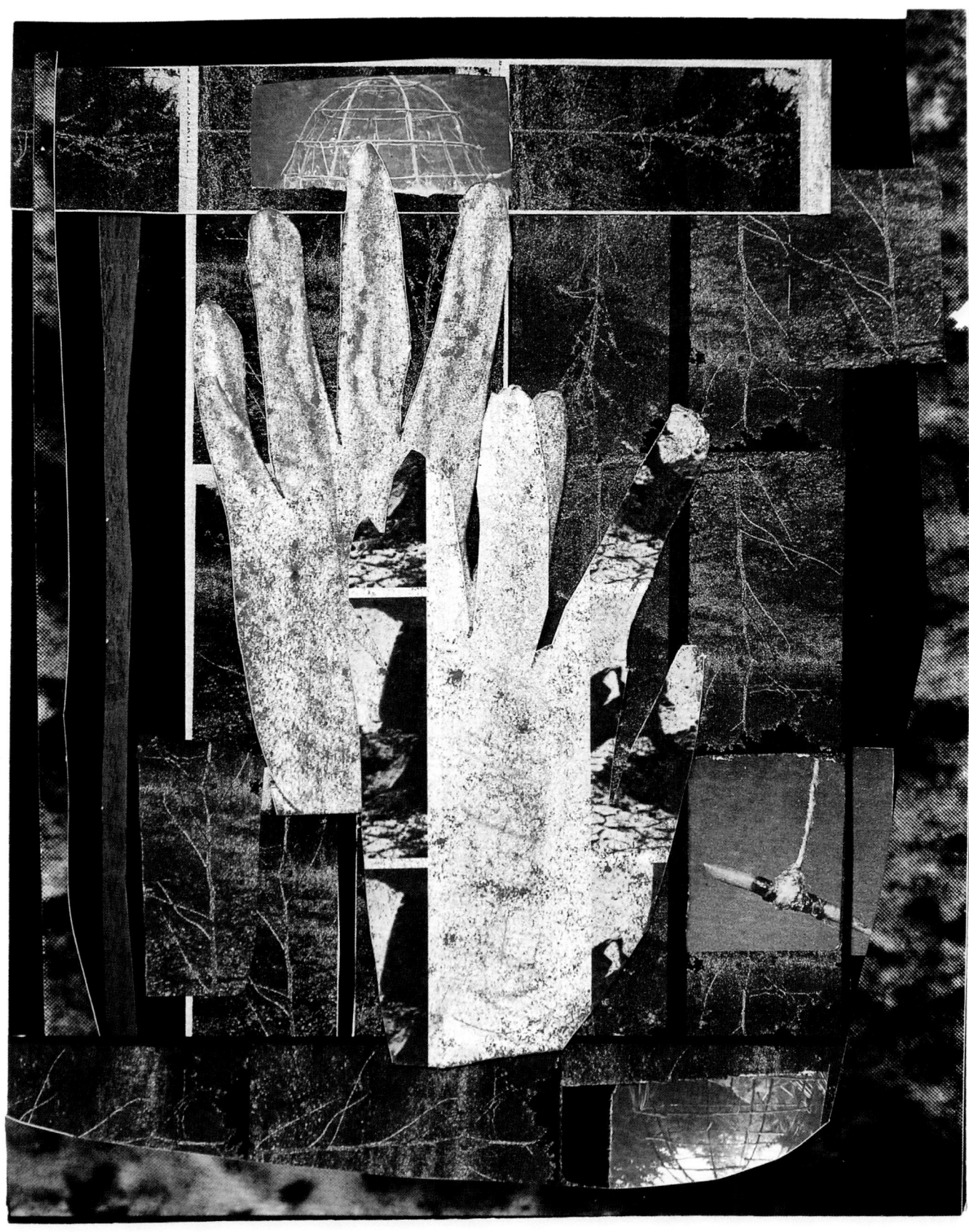

Contact, 2020

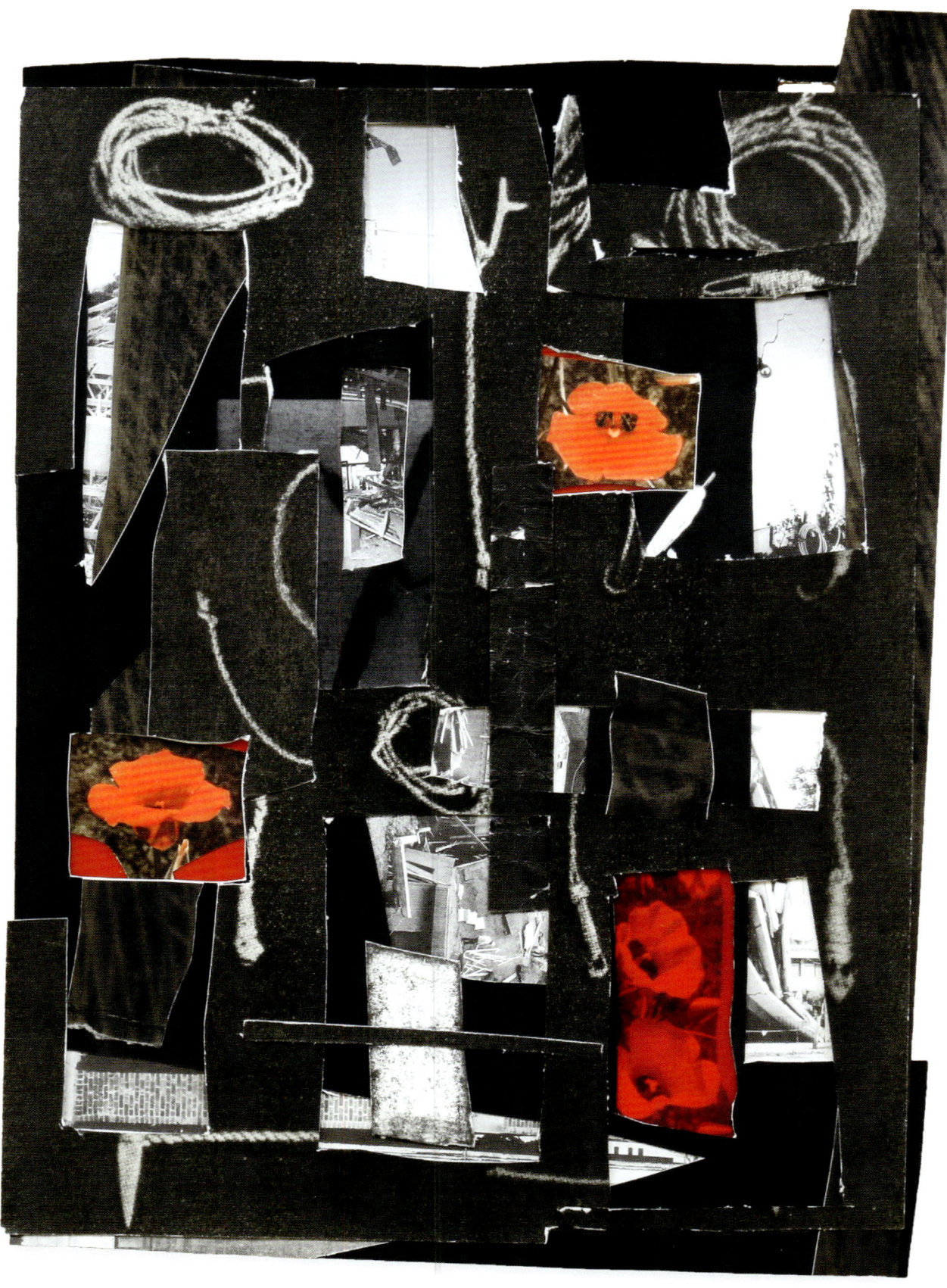

Wounds, 2020

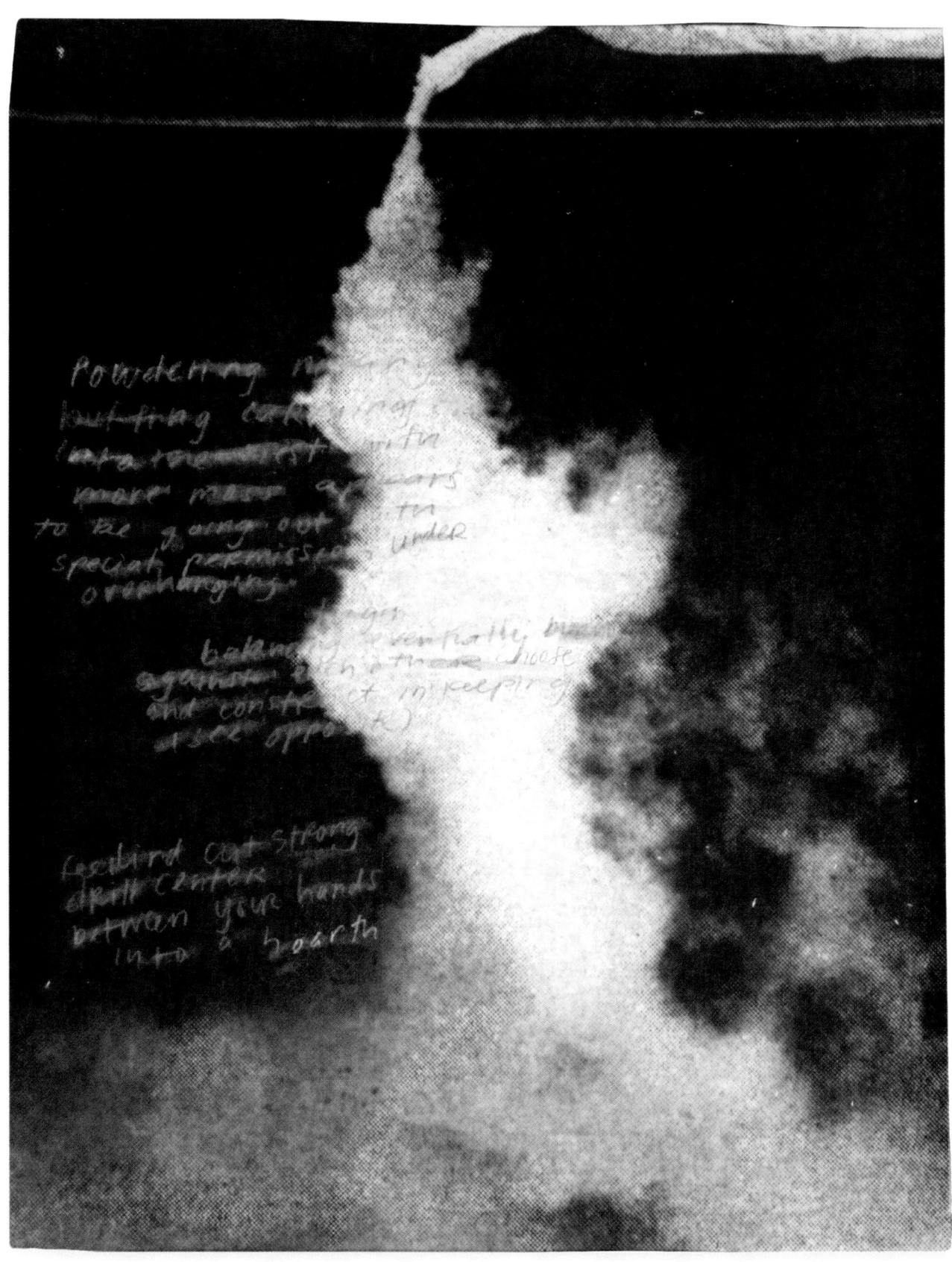

Between your hands into a hearth, **2019**
All works courtesy the artist

Baldwin Lee
Southern Journeys

Casey Gerald

The afternoon I spoke with Baldwin Lee about his photographs, I thought of Little Richard.

Specifically, a short clip from a 1973 documentary about Jimi Hendrix, whose early career included a stint in Little Richard's band. In the clip, Little Richard holds court from a piano bench. He wears a periwinkle-blue jumpsuit. A gray, sequined headband keeps his wild curls at bay, kinda. His face is beat. As the clip opens, Little Richard's fantastic face and hair fill the frame. *He was a star*, he says of Jimi. He lifts his hands high and wide as the camera pans out . . . then lifts his eyes to the ceiling, swivels on the bench, turns back to the interviewer, arms still high: *When I got him, he was a star. Sly told you that everybody is a star! The only problem is, some people haven't been put in the dipper and poured back out on the world.*

Ten years later, Baldwin Lee stopped through Macon, Georgia, Little Richard's hometown. Macon was one of many southern towns Lee visited at the start of what would become an almost decade-long project. He drove a Dodge Dart Sport. In each town, he left his car and walked the streets, carrying a 4-by-5-inch view camera, searching for someone to photograph, wilting in the summer heat. Sometimes, he took his map to the local police station. He'd tell them he was a photographer with expensive equipment and hand over a highlighter so they could circle the neighborhoods to avoid. "Of course," he says in an interview with curator Jessica Bell Brown, in a forthcoming monograph published by Hunters Point Press, "I did the opposite."

Lee had received perhaps the best photography education one could ask for in the United States in the twentieth century. His father—who fought in World War II with the U.S. Army (although he was a Chinese national) and later studied architecture at Pratt Institute on the G.I. Bill—told Lee when he was five years old that he would go to the Massachusetts Institute of Technology. Lee fulfilled the prophecy in his own way, taking up photography there as a student of Minor White. Next came the Yale School of Art, where he studied with Walker Evans and earned an MFA in 1975. Lee served as Evans's personal printer, frequently stayed at the legend's house in Connecticut, and handled some of Evans's greatest negatives from *Let Us Now Praise Famous Men*. He'd spent enough time with the so-called best and brightest—or, in his words, "eggheads and all the rest"—so, in 1983, he took a two-thousand-mile road trip through the South.

On that first journey, Lee says he photographed "landscapes, cityscapes, night studies, interiors, and portraits of people— white and Black, old and young, rural and urban, well-to-do and poor." He proofed the film and realized that what interested him most were the pictures of poor Black Americans. "I was certain I had found my subject," Lee states in the interview with Brown.

I pause here to confess that I felt a little sick with worry when I first read those words. Was Lee another in the long line of photographers, preachers, politicians, et cetera, et cetera, who seized upon the *wretched of the earth* as subject-cum-spectacle-cum-cash-cow? Then, I spent more time with one image—of a woman with her wigs.

I can't tell you how many times I've come back to this photograph. I come back because it reminds me of my mother, who dragged little me to wig shops all over Dallas, and because I have known and loved so many other women who also loved their wigs. I know one thing thanks to them: there's not a chance in hell this woman trotted out her wigs for some strange camera-toting man unless she liked him. Unless *she* trusted him a little bit. And since she trusted Baldwin Lee enough to show her wigs,

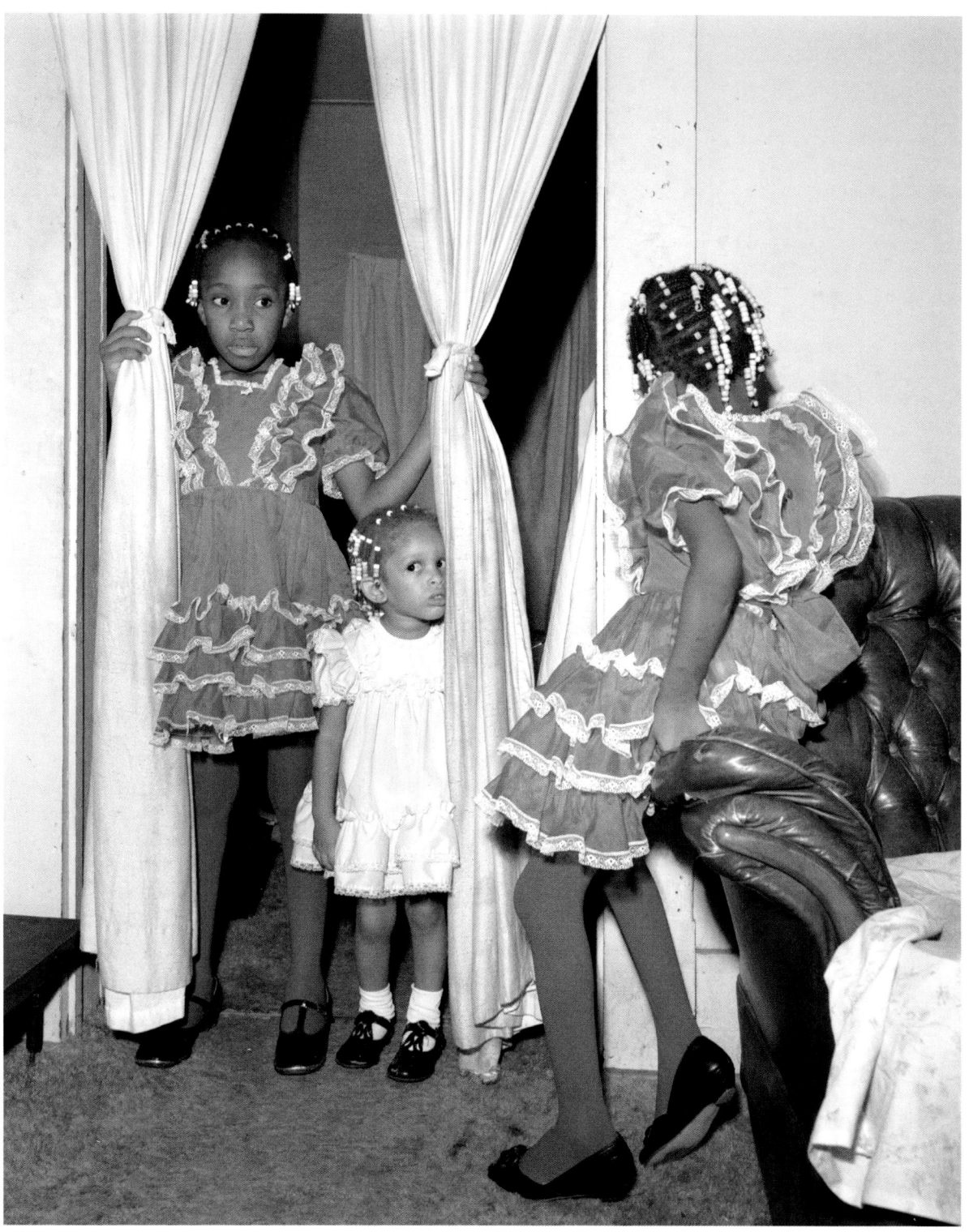

I was inclined to trust him enough to call and ask *why*. Why these people, this project?

"The kind of photography that I was most interested in was the kind that involved going outside, involved physically and psychically and mentally and emotionally stepping into an unknown world, an unknown situation," he explains. "It wasn't just for entertainment, amusement, or diversion, there was a real mission. I discovered I was a political being."

He'd been put into the dipper, you could say. He stayed there from 1983 to 1989, on the back roads of Tennessee (he'd already moved to Knoxville), Kentucky, Missouri, the Carolinas, Florida, Georgia, Alabama, Mississippi, Texas, Arkansas, and Louisiana. What he poured back out on the world is a collection of roughly ten thousand images, most of which have never been seen. It is a body of work that the photographer Barney Kulok, the founder of Hunters Point Press, counts "among the great bodies of work of twentieth-century American photography."

Lee's mission-speak led me to wonder whether Evans had inspired him to do his own take on *Famous Men*.

"I didn't go in with some simple pronouncement that I wanted to expose the injustice that Black Americans had to endure. It's not some kind of dumbass, do-gooder kumbaya," Lee says. "It's not any of that shit. It's just simply that what people are doing, what's going on, is important." He adds that it's about being fair to people, which isn't "any earthshaking thing."

It's no small thing, either. I do not take for granted that a photographer with Lee's talents and moral clarity dedicated nearly a decade to this proposition. Without *both*, this work might not exist—and if it did exist, it would not hold such power. Lee's images succumb to neither exploitation nor sentimentality, which is most evident in his photographs of children. Childhood is nothing if not an exercise in being looked down on by adults, yet the children here seem to recognize that the man who stands before them takes them seriously. That may be my highest praise: Baldwin Lee took people *seriously*.

"The world only becomes interesting if you get into the real specifics of it that make it individual and unique," he says of his approach. Take another example, an image that Kulok calls one of Baldwin's greatest. Here, in this untitled photograph from the mid-1980s, Lee has captured (in my mind) a beautiful young Black Jesus, standing tall and whole, playfully rejecting the cross and the lynching tree.

Lee listened from his garage in Knoxville as I rattled off my thoughts. I was reminded of the hecklers at the foot of Jesus's cross yelling, "If you are the son of God, if you're so big and bad, come down, save yourself."

"Photography is not wordless literature," Lee tells me. He considers it closer to sculpture, or improvisational theater. Between Lee and his subjects there is "an absolute imprecision of both of our abilities that sometimes results in something miraculous that is infinitely better than anything I had wanted. And that's when the hair on the back of your neck stands up, and that's when your pulse quickens, and that's when you say, Oh, dear God, please don't let me fuck this exposure up." How rare, how wonderful, that someone looked carefully enough to see these Black women and Black men and Black children not as symbols, not as props, but as stars. "I saw myself as a talent agent," he adds.

So, why did Lee stop photographing? He retired from the University of Tennessee, where he taught photography for more than thirty years, and doesn't use a camera aside from the one on his iPhone. He speaks of his guilt, knowing that he had safe harbor when many of the people he photographed did not. He speaks of the work becoming predictable and repetitive.

He compares it to the arc of an athletic career. "You think that the trajectory you're on is going to go on forever. And it doesn't. It's finite. Because if it was to continue indefinitely, if it was always good, it would be no good. If all things are good, nothing is good."

I think again of Little Richard. At the end of that 1973 clip, Little Richard laments that he was never allowed to speak to Jimi Hendrix before he died. "I had something to tell him," Little Richard cries, pushing hair away from his forehead. "And I never did, so now I have to talk about it and let him know: it was good." Baldwin Lee is still with us. His photographs are with us too. Let us now say: It was good, Baldwin Lee. It was good.

Casey Gerald is the author of the memoir *There Will Be No Miracles Here* (2018).

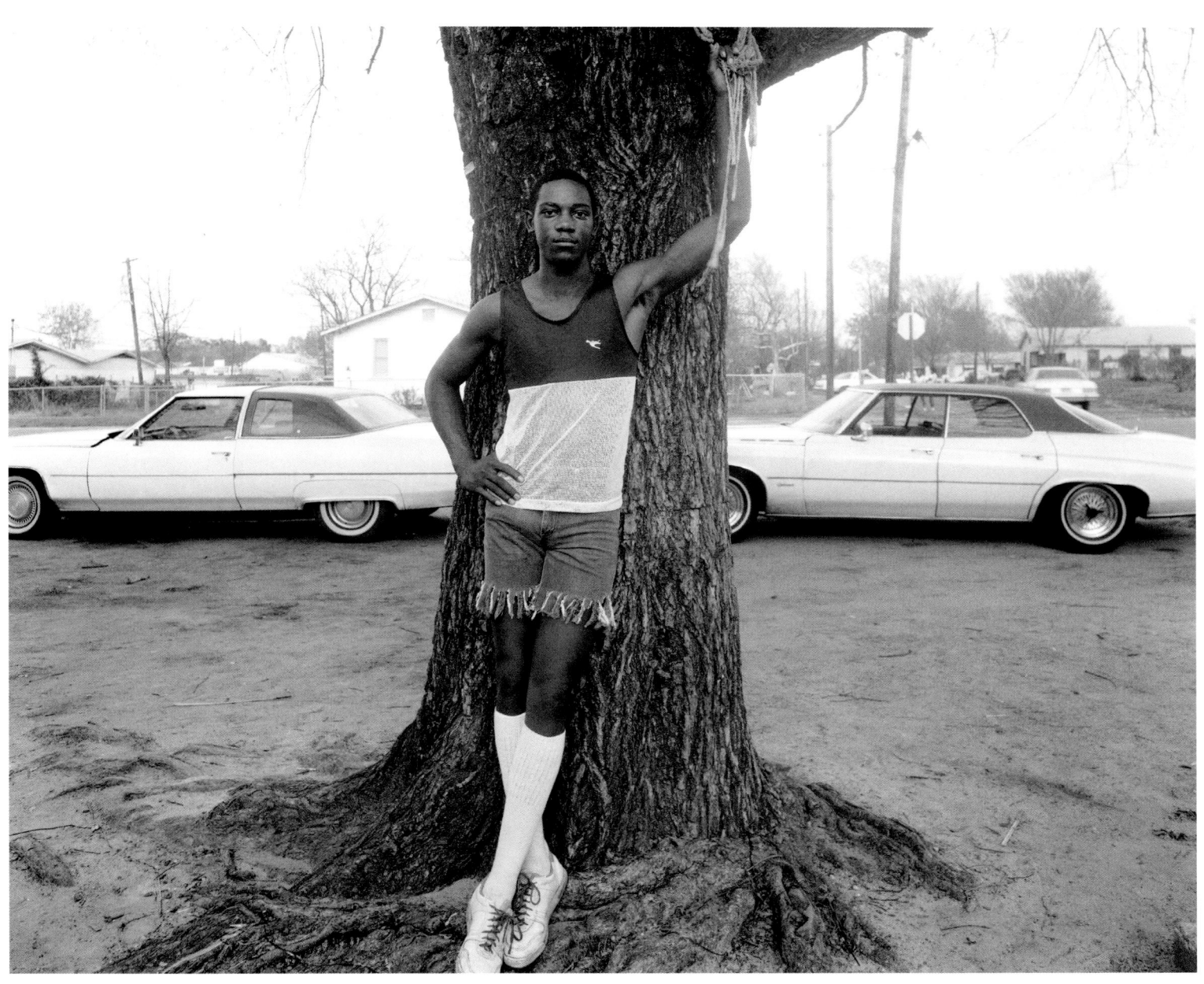

Untitled, mid-1980s

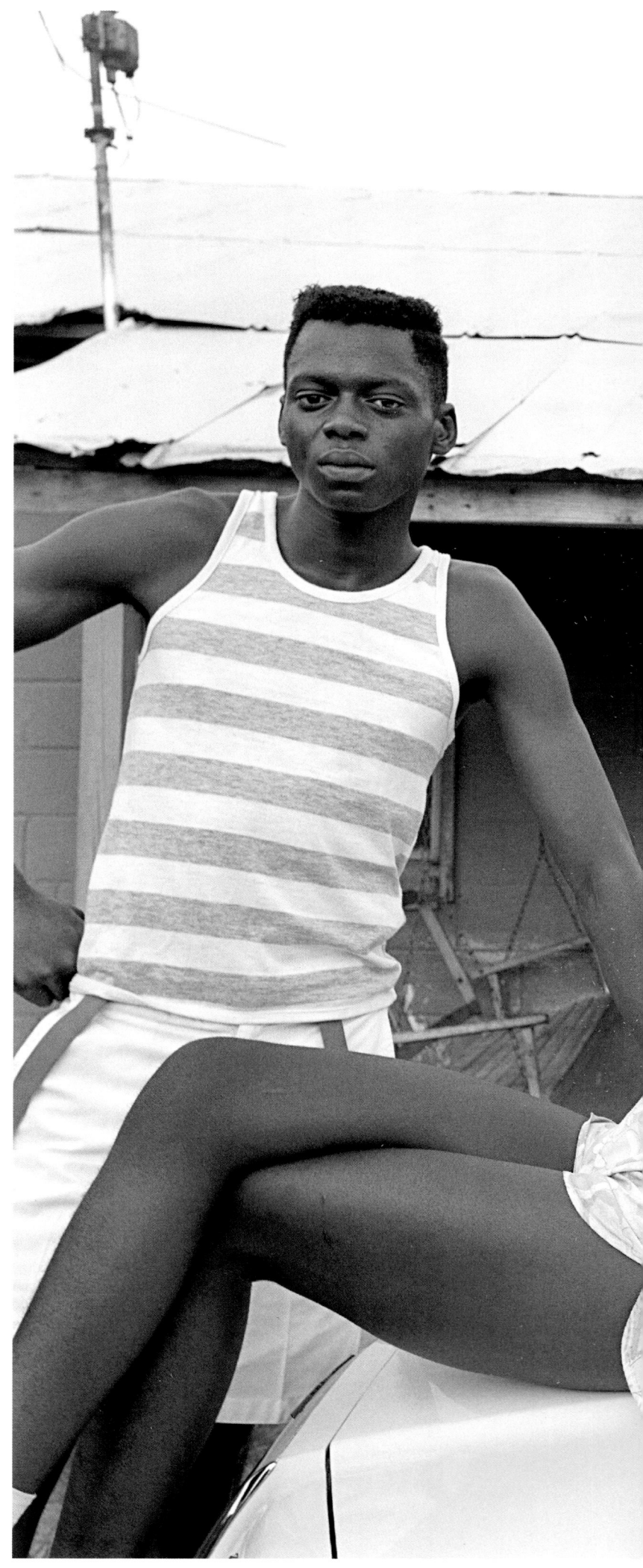

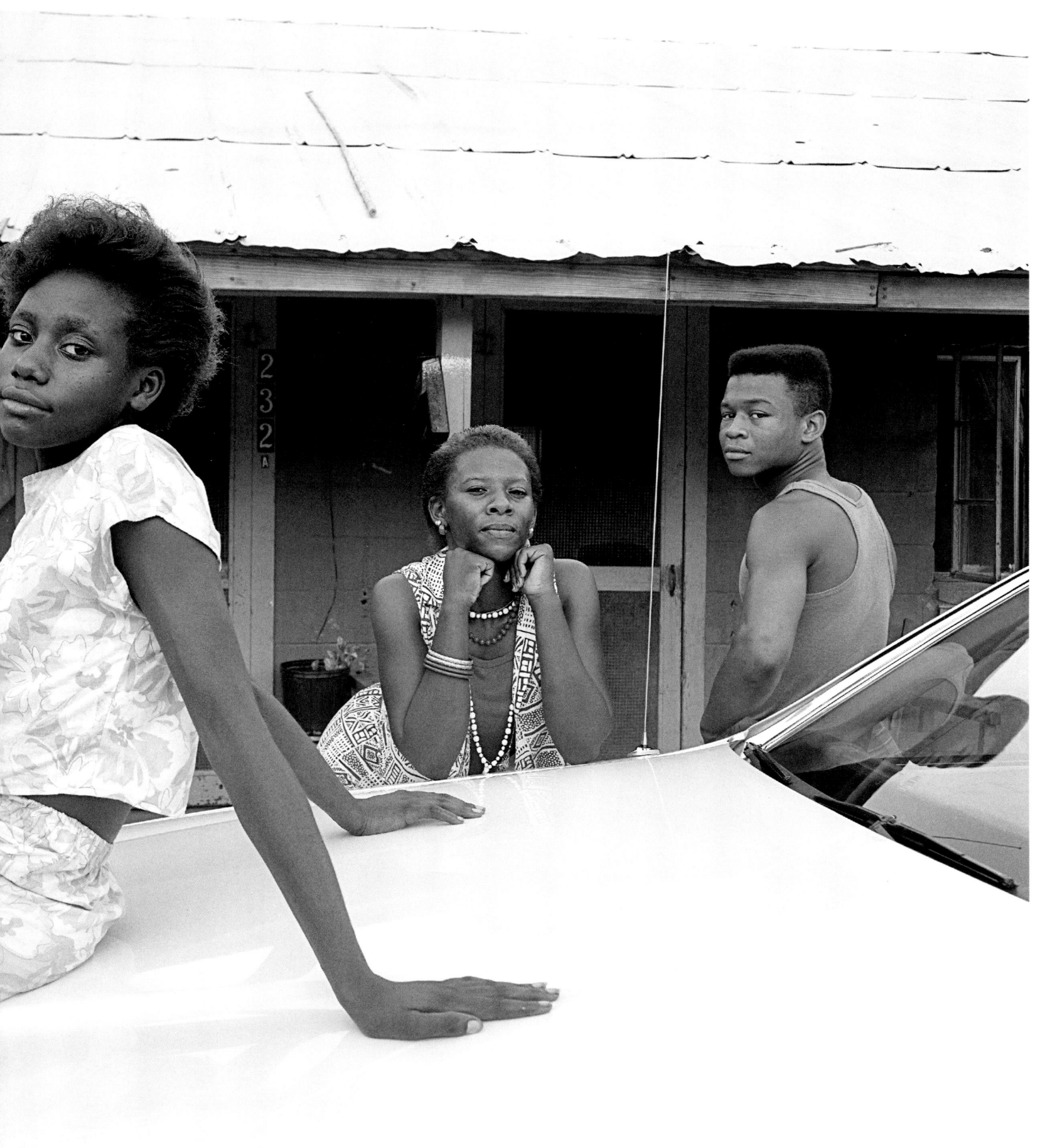

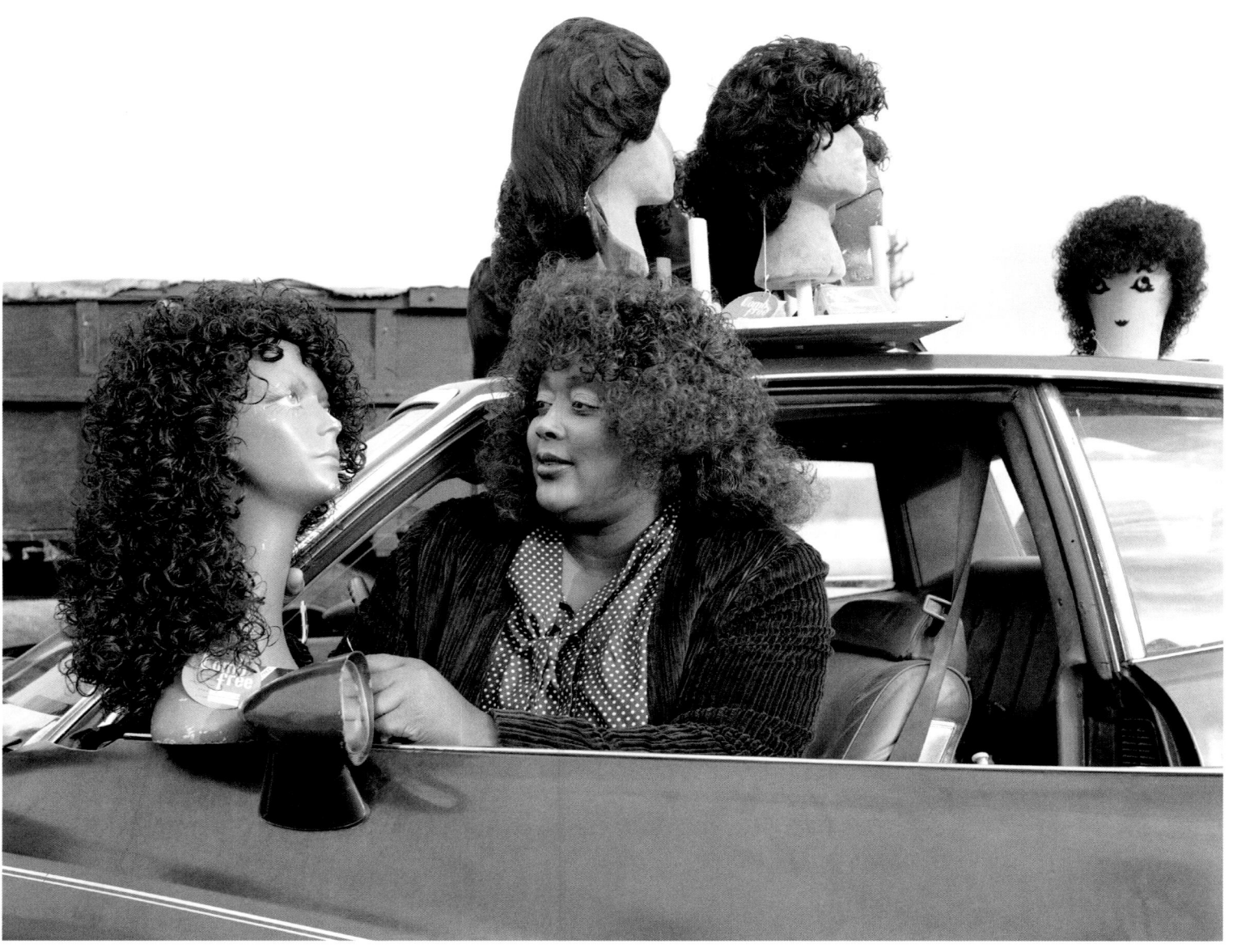

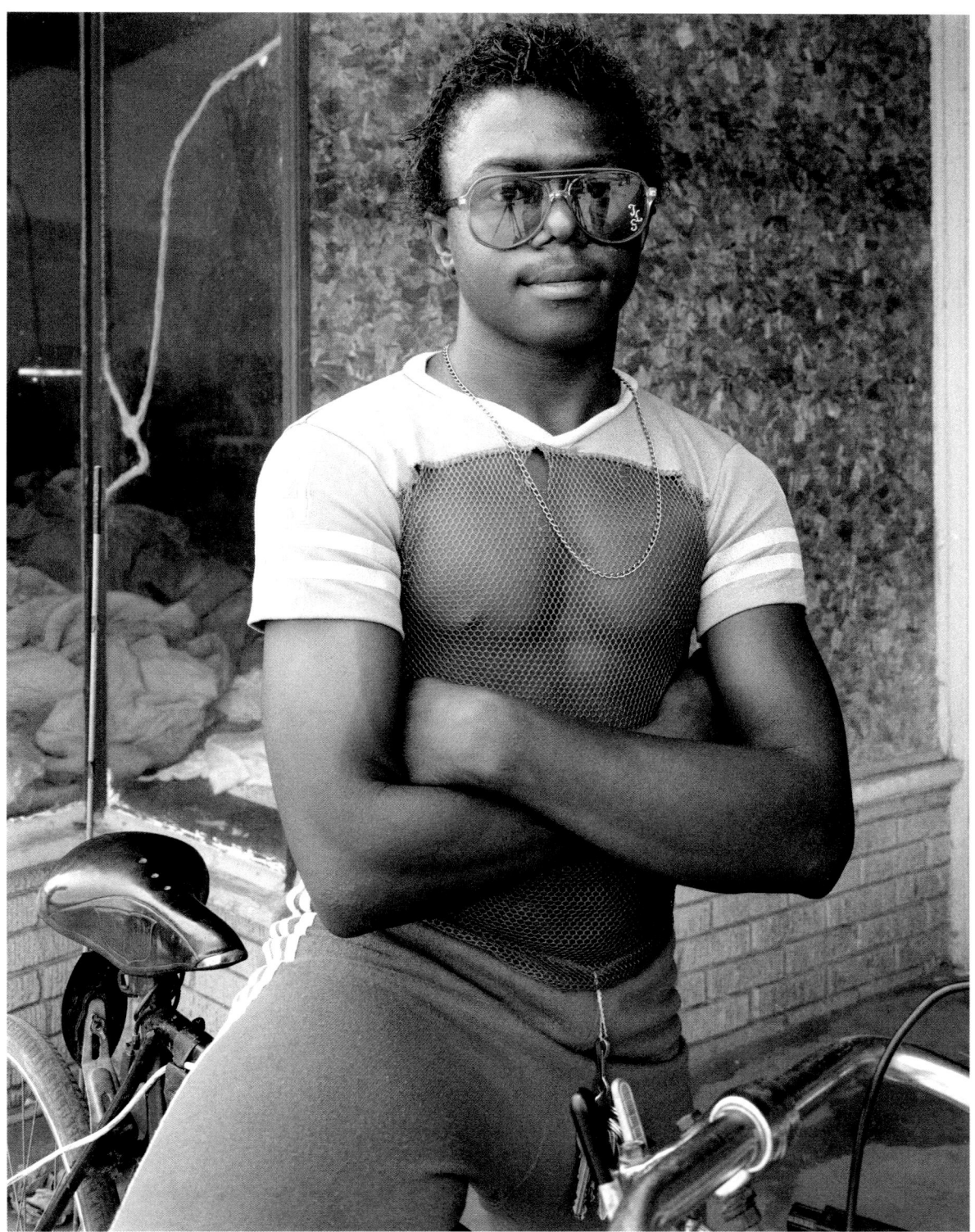

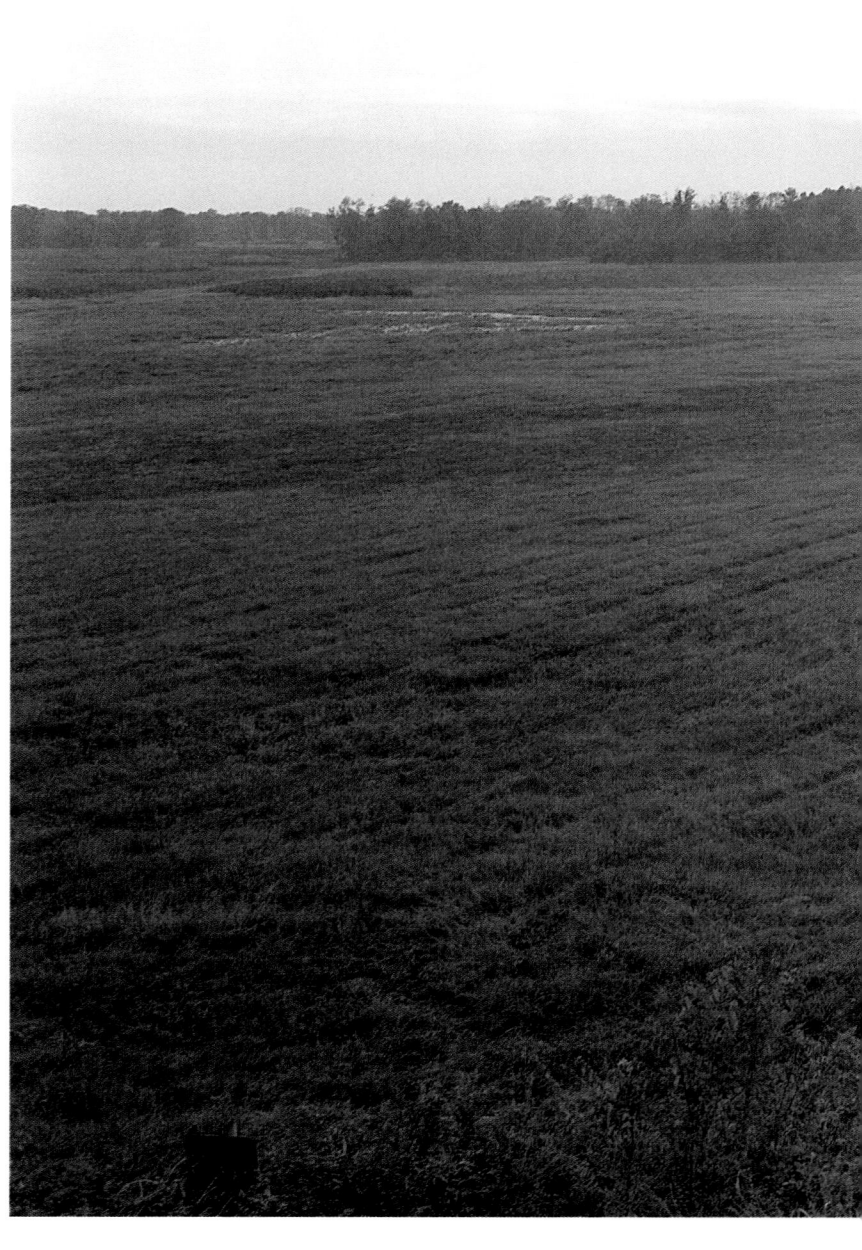

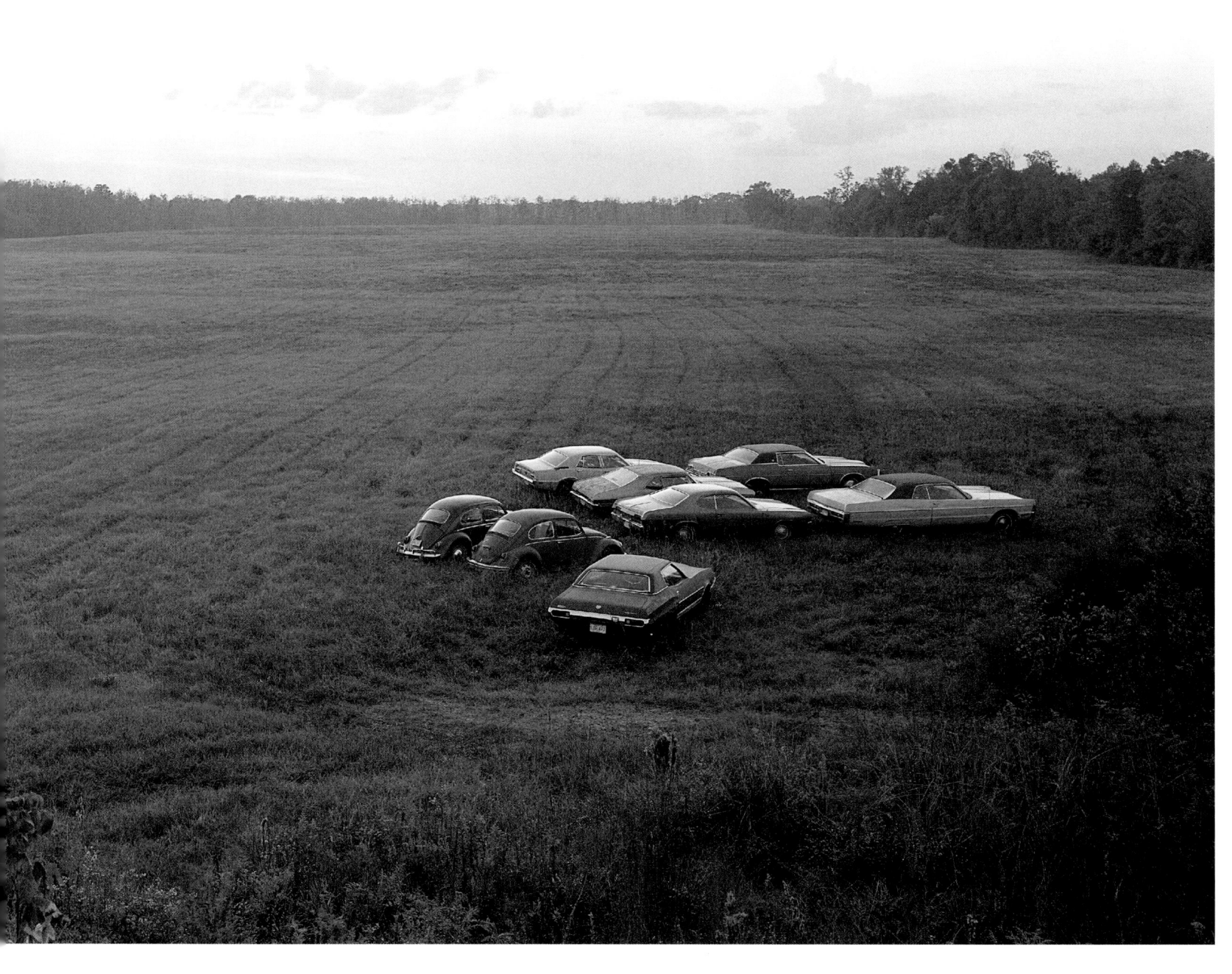

In 2008, after hustling for more than a decade in New York as a fashion photographer, Juan Brenner returned to Guatemala, where he was born in 1977, to devote himself to documenting the country's history as seen through its resilient population and mountainous geography. His urge to discover and say something new led him to his native country's Western Highlands, a region whose majestic, earth-exuded energy and Indigenous societies marked by years of oppression and civil war exerted a strong pull on him. "I instantly fell in love with the territory and its people," he told me.

If Brenner's first documentary project about the Guatemalan Highlands, *Tonatiuh* (2017–19), fit into a familiar category— a nuanced examination of the trauma and lingering scars of colonization—his latest project entices for different, less orthodox reasons. The ongoing series, titled *Genesis*, which Brenner began in 2018, captures present-day life in the K'iche', Kaqchikel, Mam, and Tz'utujil communities of Guatemala, all descendants of the Maya. The photographs show, among other things, dentures, fragments of a crucifix, a shamanic altar, shiny caskets, wildflowers on the edge of a highway, and fake gold necklaces. Any temptation to label a tableau as timeless or quaint is quickly shattered by the intrusion of a cell phone, a pair of Nike shoes, a jewelry pendant in the shape of an AK-47, or a hip-hop-style grill. These still lifes and portraits celebrate the emergence of a novel, affluent aesthetic informed by both local roots and outside influences. Youth and the array of metallic objects his subjects love to covet and flaunt, whether actually precious or not, enthrall Brenner in equal measure.

Gold, of course, has a long, fraught history in the region, and the intention to plunder it is why the Spaniards invaded the Americas to begin with. But the metal's story isn't sufficiently linear or tidy for its current boom to be a case of conscious reclaiming. As Brenner recounts it, for instance, the elite of the Maya empire embellished their mouths with bone, conch, and jade, rather than gold. In fact, the widespread oral use of gold didn't start until the 1950s, through dentistry; further complicating matters, the metals being used ornamentally in the area today are actually alloys from China. Brenner sees the grills as an example of incidental circularity. While people in the mountains are highly conscious of their Maya roots, the mouth embellishments are in no way connected to their heritage or the conquistadores' material greed, instead serving mainly to signal purchasing power and a specific, thoroughly modern but ultimately foreign aesthetic.

What could be framed in terms of consumerist demise and a loss of cultural purity Brenner views more optimistically as the long-overdue advent of a newly emancipated Indigenous society. Considering a dependence on remittances from the United States, continued church dominance, and the rising role of drug-money laundering, the ability to buy imported goods seems like a relative measure of progress. But with the rich, incisive sweep of *Genesis*, Brenner counters the stereotype of the destitute, perennially exploited Indian. His images show a nation confidently embracing modern signifiers to project status, fluency in the global parlance of TikTok and pop culture, and a taste for opulence. In this telling, bleached hair, done-up nails, and other Generation Z markers are a potent retort to the patronizing expectation that Indigenous people "preserve" their traditional garb and customs.

Regarding how he navigates his own position vis-à-vis largely Indigenous communities, Brenner says, "I see myself as an observer. I'm mestizo [part European, part Indigenous] but don't even know what community my ancestors are from. I will never really understand my subjects' struggle, but I'm in a position that allows me to tell stories." The project is about "a generation that is moving on. Thanks to globalization, communication, technology, and fashion, this is the first time people in the Highlands are fully interacting and on more equal terms with the wider world," says Brenner. "*Genesis* is about the future. I can't predict what's going to happen, I can only document what's going on now, and, to me, it looks like a decisive tipping point."

Juan Brenner
Genesis

Suleman Sheikh Anaya

All photographs from the series *Genesis*, Guatemala, 2018–ongoing
All photographs courtesy the artist

Suleman Sheikh Anaya is a writer based in New York and Mexico City.

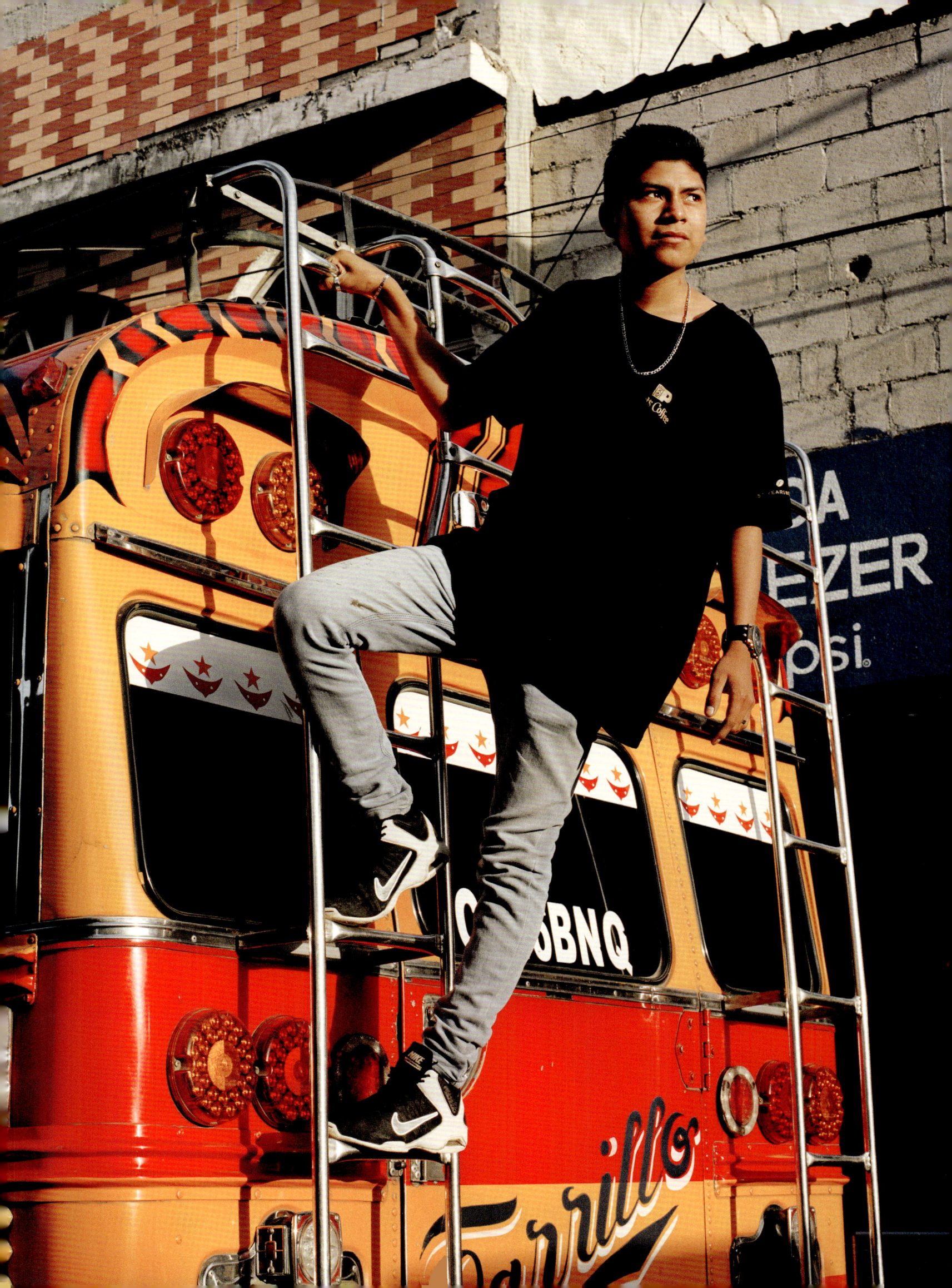

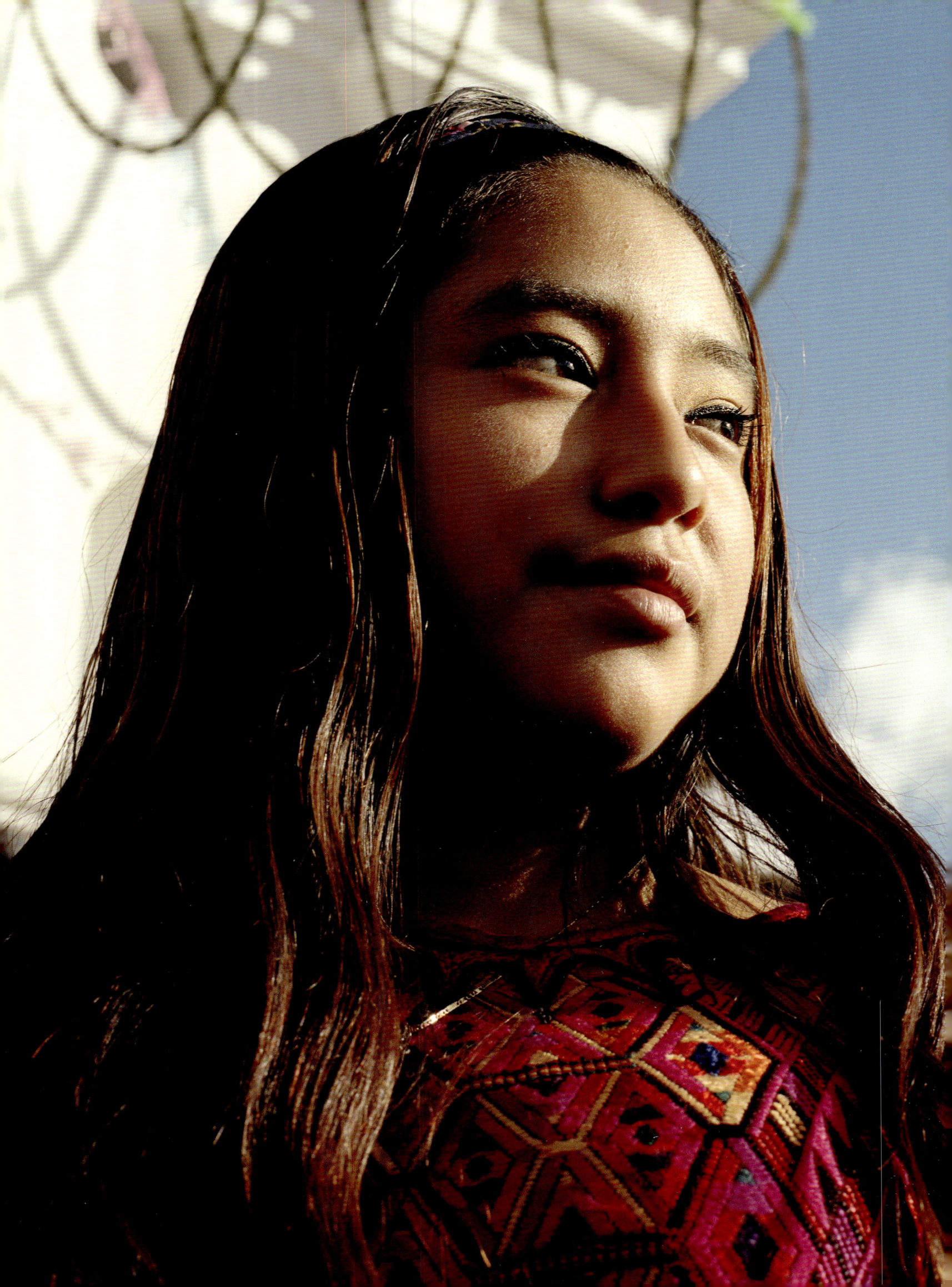

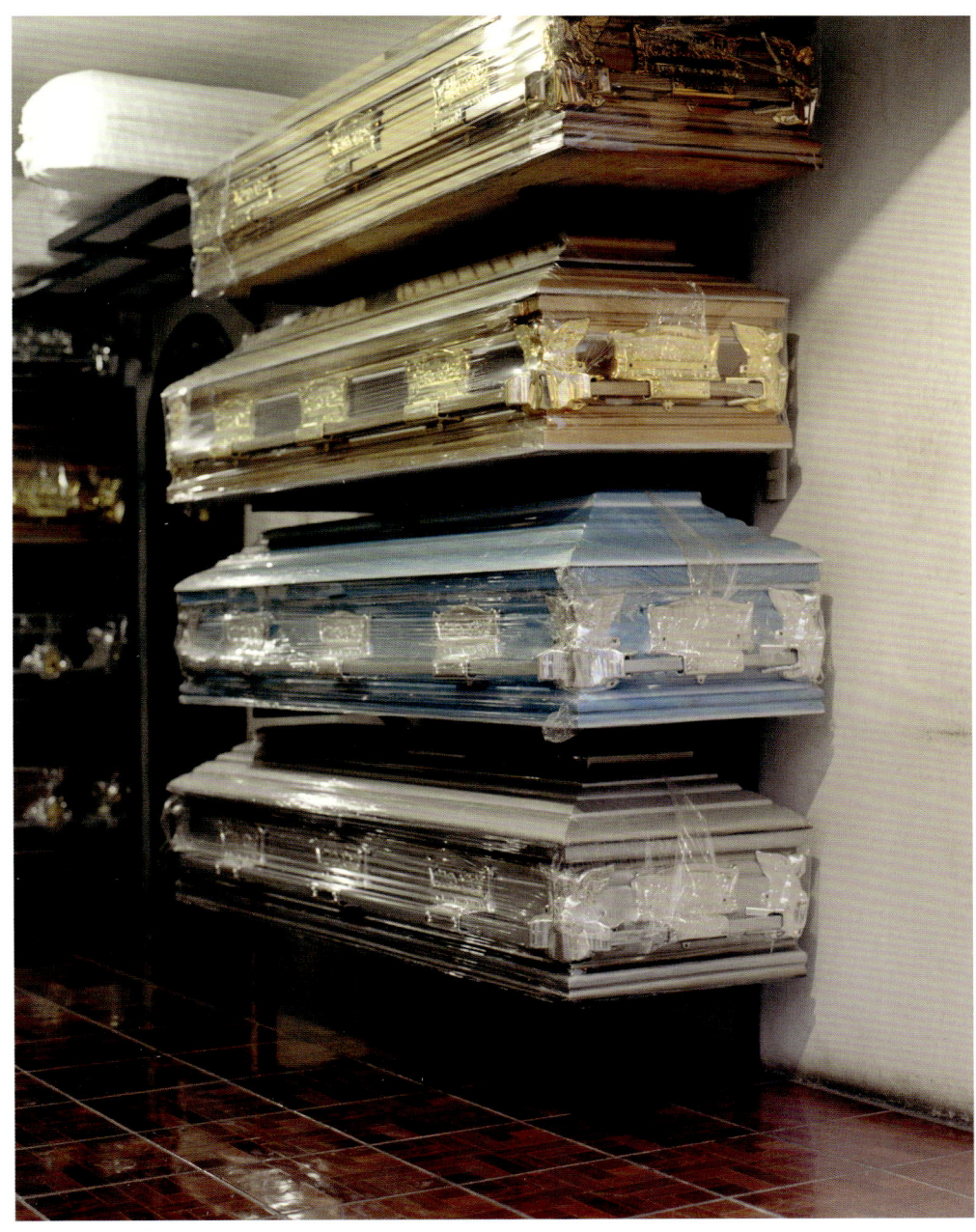

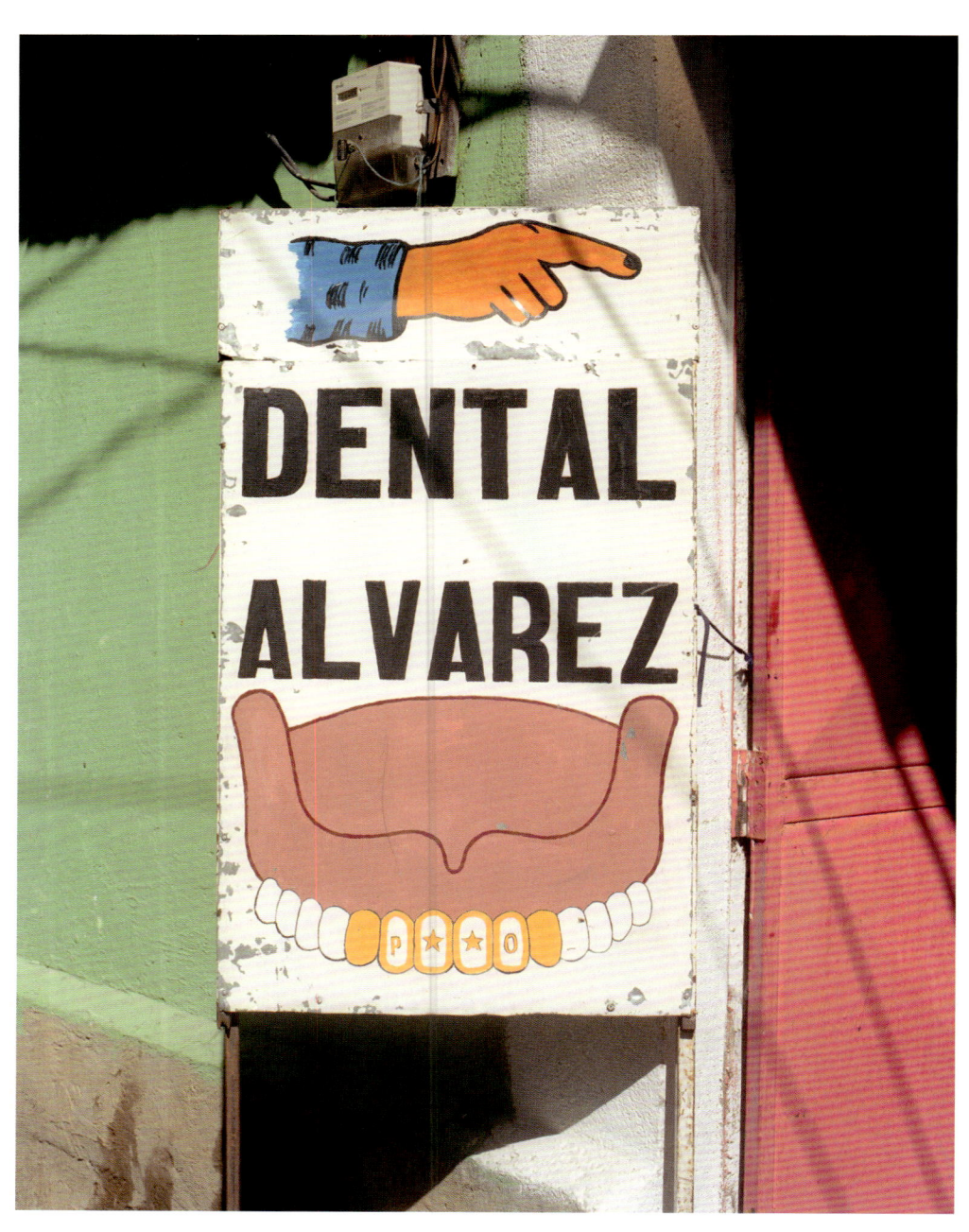

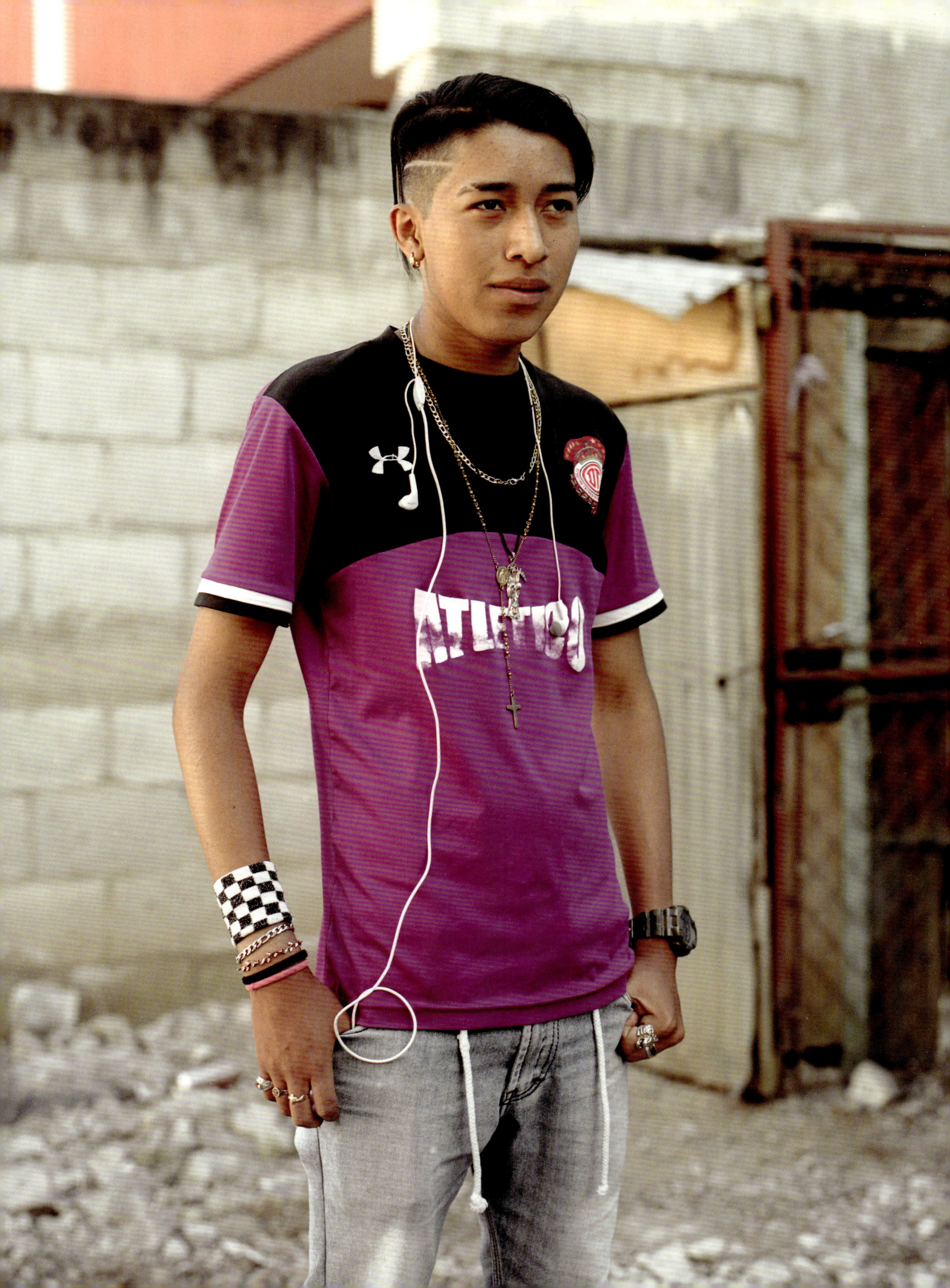

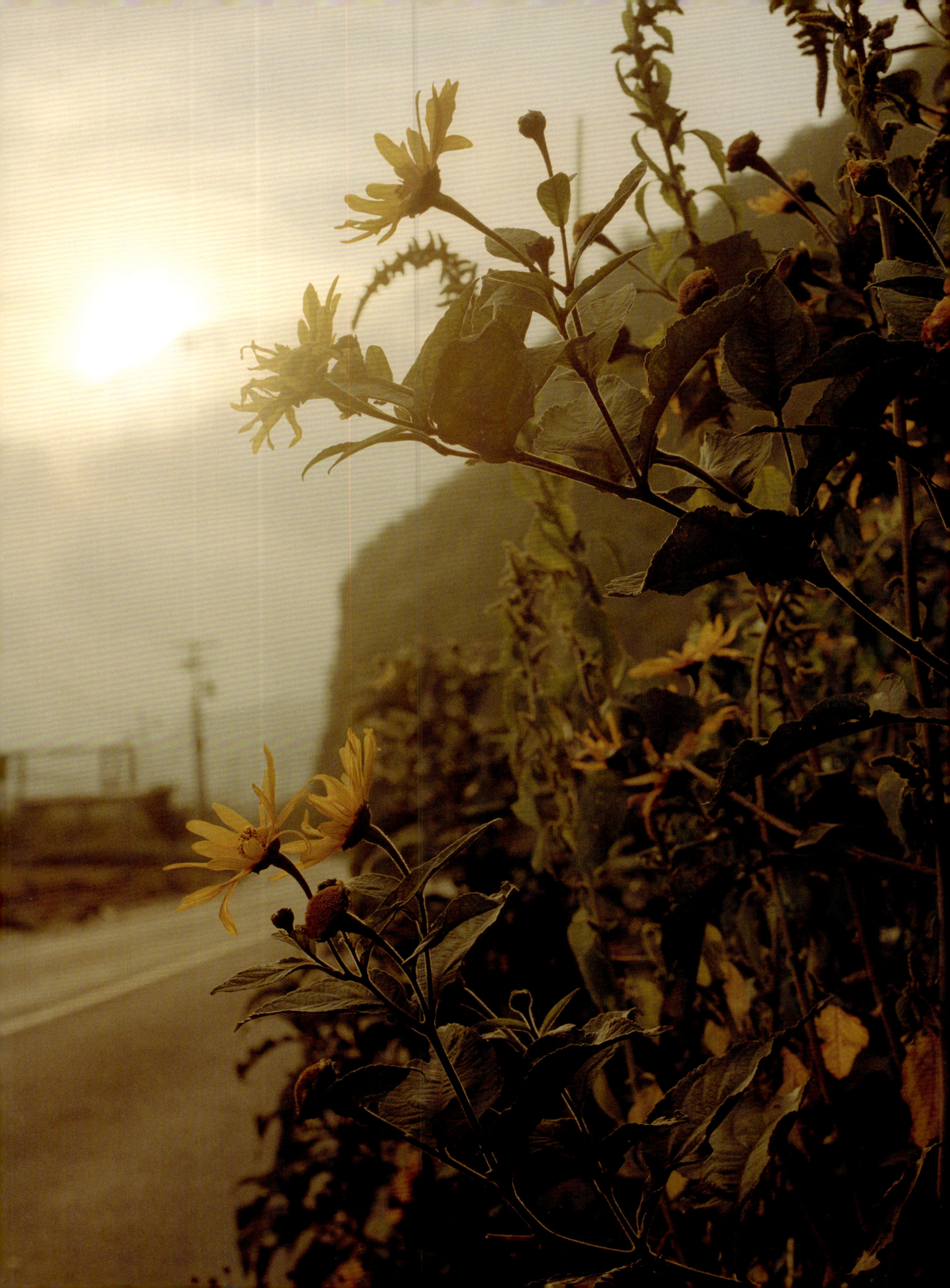

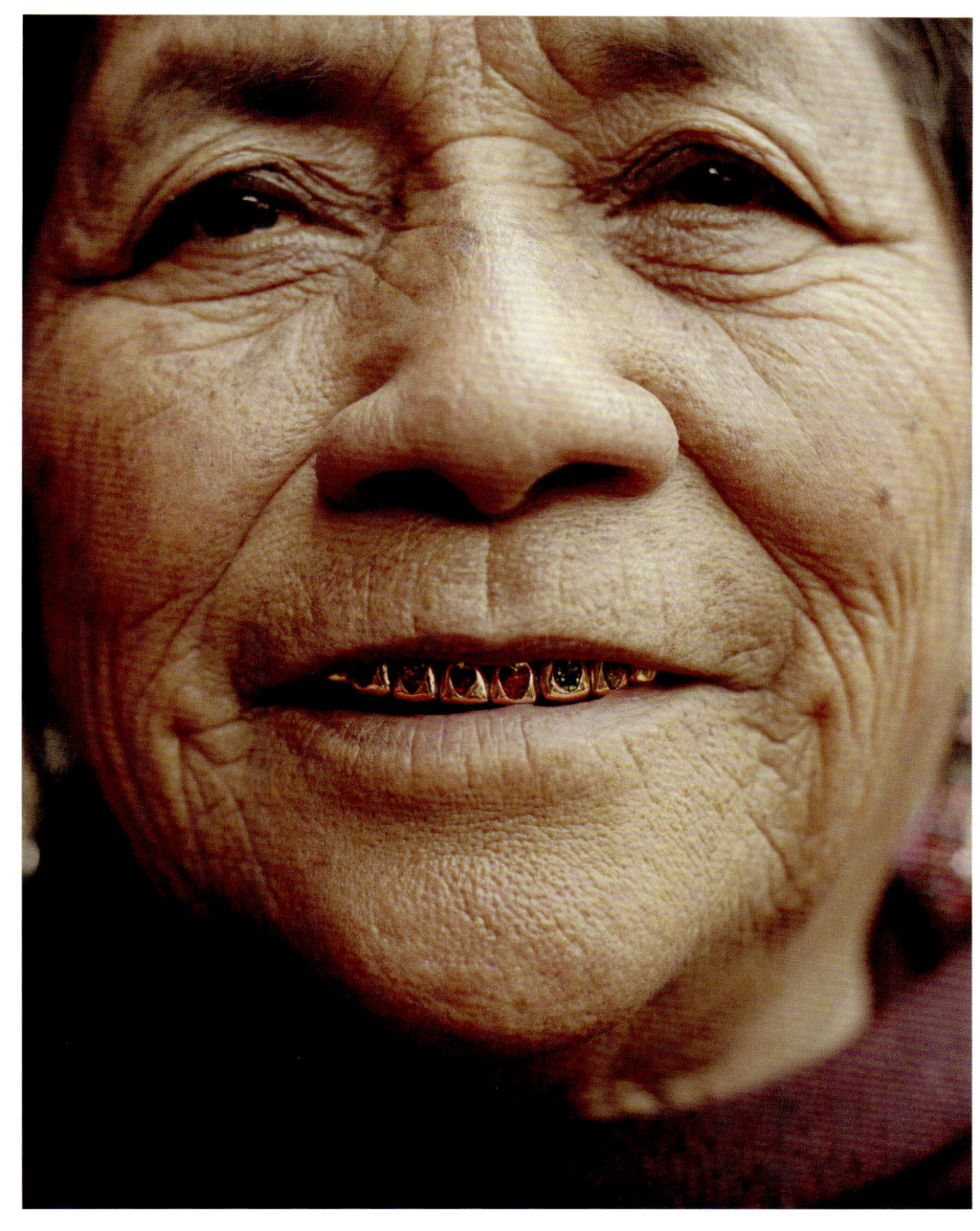

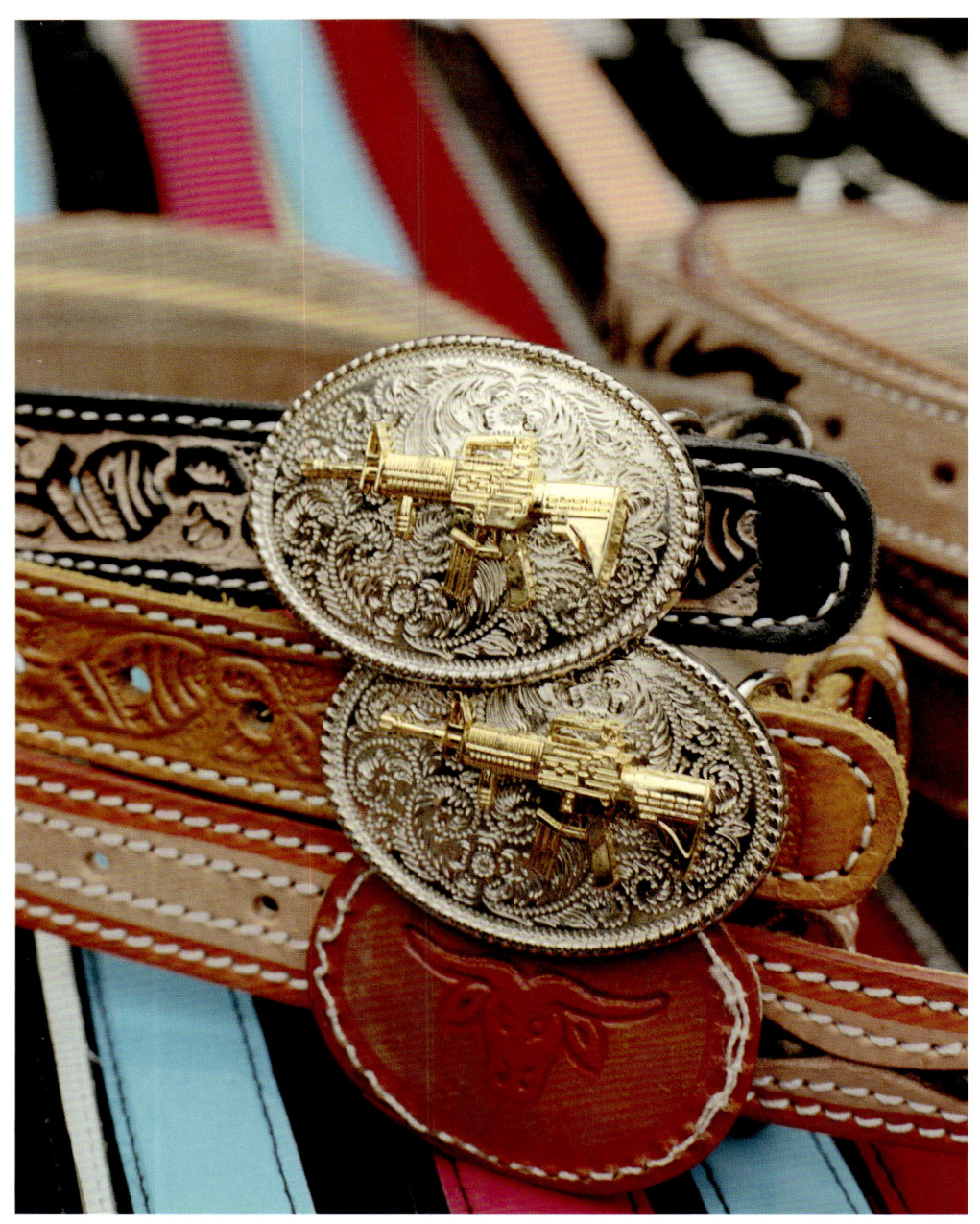

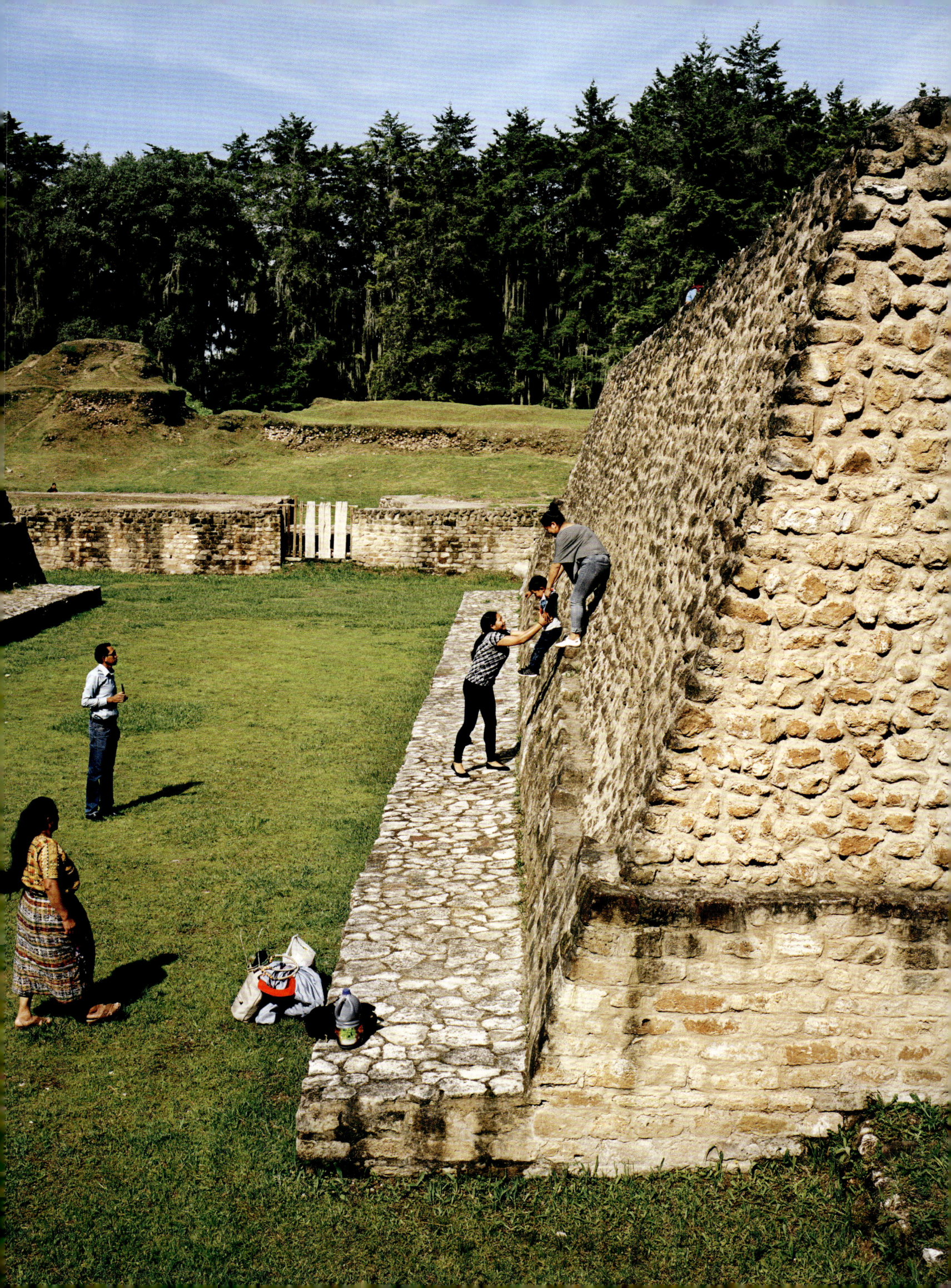

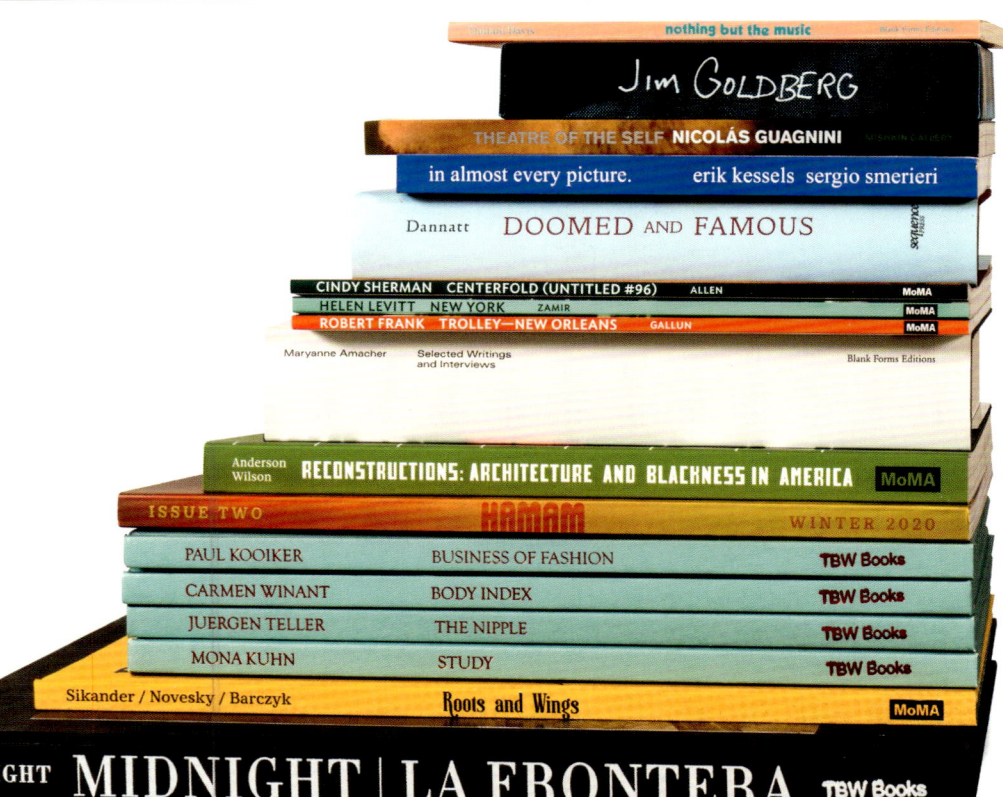
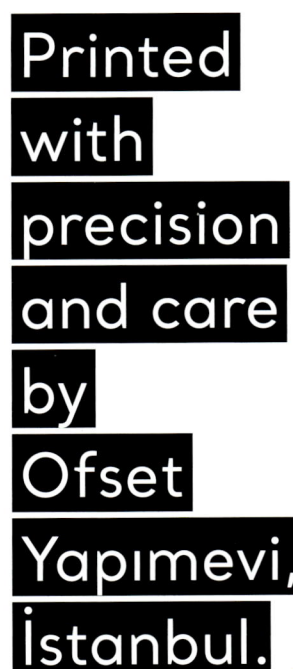
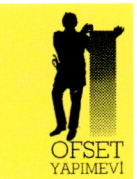
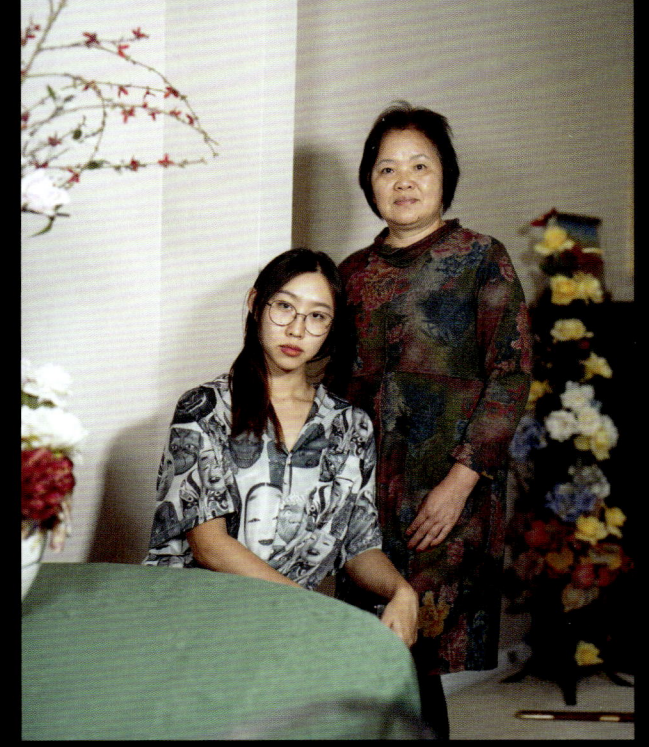
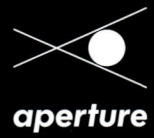
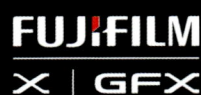

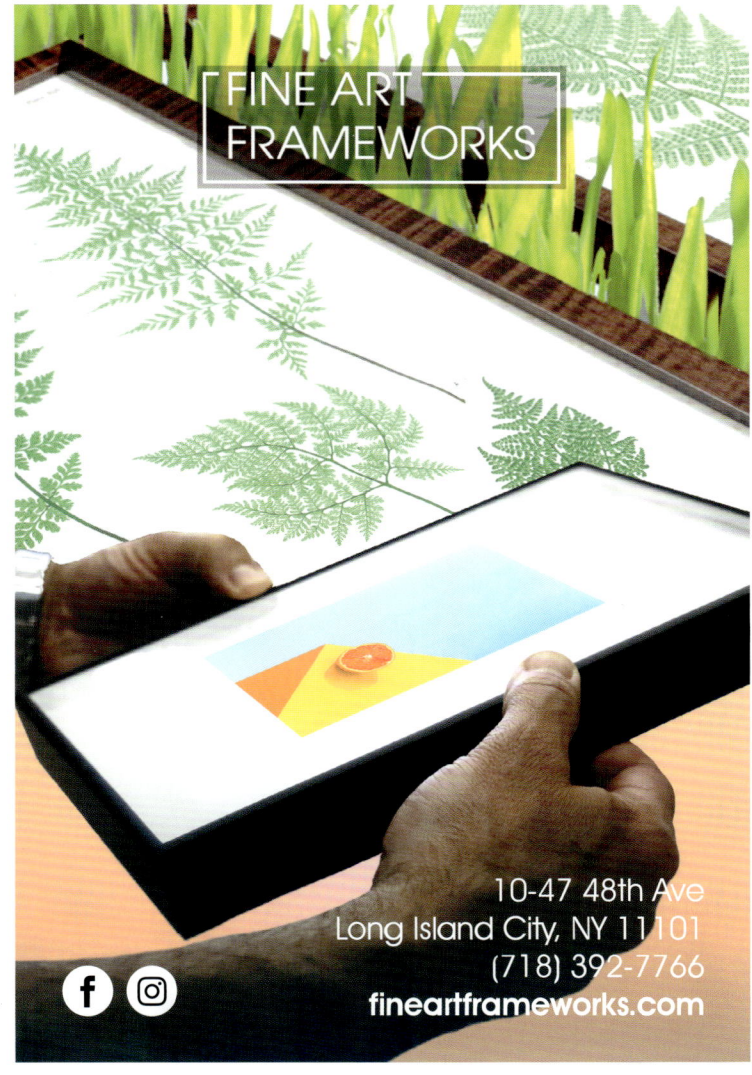
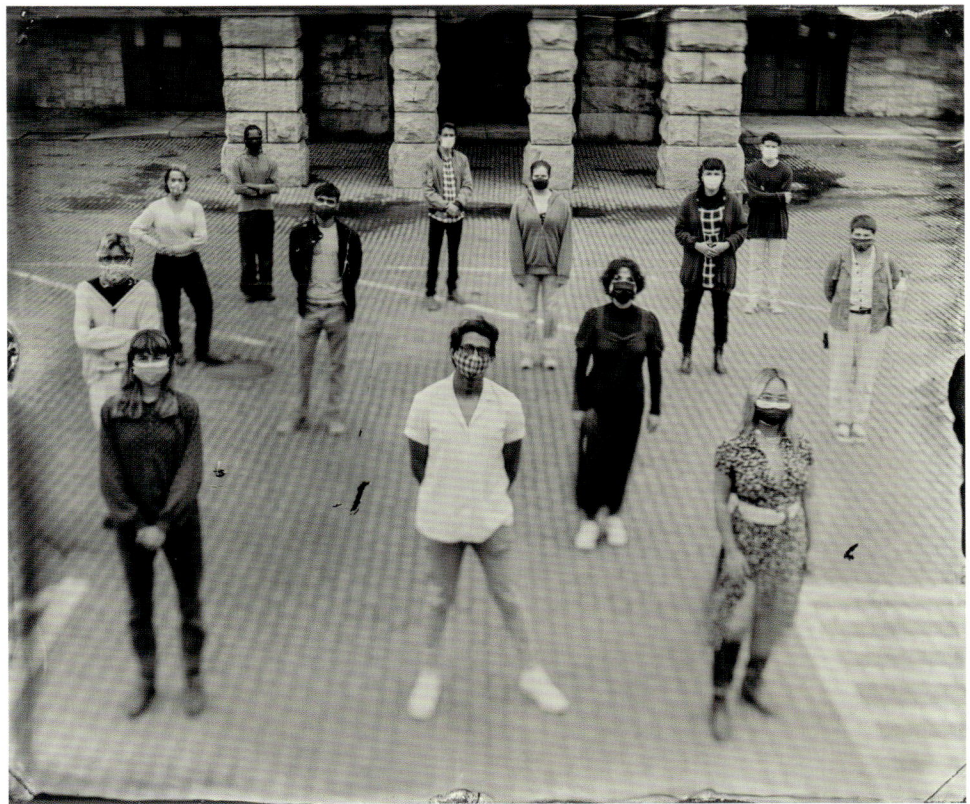

Endnote
Akwaeke Emezi

Akwaeke Emezi splits open new worlds. The best-selling author of four critically acclaimed books, Emezi has rapidly made their mark on the literary scene, while finding new, aching language—in short films as in their books—to narrate their experience as an *ogbanje*, defined in Nigeria's Igbo ontology as a reincarnating spirit born into a human body.

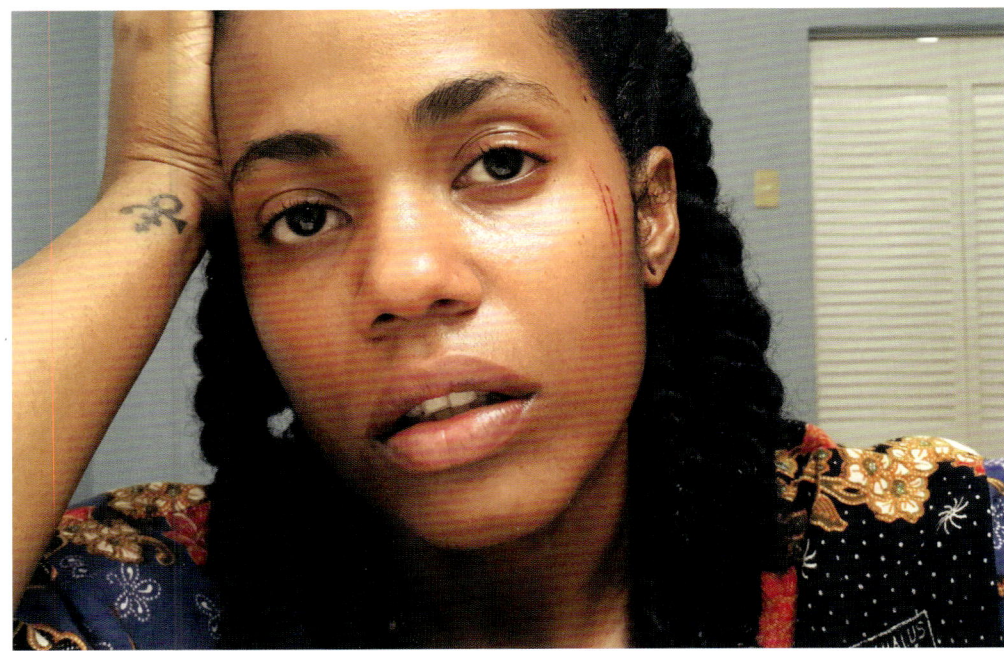

Still from Akwaeke Emezi, *Take the Mark*, **2017**
Courtesy the artist

How do you bridge your literary and film work? Do these media feel part of one consistent language?
I think of the different media as different containers for my thinking. Much of my video art is a documentation of ritual. My entire body of work, including my book *Freshwater* (2019) and my memoir, *Dear Senthuran* (2021), as well as the video art, is trying to process embodiment. It's thinking about a personal mythology and about being a nonhuman, an ogbanje, a deity's child.

In your memoir, you write about shifting between various masks. Do the images in your film *Take the Mark* (2017) represent your face as an ogbanje?
Part of the mythology of an ogbanje is the belief that to "take the mark" exposes the spirit behind the child. Scarring the child is meant to sever the connection that the child has with their spirit cohort. It is an attempt to change your fundamental

nature. To force your spiritual family to abandon you. To isolate you.

In *Take the Mark*, I thought, All right, so I'm going to mark myself. I'm going to reclaim this ritual of cutting because my cohort is not like other cohorts. The function of the ritual can be changed. The context of an ogbanje can be changed. I'm going to expose myself, because what are you going to do? You don't have any power over me. I don't need to hide from you.

I did the ritual in Trinidad when I was living there. At midnight. It was a hugely important part of coming into myself.

Does an image ever become a launching pad for a literary piece?
No. What happens is when I'm writing, I see things visually first before I see them in words.

Are any of the photographs or other art that you live with helpful totems to have in your home?

I live with a lot of art, because I really like collecting. I started a little hobby of looking for artists on Instagram, searching for their work, and building a collection that way. One of my friends who is an artist helps me think about what to add to my collection. She observes the kinds of images I'm drawn to, and she's noticed that I'm really drawn to portraiture— like, heavily.

Who are some of your favorite portrait artists?
My sister Yagazie Emezi takes such striking portraits. For Christmas, she gifted me an untitled portrait from her series *The Beauties of West Point* (2017). We're trying to do more work together, where she gets to take portraits of me, because, unbelievably, no one has commissioned her to do it yet! This is ridiculous. My girl is shooting for the *New York Times*, like, all the time. Pair us together!